ENEMY AT THE GATES

ENEMY AT THE GATES

PANIC FIGHTERS OF THE SECOND WORLD WAR

JUSTO MIRANDA

FONTHILL

'Everyone is a pacifist between wars. It is like being a vegetarian between meals.'

Colman McCarthy

'A city is well-fortified which has a wall of men instead of brick.'

Lycurgus

Fonthill Media Language Policy

Fonthill Media publishes in the international English language market. One language edition is published worldwide. As there are minor differences in spelling and presentation, especially with regard to American English and British English, a policy is necessary to define which form of English to use. The Fonthill Policy is to use the form of English native to the author. Justo Miranda was born in Spain, lives in Madrid, and chose to write the book in British English.

Fonthill Media Limited
Fonthill Media LLC
www.fonthillmedia.com
office@fonthillmedia.com

First published in the United Kingdom and the United States of America 2019

British Library Cataloguing in Publication Data:
A catalogue record for this book is available from the British Library

Copyright © Justo Miranda 2019

ISBN 978-1-78155-766-2

The right of Justo Miranda to be identified as the author of this work has been asserted by him in accordance with the Copyright, Designs and Patents Act 1988.

Typeset in 10.5pt on 13pt Minion Pro
Printed and bound in England

Contents

Introduction

The economic principle of supply and demand—a fundamental law of nature that manifests itself when everyone wants the same thing at the same time—also impacts governments, especially those in small countries lacking the industrial infrastructure to make their own weapons, who are only able to exist in peacetime.

Military technology advanced slowly during the years 1920 and 1930, limited to improve the designs of the First World War. In this period of strong economic depression and serious social upheavals, several philosophies of aeronautical design coexisted. The manufacture of aircraft using wood and fabric, preferred by the British, competed with the French monocoque system, based on plywood. The Americans began to put on the market its expensive all-metal aircraft, arguing that its durability and structural resistance made up for the price difference. The Dutch specialised in fabric-coated steel tube structures and the British began experimenting with stainless steel structures in their naval aircraft.

Monoplanes were still considered unsafe and failed to prevail because of the poor quality of the aerodromes of the period, which were unprepared for high-speed landings, usually without flaps. The biplane fighter (with a liquid-cooled in-line engine) and the multiplace bomber (with air-cooled radial engines) were the designs preferred by the main powers.

Still, in 1939, most air forces continued using the combat tactics of 1918. The standard formation for the fighters was the triangular patrol. In this formation, the leader gave his orders based on gestures, so that all the planes had to fly very close, trying to avoid a collision and without paying due attention to the enemy. This situation changed with the development of radio telephony, which allowed more effective formations. During the Spanish Civil War, the Germans devised the *Schwarm* system of two pairs, with aircraft flying at different heights to increase their field of vision.

In 1939, the bombers, derived from civilian aircraft, were initially conceived for air police functions in the extensive colonial empires and adequate to quell indigenous insurrections with a few small-calibre bombs. These aircraft were capable of accommodating a large number of crew members, and the spaciousness of the fuselage (without any equipment) enabled them to be used as transport.

The Spanish neutrality during the First World War allowed the enrichment of the country, with the export of food to a devastated Europe. In the mid-1930s, Spain had large reserves of gold, but the Republican government considered it unnecessary to modernise the *Aviacion Militar* (equipped with obsolete French planes), refusing the acquisition of Hawker Fury and Boeing 281 fighters.

At the outbreak of the Civil War, the democracies grew horrified by the revolutionary excesses and refused to supply arms to either side. Consequently, both of them had to sell their soul to the devil in association with Hitler, Mussolini, or Stalin. The Spanish War served to perfect many of the technologies used during the Second World War, such as the monoplane fighters with a retractable undercarriage, enclosed cockpit, 20-mm cannons, radio, and oxygen equipment; long-range bombers with 1,000-kg bombs or dive bombers with 500-kg bombs were military secrets still in the experimental stage. Yet its use in real conditions of combat was only useful for international observers to learn the wrong lessons.

The French proved that their planes were technically inferior to their German counterparts, and despite having the opportunity to carefully study a Messerschmitt Bf 109 and a Heinkel He 111 captured by the Republicans, they refused to reform their aeronautical policy until it was too late. The Russians lost their opportunity to take advantage of the tactical experience gained by their pilots against German aircraft because of purges that eliminated a considerable number of them. Therefore, they continued building biplane fighters, along with the British and the Italians. The Czechs and Poles did not have time to apply what they had learned, while the British observed, remained silent, and decided that they were not prepared, starting a policy of appeasement and massive rearming.

The Germans drew the wrong conclusions, which would cost them the next war; the decision not to manufacture four-engine strategic bombers prevented them from destroying the Russian factories located behind the Urals in 1942. The success of the He 111 and Do 17 against the primitive interception means of the Spanish Republicans made them believe that they could operate without a fighter escort. They also did not take any actions to equip the Bf 109 that flew over London with detachable fuel tanks, even though the system had been successfully used in Spain.

The precision of the *Stuka* attacks led them to build the next generation of bombers to act as dive bombers, with pernicious effects in the production of the Ju 88 and devastating results in that of the He 177. The Americans, on their part, did not attach enough importance to oxygen equipment in their fighters; in the end, they had to adopt the British system.

The Third Reich annexed Austria in March 1938 and the Czech region of the Sudetenland in October. In March of the following year, it was the remainder of Czechoslovakia. The war in Spain ended in April, with the victory for the side supported by Germany. Europe was relentlessly rushing towards a war that no one could stop.

After the Munich Agreement, the French and British realised that they were unprepared. The Hawker Fury biplane fighters of the RAF hastily received camouflage paints to be used as emergency fighters in the face of the shortage of Hurricanes and *l'Armée de l'Air* did the same with its obsolete Dewoitine D.510 and Loire 46 fighters. The countries lacking a sufficiently advanced aeronautical industry encountered many difficulties to get supplies of fighter planes in the international market.

The demand for modern fighters shot up and the supply retreated until it disappeared completely when all European countries demanded some kind of protection against the threat of the Luftwaffe. Latvia did not receive any of the thirty Morane-Saulnier 406 fighters ordered in 1939. The same happened with the thirteen Moranes that Lithuania had already paid to the French Government or with the twelve Spitfires that Estonia had been waiting for since July 1937. When the *Stukas* arrived, Poland had only received one Hurricane and Belgium fifteen.

Then the demand for fighters went to the North American industry, but it turned out that the production capacity of Curtiss and Boeing was saturated by the enormous orders of planes made by French and British. After the Molotov–Ribbentrop Pact, Americans banned the export of sixty Seversky EP-106 and 144 Vultee V-48 fighters to Sweden, fearing that their technology would fall into the hands of the Soviets.

The panic increased. Left to their own devices, the weak countries had three options only: to improve the fighters at their disposal; to develop new fighters from advanced trainer planes; or to build them from scratch creating their own 'panic fighters'. Sweden and Finland tried the last solution with average results due to their lack of experience. The old Swiss and Finnish Morane 406 were equipped with more powerful engines in an attempt to expand their operational life. Australia, Peru, and Thailand bought fighters based on the North American Texan trainer. Britain, Lithuania, and Latvia modified their Miles Master, Irbitis I-16, and Aviotehas trainers to use them as emergency fighters.

Other countries that managed to remain neutral or were attacked later had time to develop advanced fighters. However, in most cases, the rapid advance of the German, Soviet, and Japanese armies prevented the 'panic fighters' to surpass the phase of projects or prototypes.

The subject has never been specifically treated in the aeronautical literature and I have tried to fill this gap with the compilation of many practically unknown projects that are included in the present book. Between December 1936 and June 1942, the Messerschmitt and Mitsubishi fighters took over much of the world without encountering any effective opposition. This is the story of those who tried to oppose them.

Justo Miranda
Madrid, February 2018

1

The German Aggressor
(September 1938–February 1943)

The Luftwaffe was originally conceived as a tactical air force to support the operations of the *Wehrmacht*, by acting as long-range artillery. Its *modus operandi* was to destroy the enemy air force on the ground, bombarding its airfields by surprise, while the *Stuka* dive bombers neutralised the strong points of the ground defences, previously located by reconnaissance aircraft. Then the medium bombers, escorted by Messerschmitt Bf 110 heavy fighters, would attack the capital city of the enemy, forcing its surrender.

The aerial superiority required for this tactic to work well was achieved by using single-engine fighters, with their performances exceeding those of the enemy interceptors. After the failure of the Heinkel He 51 in Spain against the Soviet Polikarpov, the *Reichsluftfahrtministerium* requested the design of an air superiority fighter powered by the most advanced in-line engine available.

In the summer of 1936, the Messerschmitt Bf 109 won the fighter contest for the re-equipment of the *Jagdflieger*, becoming the spearhead of all conquests made by the Third Reich until February 1943. It was only overcome after the arrival of large quantities of North American P-51 fighters to Europe during the second half of 1943.

When the Germans tried to use the Luftwaffe for strategic purposes, without the support of the *Wehrmacht*, they failed in their attempts to destroy the RAF, the Soviet industry, and the Allied convoys over the Atlantic Ocean. The main cause was the decision not to build heavy bombers, to increase the production of medium bombers Heinkel He 111, Dornier Do 17, and Junkers Ju 88, as well as the failure to use the Messerschmitt Bf 110 as an escort fighter. Germany was not prepared for a long war and when the *Blitzkrieg* stalled, their industrial capacity turned out to be insufficient.

German 'Panic Fighters'

Readers interested in this topic can find detailed descriptions of the Lippisch 8-334 project (Me 334) in my book *The Ultimate Piston Fighters of the Luftwaffe*, published by Fonthill Media Ltd in 2014.

Descriptions of the projects Arado E-581, Blohm und Voss P.217, Henschel P.135, Horten Ho.X, Lippisch P.13, Lippisch P.15, Lippisch P.20, and Messerschmitt P.1111 are in *The Ultimate Flying Wings of the Luftwaffe*, published by Fonthill Media Ltd in 2015.

Descriptions of projects Focke-Wulf Fw 190 A-8 *Rammer*, Bachem Rocket Fighter (early), Blohm und Voss P.186.01-01, Blohm und Voss BV 40, Blohm und Voss/ Stöckel *Rammschussjäger*, DFS *Eber*, DVL *Jagdsegler*, Focke-Wulf *Rammjäger*, Gotha P.54 *Rammer*, Lippisch *Rammer*, Messerschmitt Me 328 Series, Messerschmitt P.1103, Messerschmitt P.1104, and Zeppelin *Rammer* are in my book *Axis Suicide Squads: German and Japanese Secret Projects of the Second World War*, published by Fonthill Media Ltd in 2017.

Also, descriptions of projects Focke-Wulf Ta 183, Focke-Wulf *Volksjäger*, Focke-Wulf *Volksflugzeug*, Focke-Wulf Ta 283, and Focke-Wulf *Triebflügeljäger* are in my book *Focke-Wulf Jet Fighters*, published by Fonthill Media Ltd in 2018.

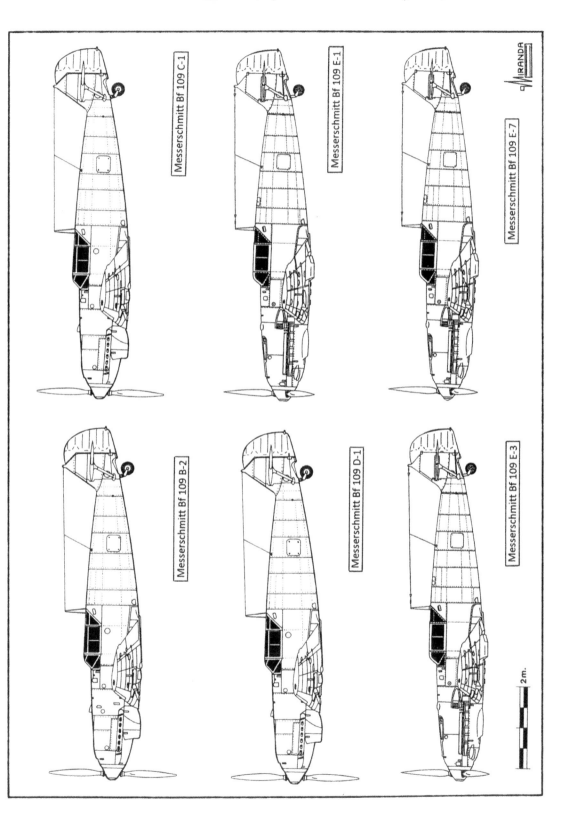

Messerschmitt Bf 109 C-1

Messerschmitt Bf 109 E-1

Messerschmitt Bf 109 E-7

Messerschmitt Bf 109 B-2

Messerschmitt Bf 109 D-1

Messerschmitt Bf 109 E-3

2 m.

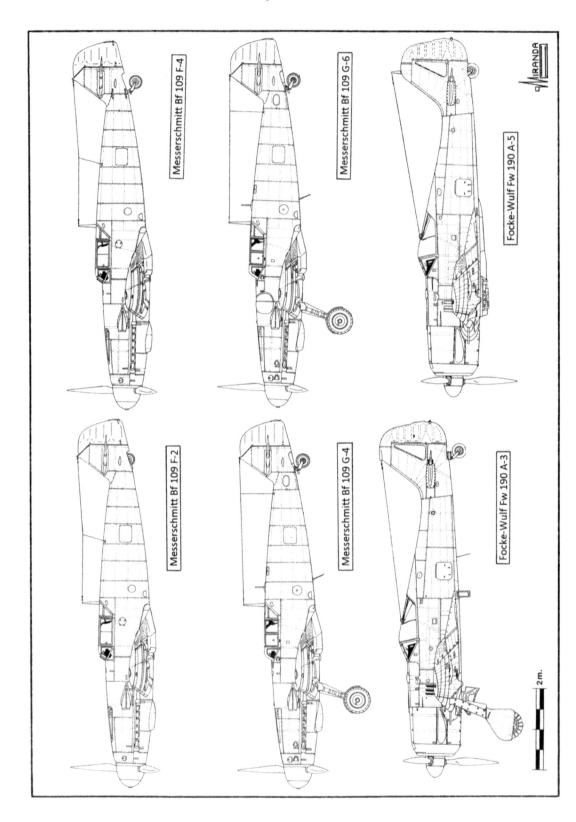

Messerschmitt Bf 109 F-4

Messerschmitt Bf 109 G-6

Focke-Wulf Fw 190 A-5

Messerschmitt Bf 109 F-2

Messerschmitt Bf 109 G-4

Focke-Wulf Fw 190 A-3

2 m.

2

Czechoslovakia
(1 October 1938–15 March 1939)

Alarmed by the rapid development of the new German monoplane fighters, the Czech Ministry of National Defence (MNO) issued the 23-308 Type I specification on 1 January 1936, calling for a single-seat monoplane fighter with retractable undercarriage, powered by the 1,000-hp Avia HS.12-1000 Y in-line engine, an advanced version of the French Hispano-Suiza 12Y-37.

When it was learned that the Messerschmitt Bf 109 B-1 had entered service in February 1937, the design team of the firm Avia, under the leadership of Ing. František Novotný, presented the Avia B-35 project. On 22 May, the MNO approved the construction of two prototypes, temporarily equipped with a fixed undercarriage to gain time. A wooden mock-up, with a three-bladed propeller and retractable undercarriage, was also approved and displayed at the National Exhibition in Prague.

At the end of 1937, the construction of the prototype B-35.1 began. It flew for the first time on September 1938, powered by an 860-hp Hispano-Suiza/Avia HS.12Y drs engine, driving one Avia 232A wooden propeller. In a second test, carried out on the same day but with one M-100 metal propeller, the B-35.1 reached a maximum speed of 485 kph.

The prototype was 2,200 kg in gross weight, had a 500-km range, a 13-m/s rate of climb, and a ceiling of 8,500 m. The wings, spanning 10.85 m, were built in wood/plywood bonded to an outer duraluminium skin and housed two fuel tanks in the wing roots. The fuselage, 8.5 m in length, was built in welded steel tube with dural panelling forward and plywood/dural aft. It housed the engine, armament, cockpit, and a third fuel tank.

Armament tests were carried out later with a *moteur-cannon* HS.12Y crs, with one 20-mm HS.404 cannon firing through the hub of the Letov Hd 43 propeller, as well as two ČZ Strakonice vz. 30, 7.92-mm synchronised machine guns. The B-35.1 was destroyed in an accident on 22 November 1938.

The B-35.2 made its first flight on 30 December 1938, powered by an HS.12Y drs, driving one Avia 232B wooden propeller. It differed from the B-35.1 in the wooden structure of the fuselage, designed to facilitate the construction, and in the wing chord, reduced to 215 cm to facilitate manoeuvrability at high speed. No armament was installed.

After the German annexation of the Sudetenland in October 1938, the MNO ordered the urgent construction of ten pre-production units (B-35.3 to B-35.12) with a retractable landing gear.

The B-35.3 (equipped with a Messier retractable undercarriage, a wooden propeller, and two machine guns, flew for the first time on 20 June 1939) reached 535 kph. It differed from the B-35.2 in the wings, designed to facilitate production, with straight leading edge and 223-cm chord. It was 2,462 kg in gross weight, with a 940-km range, 13.5-m/s rate of climb and 9,500-m ceiling.

The pre-production B-35 would have performed better in combat than its contemporaneous Fokker D.XXI, Polikarpov I-6 Type 10, Heinkel He 112 B-0, Messerschmitt Bf 109 B-2 and C-1, and Morane Saulnier M.S.406; it also would have fought on equal terms with the Messerschmitt Bf 109 D-1, the Dewoitine D.520, and Hawker Hurricane Mk I.

The construction of the B-135 'panic fighter' would have started in May 1939, but it was cancelled after the German annexation of Bohemia-Moravia on 15 March 1939.

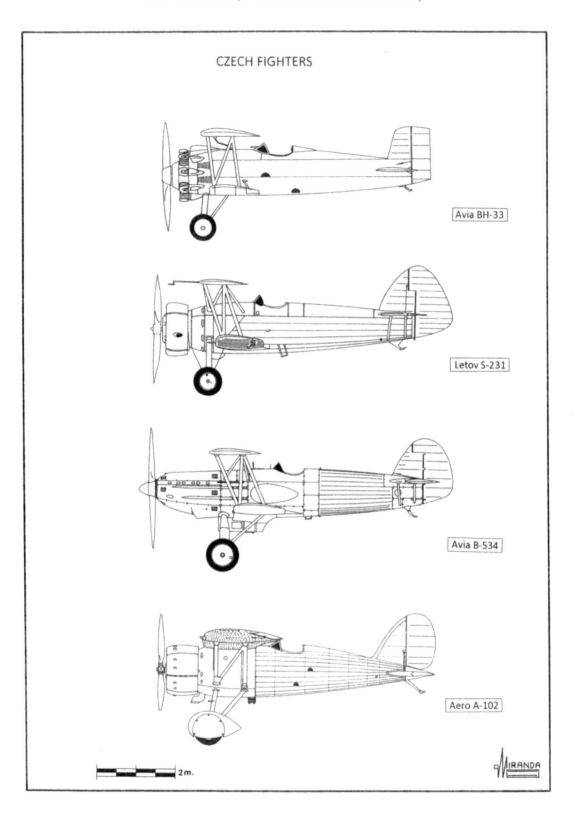

CZECH FIGHTERS

Avia BH-33

Letov S-231

Avia B-534

Aero A-102

2 m.

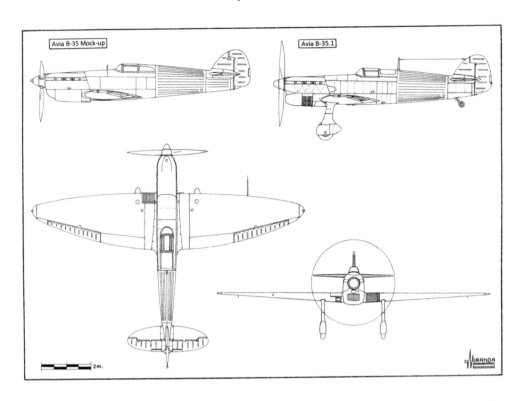

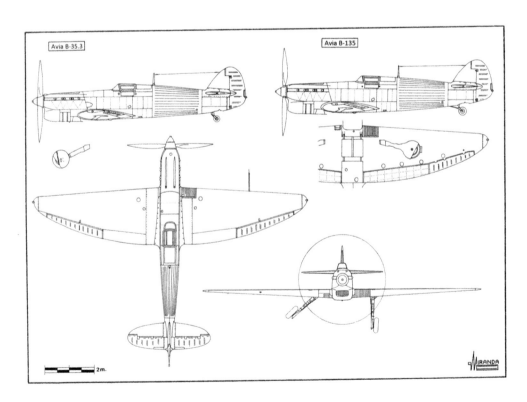

3

Poland
(1 September–6 October 1939)

At the outbreak of the Second World War, the Luftwaffe attacked Poland with 2,300 modern combat aircraft.

The Polish Air Force only had 240 fighters and succumbed after just thirty days of fighting, hopelessly waiting for the squads of Moranes, Hurricanes, and Battles with which their false French and British allies had promised to help. Such was the trust of the Polish Government in its Western allies that they had sold its most modern PZL P.24 fighters to Greece, Turkey, Romania, and Bulgaria, retaining the obsolete models P.7a, P.11a, and P.11c for the defence of the country.

The origin of this dangerous decision appears to be in the *douhetiste* mentality of the general Ludomil Rayski, commissioned to lead the Polish Air Force procurement programmes since 1936. The writings of Giulio Douhet had convinced many influential persons in the mid-1930s that future wars would be won from the air by large fleets of bombers. Yet the combat experience gained in Spain and China clearly indicated that the bombers had to be escorted by fighters to be effective.

The limited range of the fighters of the time restricted the territorial ambitions of the countries to over 300 km beyond its borders. However, Germany dreamt of the Urals, Italy dreamt of Egypt, and Japan dreamt of China. Trying to overcome that limit was how the concept of 'strategic fighter', with powerful weapons and a high range, was conceived. France, Germany, Poland, and Japan invested large resources, with a more ideological than a scientific basis.

By the end of the 1920s, Polish strategists believed the expansion of their accesses to the sea through the annexation of German East Prussian territories feasible. The lessons derived from the war against the Soviets in 1920 were all wrong, as well as the belief that Germany was a country definitely defeated. Erroneously, the Poles decided to devote a large part of their resources to the creation of a modern attack force, consisting of fast-bombers and long-range 'strategic-fighters' to force the future annexation of new territories.

The manufacture of the new single-engine fighters PZL P.50 and P.55 had to be delayed in favour of the twin-engine PZL 'strategic-fighter' P.38 *Wilk*. The expansionist policy carried out by the USSR and the Third Reich in Manchuria, Spain, Finland, Austria, and Czechoslovakia alarmed the French and British, forcing them to suspend the export of fighter aircraft and engines to small European countries that needed them. At the beginning of 1939, Poland was like a blind man between two monsters.

After the invasion of Czechoslovakia in March, General Józef Zając received the command of the Polish Air Force and commissioned the urgent production of 400 PZL P.11g *Kobuz* fighters powered by a Bristol Mercury VIII engine. In June, the Polish Government began negotiations for the acquisition of the Seversky P-35 and Curtiss P-36 fighters. In August, after the French refused to export their few Dewoitine D.520, an agreement was signed for the acquisition of 160 Morane-Saulnier M.S.406s that were finally retained in Le Havre after the German occupation of the Polish ports.

The British agreed to export only ten Hurricane Mk Is, one Spitfire Mk I, and 100 Battle bombers, but only the Hurricane L2048 arrived to Poland before the German invasion. At the end of August, the Dornier Do 17P-1 of the Luftwaffe began to carry out reconnaissance flights over Poland at an altitude that the PZL P.11c of the *Zasadzki patrols* could not reach.

On 1 September 1939, the Luftwaffe had 1,090 Messerschmitt Bf 109s, but most remained in Germany after the declaration of war made by French and British on the third day of the month.

The invasion of Poland only involved 429: thirty-six Bf 109 B-2s (462 kph) of the JGr 101, seventy-six Bf 109 C-1s (467 kph) of the I/JG21, forty Bf 109 D-1s (571 kph) of the JGr 102, and 277 Bf 109 E-1s (547 kph) of the I/JG1, I/LG2 and I/JG 21. None of them were still armed with the 20-mm cannons used by the seventy-four Bf 110 C-1s and eight Bf 110 B-1s that were escorting the main force of bombers, formed by 367 Dornier Do 17s and 444 Heinkel He 111s.

On the day of the invasion, the Polish Air Force had fewer than 400 first-line aircraft and only fifteen fighter squadrons equipped with thirty PZL P.7as, twenty PZL P.11as, and 111 PZL P.11cs. There were seventy-five more units of the PZL P.7a in second-line reserve units and fighter schools, along with one PZL P.11g, one PZL P.24 IV, and two PZL P.50 prototypes.

With a maximum speed below the theoretical of 380 kph for the P.11c and of 327 kph for the P.7a, these outclassed aircraft were not only slower than the German fighters, but they did not even match the cruising speed of the bombers. Fortunately for the Poles, the Luftwaffe pilots had orders to fly at medium level to safely identify targets. Confident in the protection of the escort fighters and the ability of their rear gunners, the German bombers did not avoid combat, so even the PZL P.7a had its opportunity, managing to shoot down two He 111s, one Do 17, two Bf 110s, and one Hs 126, losing in exchange 70 per cent of its forces.

The Vickers E Mod. 1933 machine guns of the P.7a had a low rate of fire and tended to clog very often. They were mounted very low on the fuselage sides and the pilot could not watch the tracer bullets' trajectory. These had been replaced by the indigenous FK Wz.33A in some planes.

The P.11a had much better visibility from the cockpit with one more powerful engine. However, the armament was the same and no match for even a Dornier in performance.

The P.11c was designed with two additional Wz 36S machine guns located in the wings, but at the start of the war, they had only been installed in one-third of the aircraft. Despite their limitations, Polish fighters were cleverly used by the Pursuit Brigade *(Brygada Pościgowa)* during the Warsaw defence. Its high-wing configuration allowed them to take off from short airstrips, operating in small groups from numerous improvised airfields located around the capital; they also frequently changed base to avoid the photo-reconnaissance of the Do 17 P-1 *Fernaufklären*. Its good rate of climb allowed them to quickly attack from below the bombers flying at medium level.

The P.11c could dive at 600 kph and it was superior in a dogfight to the Bf 109 and the Polikarpov I-16 Type 10. Its great structural robustness let them carry out manoeuvres at high *g*, for which the pilots had been superbly trained. However, its armament was insufficient to destroy the He 111. When firing too long a burst, the excessive heat blocked the synchronisation device and the bullets struck the propeller blades.

The malfunction of the machine guns forced Lt Col. Leopold Pamula from 114 Sqn to ram a German fighter (possibly a Bf 109 B-2 of the JGr 101) over Łomianki. Between 1 and 26 September, the Polish fighters shot down 110 to 160 German and Russian aircraft in combat. The Luftwaffe lost 285 aircraft for various reasons, and another 279 were damaged. The Polish Air Force lost 118 fighters.

Chronology of the Disaster

On 10 May 1934, the German Government officially recognised the existence of the Luftwaffe. In April, the *Reichsluftfahrtministerium* decided to update the concept 'strategic fighter' that had been developed in Germany during the First World War.

In July, the Polish Government approved the development of the PZL P.37 Łos medium bomber. In September, the Polish Department of Aeronautics approved the design of the 'strategic-fighter' PZL P.38 *Wilk*. On 31 October, the French Air Ministry issued a specification for a multiplace *léger de défénse*, Potez 63, the French version of the so-called 'strategic-fighter'. On 28 May 1935, the Messerschmitt Bf 109 V1 prototype performed its first secret flight. The prototype of the dive bomber Junkers Ju 87 V1 *Stuka* flew on 17 September.

All the work of design of the German 'strategic-fighter' Messerschmitt Bf 110 was carried out during the summer of 1935. In October, the prototype Dornier Do 17 V1 was demonstrated at Bückeberg and the Polikarpov I-16 Type 5 at the Milan International Aeronautical Salon. On 6 November 1936, the Condor Legion was created and the Polikarpov I-16 Type 5 entered combat in Spain.

On 10 January 1937, the Heinkel He 111 V4 prototype was revealed to the world. In February, the Bf 109 B-1 (462 kph) entered service with the JG 132 *Richthofen*, and the Ju 87 A-0 performed its first bombing mission in Spain. From 23 July to 1 August, the Bf 109 V13 with DB 600 engine and the Do 17 (450 kph) were presented to the international press during the fourth International Air Show at Dübendorf. In November, the Bf

109 V13, with DB 601 engine, reached the world speed record with 611 kph, and the Polikarpov I-16 Type 5 entered combat in China.

In January 1938, the He 111 E was revealed, the government of Yugoslavia ordered twelve Hawker Hurricane Mk I, and the PZL P.37 bomber entered service. On 13 March, Austria was annexed by the Third Reich, and the Polikarpov I-16 Type 10 entered combat in Spain. During the spring of 1938, the Bf 109 C-1 (467 kph) and the Bf 109 D-1 (571 kph) entered service. In May, the prototype PZL P.38 *Wilk* carried out its first flight equipped with two provisional Ranger engines.

In July, the Bf 109 D-1 was revealed as the fastest service fighter in the world. The Messerschmitt Bf 110 B-1 was revealed during the official visit of the French Chief of Air Staff *Général* Vuillemin in August. On 28 September, the Munich Agreement was signed. The Hawker Fury, Gloster Gauntlet, Hawker Demon, Dewoitine D.510, and Loire 46 were painted in camouflage to be used as 'emergency fighters' due to the shortage of modern fighters still in production. The RAF has only six squadrons of Hurricanes and three Spitfire fighters.

In October, the *Wehrmacht* occupied the Sudetenland, and the Polish Department of Aeronautics published the *Sokół* emergency fighter programme specification. In December, the Bf 109 B-2 was revealed, the Government of Romania placed an order for twelve Hawker Hurricane Mk I, and Polish preparation of the Plan W for the defence against the USSR was completed.

The first flight of the PZL P.38 prototype, powered by two *Foka* II engines, was made in January 1939. The delay of its mass production prevented the conversion of the fifteen squadrons of PZL P.11c scheduled for that year. The PZL P.50/I was officially presented, and the Bf 109 E-1, capable of flying at 547 kph, entered into service in February. On 15 March, German invaded the remainder of Czechoslovakia, and the Polish Government completed the preparation of Plan Z for the defence against Germany. Hitler decided to invade Poland on 23 May. In June, the Polish pilots testing the Seversky EP-1 considered it faster and more manoeuvrable than the PZL P.50/I.

During August, the Polish Government tried to acquire, without success, Dewoitine D.520, Morane 406, Hawker Hurricane Mk I, Supermarine Spitfire Mk I, Seversky P-35, and Curtiss P-36 fighters, as well as Fairey Battle bombers. The Dornier Do 17 P-1 began their missions of reconnaissance on Poland flying at 7,000 m; the PZL P.11c took nine minutes to reach that altitude, but they were slower than the German aircraft and could not reach them.

On 23 August, the Molotov–Ribbentrop Pact was signed, allowing the Third Reich access to resources of petroleum in Romania and Hungary, and the Soviets regained the territories lost in 1920. The mobilisation of the Polish Army began.

On 1 September, the German invasion took place, with 429 Messerschmitt Bf 109s (types B-2, C-1, D-1, and E-1); eighty-two Messerschmitt Bf 110 B-1s and C-1s; twenty-one Heinkel He 46s; eight Fieseler Fi 156s; thirty-seven Henschel Hs 123As; 111 Henschel Hs 126 A-1s; 273 Junkers Ju 87 B-1s; ten Junkers Ju 87 C-0s; 447 Dornier Do 17s (types E, F-1, Z-2, and P-1); 302 Heinkel He 111s (types E, H, and P); twenty-one Heinkel He 60 Cs; eight Heinkel He 115s; twenty-seven Dornier Do 18 Ds; and 495 Junkers Ju 52/3ms. On 17 September, the Red Army occupied the eastern regions of Poland.

The *Sokół* Emergency Fighters Programme

After the Third Reich annexation of the Sudetenland, the Polish Air Force was pressing for 170 per cent reserves of fighters, facilitating the reactivation of the *Sokół* project, which had been dismissed a year earlier in favour of the PZL P.50.

At the beginning of 1939, the Polish Department of Aeronautics issued the *Sokół* specification, calling for a Plan Z single-seat fighter powered by one 660–730-hp Gnome-Rhône 14M-05 *Mars* double-row radial engine, armed with four 7.7-mm KM Wz36 SG machine guns and equipped with a Walter *Iskra* R/T device and full oxygen installation.

The PZL firm proposed two *Sokół* versions with an all-metal construction, a semi-monocoque fuselage structure, and a PZL two-blade, adjustable pitch airscrew— the P.45/I with a fixed undercarriage and the P.45/II with a retractable undercarriage. Both versions used structural solutions based on the PZL 19 Challenge tourer wings, spanning 12.14 m, with 10.3 aspect ratio and 14.3-sq. m surface. Each wing panel housed one 175-l fuel tank and one flap. A third flap was located in the belly fuselage. The estimated maximum speed of the P.45/II was 520 kph and the gross weight was 1,940 kg. The construction of the P.45/I had still not concluded in September 1939.

The design proposed by the firm R.W.D. was very similar to the Fokker D.XXI and used the same construction system, with all-wood wings, spanning 10.5 m without flaps to simplify production. The fuselage, with a welded chromium-molybdenum tubular structure, had a coating of light metal sheets in the front section and fabric in the rest.

The Letov three-blade fixed-pitch airscrew foreseen for the original design was to be replaced by another model after the invasion of Czechoslovakia. This version of the *Sokół*, called R.W.D. 25, would have an estimated maximum speed of 450 kph and a gross weight of 1,800 kg. The construction of the prototype, which started in July 1939, could not be completed.

Design Number 42, proposed by the firm PWS early in 1939, would be totally built of wood/plywood, with inwards retractable landing gear, a 9-m wingspan, and a 16-sq. m wing area. It was to be armed with two machine guns in the wings and two more in the nose. Its estimated maximum speed would be 520 kph and its gross weight 1,900 kg.

PZL P.50 *Jastrząb*

Designed at the end of 1936 as a successor to the PZL P.11, the P.50 was a small monoplane with an elliptical wing and appearance like that of the American Seversky P-35.

The original specification required a highly manoeuvrable interceptor for the close defence of specific targets, propelled by an 840-hp Bristol Mercury VIII air-cooled radial engine and armed with four 7.7-mm machine guns: two WZ.36 G in the nose and two WZ.36 SG in the external wing panels.

The manufacture of 300 aircraft, under the denomination P.50A *Jastrząb I*, started in 1938. Delivery of the first fifty machines was expected by September 1939. The Aviation Command planned an expansion programme that was to end in 1941, with fifteen squadrons equipped with P.50 A to and a reserve of 150 aircraft. The manufacture, under licence of the Mercury VIII, began in the PZL-W.P.I aero-engine plant at Warsaw-Okęcie.

The prototype P.50/I was completed in September 1938. It was a fully metallic plane, with a 2,500-kg gross weight, equipped with one Hamilton/PZL three-blade variable-pitch airscrew. The wings, spanning 9.7 m, housed the Dowty retractable undercarriage, flaps, and Handley-Page automatic slots.

During its first flight in February 1939, it showed instability at low speed and tail flutter in dive. The prototype was under-powered, with a low rate of climb, and the top speed was only 430 kph. The test pilots reported that their flight characteristics were inferior to those of the Seversky EP-1.

In August, the P.50/I managed to fly at 500 kph thanks to the amendments to the carburettor air intake, tail unit, and wing/fuselage fillets. In April, General Zając cancelled the production programme and ordered using the Mercury VIII available in the PZL P.11g *Kobuz* emergency fighters.

The basic *Jastrząb* airframe was adapted for many more powerful engines, like the indigenous 1,200-hp PZL *Waran*, lengthening the fuselage up to 8.2 m. Attempts were made to obtain either 1,050-hp Pratt & Whitney Twin Wasp, 1,400-hp Gnome-Rhône 14N 50, 1,145-hp Bristol *Taurus* III, and 1,375-hp Bristol Hercules radial engines.

The new aircraft, called P.50B, would have been a strike fighter armed with two 20-mm Wz.38D cannons in the wing roots and two 7.7-mm Wz.36 G machine guns in the nose; it would also be able to carry one 300-kg bomb or one detachable fuel tank under the fuselage.

The airframe was completed in the spring of 1939, but the Gnome-Rhône 14N 21 engine acquired in France was not available on time.

The construction of other more advanced versions in 1940-41 had been foreseen:

PZL P.53A *Jastrząb II* with *Waran* or Bristol Hercules engines and PZL/Hamilton-Standard propeller.
PZL P.53B, with Gnome-Rhône 14N 51.
PZL P.56A *Kania*, with Hispano-Suiza HS.12Y-31 or Allison V-1710-23 in-line engines.
PZL P.56B with one 1,600-hp Hispano-Suiza HS.12Z.

PZL P.55

In October 1938, the design team of the firm Dewoitine, under the leadership of Robert Castello, began working on a version of the D.520 fighter, capable of flying at 700 kph.

The wind tunnel tests carried out in March 1939 in Toulouse-Banlève with a one-eighth model, proved that at least 650 kph could be reached, using a 900-hp Hispano-Suiza HS.12Y crs engine driving one Ratier airscrew of 3 m in diameter, and exceed 700 kph with the new 1,200–1,400-hp HS.12Z.

The performances of the new French 'V' engines attracted the attention of the Polish Department of Aeronautics that started contacts with the French Government to acquire a licence for manufacture of the HS.12Y-51 and HS.12Z for the future *Kania* fighters. The designer, Jerzy Dąbrowski, was also interested to propel his PZL P.55, a new fighter based on the Challenge tourer PZL P.26, with 11.25-m wingspan and 3,250-kg gross weight, sometimes described in the literature as P.62 or Dąbrowski Fighter.

In early summer 1939, the wind tunnel test showed the aerodynamic superiority of the P.55 (660 kph) against the *Kania*, and the Aviation Command favoured its production. It would have been built entirely of metal, with laminar-flow wings provided with Handley-Page slots, flaps, and outboard retractable landing gear. One semi-retractable radiator was designed, inspired by the Prestone cooling system used by French Morane-Saulnier 406 fighters.

The planned armament consisted of a 20-mm HS.404 cannon or an indigenous Wz.38C, firing through the propeller hub, and six 7.92-mm Wz.36 SG machine guns mounted in the wings. The pilot would be protected by an armoured windshield and steel plates; the cockpit was heated and equipped with oxygen and a Walter *Iskra* R/T device.

As an alternative to the French engine, the Polish Government tried to acquire the manufacturing licence for the American Allison V-1710-23. A future P.55 equipped with the Allison could not use the cannon and would be reinforced with two Wz.36G (synchronised) machine guns in the nose. The prototype was expected to fly for the first time in the summer of 1940.

POLISH FIGHTERS

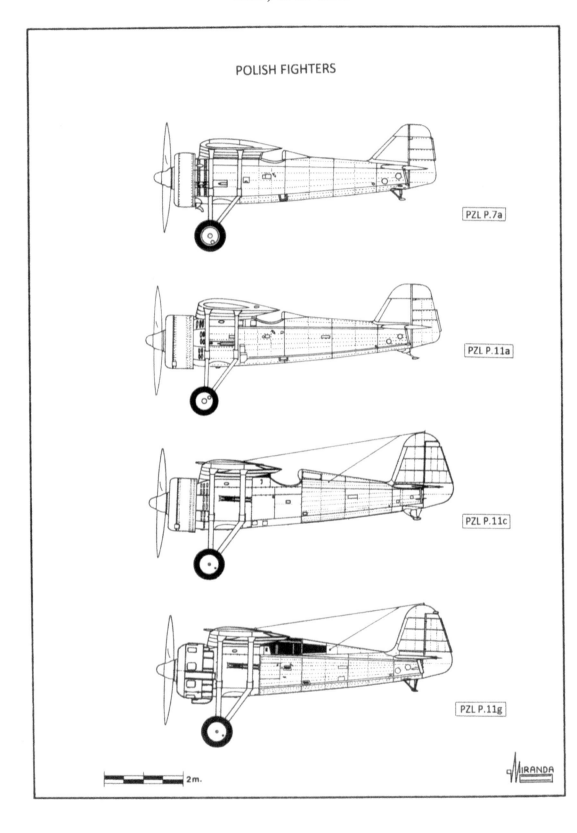

PZL P.7a

PZL P.11a

PZL P.11c

PZL P.11g

2 m.

MIRANDA

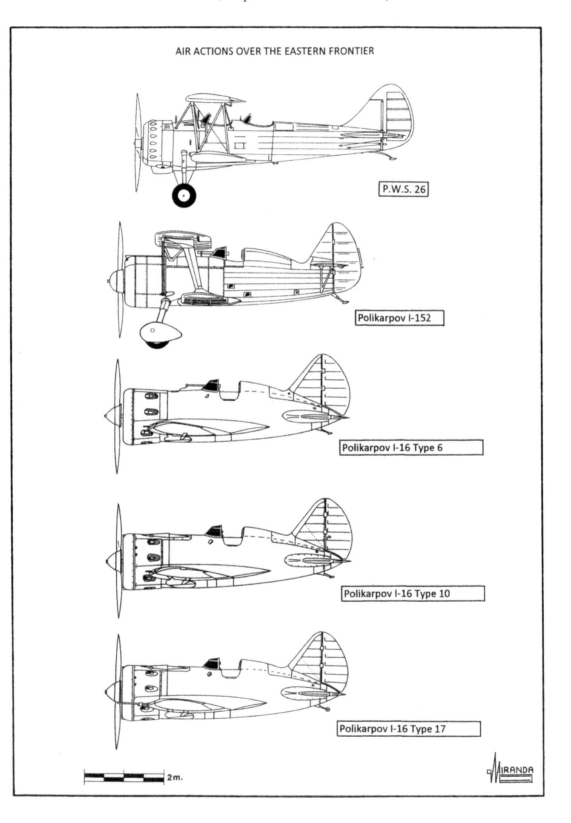

AIR ACTIONS OVER THE EASTERN FRONTIER

P.W.S. 26

Polikarpov I-152

Polikarpov I-16 Type 6

Polikarpov I-16 Type 10

Polikarpov I-16 Type 17

2m.

MIRANDA

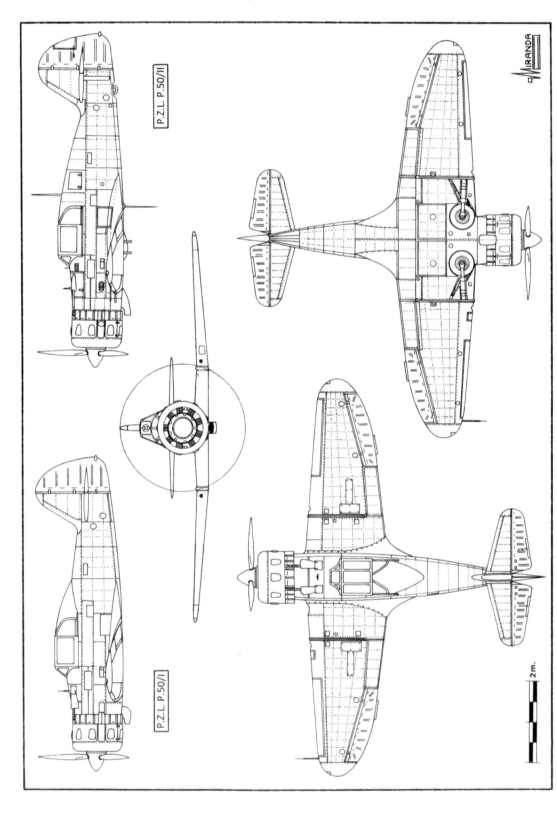

P.Z.L. P.50/II

P.Z.L. P.50/I

MIRANDA

2 m.

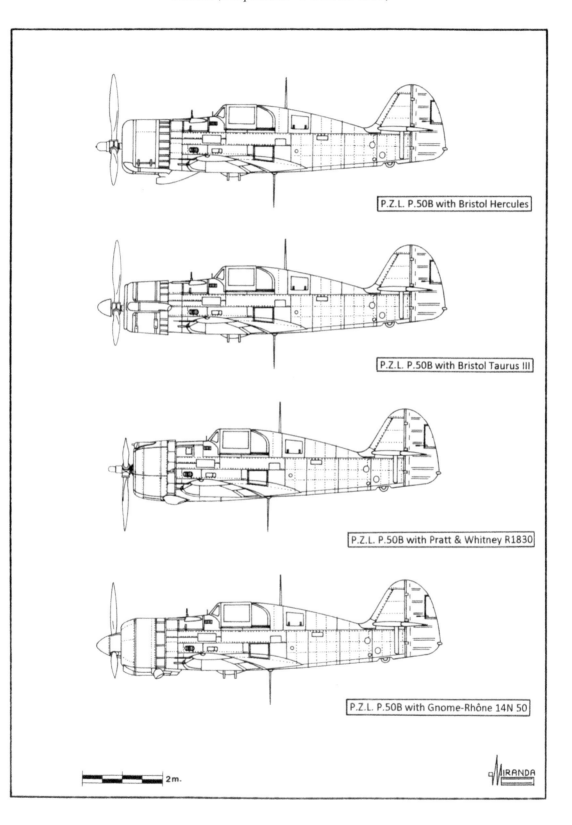

P.Z.L. P.50B with Bristol Hercules

P.Z.L. P.50B with Bristol Taurus III

P.Z.L. P.50B with Pratt & Whitney R1830

P.Z.L. P.50B with Gnome-Rhône 14N 50

2m.

MIRANDA

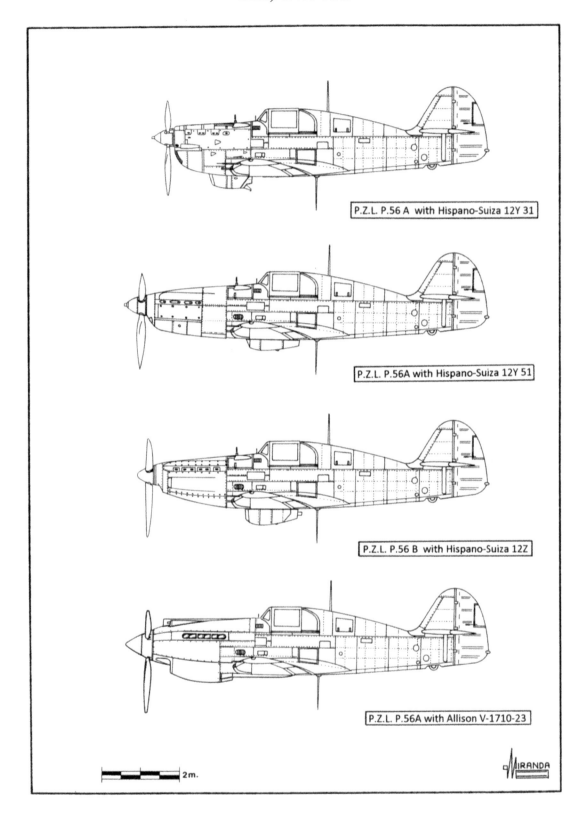

P.Z.L. P.56 A with Hispano-Suiza 12Y 31

P.Z.L. P.56A with Hispano-Suiza 12Y 51

P.Z.L. P.56 B with Hispano-Suiza 12Z

P.Z.L. P.56A with Allison V-1710-23

2m.

MIRANDA

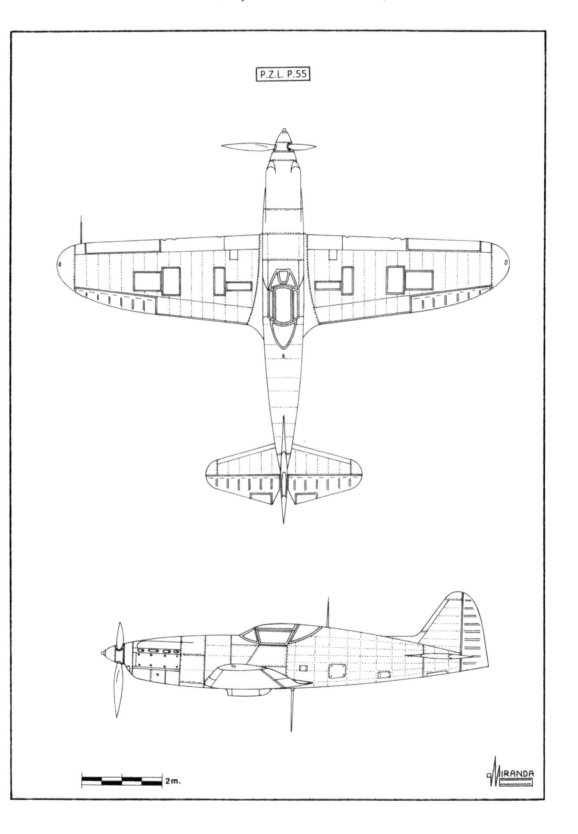

P.Z.L. P.55

2m.

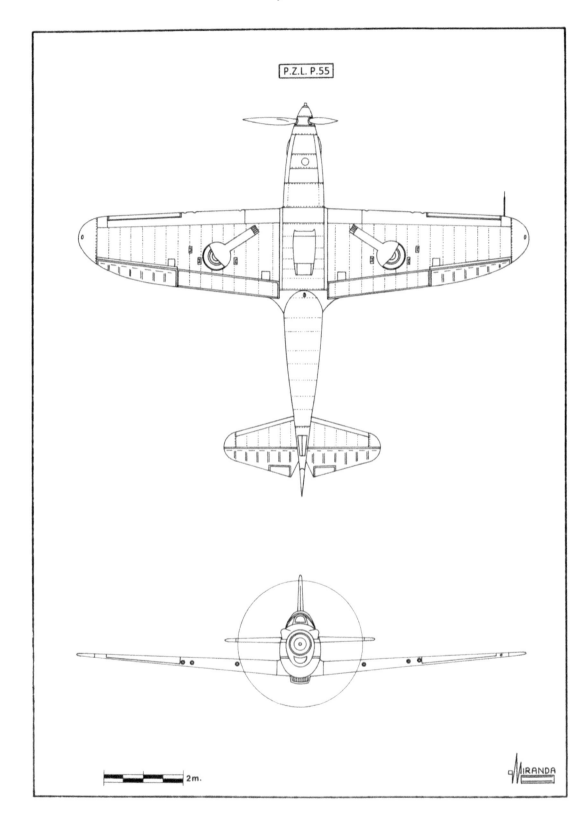

P.Z.L. P.55

2m.

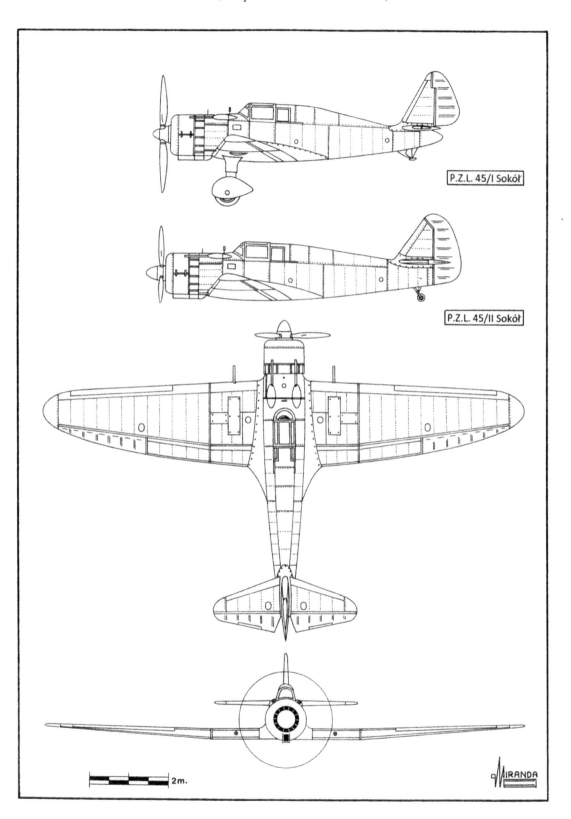

P.Z.L. 45/I Sokół

P.Z.L. 45/II Sokół

2m.

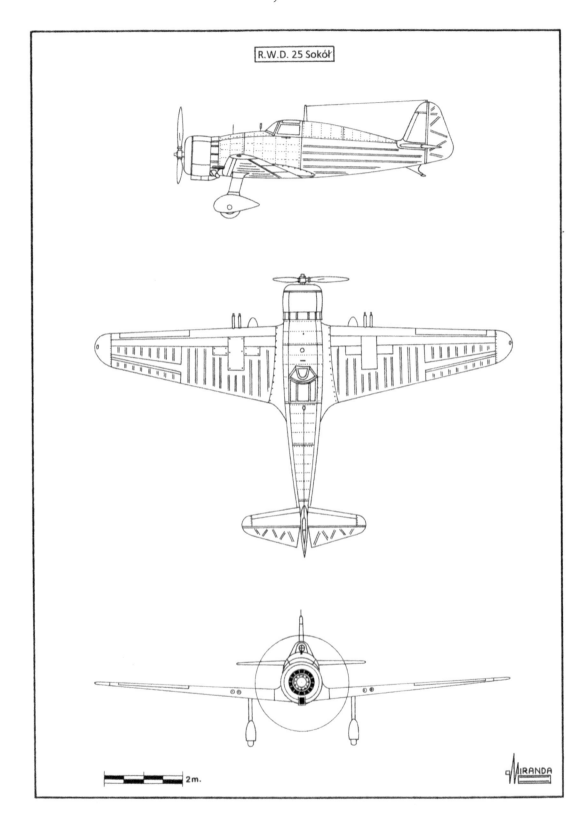

R.W.D. 25 Sokół

2 m.

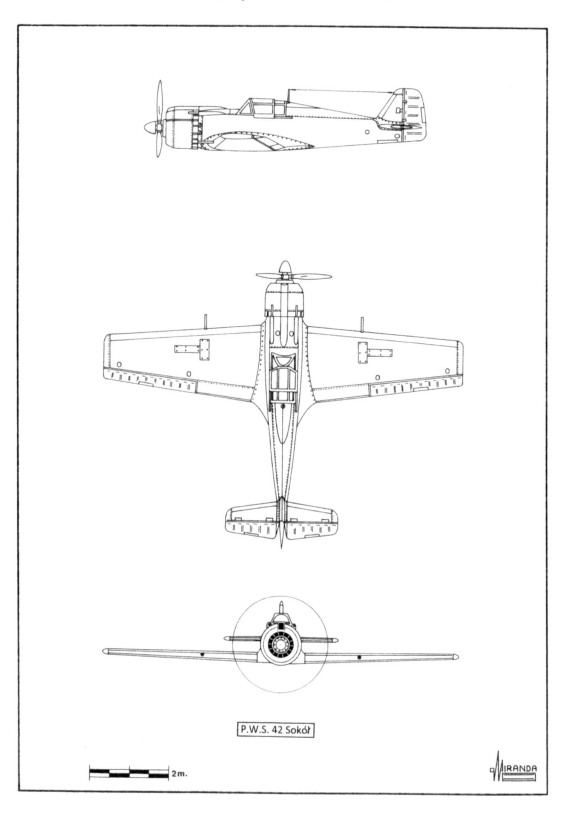

P.W.S. 42 Sokół

2 m.

4

Denmark
(9 April 1940)

After the declaration of war carried out by France and Britain on 3 September 1939, the Germans were forced to invade Norway to secure the iron ore shipping from Narvik.

The plan, Operation *Weserübung Süd*, included the capture on 9 April of the Danish Aalborg airfield in northern Jutland, for refuelling the Messerschmitt Bf 110 fighters. At that time, the Danish Naval Flying Service did not have a single modern aircraft available and had only nine Hawker Nimrod L.B.V. biplane fighters at the Avnø Naval Air Station.

On the invasion day, the four-squadron-strong Danish Army Air Service consisted of forty-five aircraft based in Copenhagen-Værløse airfield: thirteen Gloster Gauntlet II J biplane fighters, eight Fokker D.XXI monoplane fighters, twenty-two Fokker CV reconnaissance/light bomber biplanes, one de Havilland Dragonfly transport, and one Cierva C.30 autogyro.

The main action took place in Aalborg with launch of paratroopers from Junkers Ju 52/3m aircraft, but large formations of Heinkel He 111 from *Kampfgeschwader* 4, escorted by Messerschmitt Bf 110 C-1, also flew over the capital, dropping leaflets to secure the quick surrender of the Danish authorities. After the air show, which was entirely psychological, the Bf 110 of the ZG.1 and ZG.76 carried out a mission of strafing over Værløse, destroying three D.XXI and one Gauntlet and damaging three D.XXI and several Gauntlets.

The *Oberkommando der Luftwaffe* (OKL) had overestimated the danger of the D.XXI because of the publicity given to the experimental installation of two 23-mm Madsen cannons on the J-42 plane in May 1939. The Madsen 23 × 106 mm had a rate of fire superior to the 20-mm Ikaria MG-FF cannon used by the Bf 110 and to the Hispano-Suiza HS.404 cannon used by the Morane MS 406, but its powerful recoil was considered excessive to install it on the wings of a single-engined fighter.

The Danish D.XXI were armed with just two 7.9-mm Madsen machine guns that fired, synchronised with the propeller, through blast tubes located between the lower cylinders of the engine, in four and eight o'clock positions. At the outbreak of war, the Danish armed forces were partly mobilised, and their aircraft received camouflage painting.

The manufacture of a new series of Fokker D.XXI was considered and negotiations started with the Italian Government for the acquisition of twelve Macchi MC.200 fighters in April 1940. The construction under licence of twelve Fairey P4/34s and twelve Fokker G.1 heavy fighters in *Flyvertroppernes Værksteder-Klovermarken* facilities started, but none entered service before the German invasion.

In anticipation of political circumstances preventing the import of the Italian fighters, the naval shipyard *Orlogs Vaerftet* began working on the design of the OV-J-1 *Marinejager*. It was a single-seat light fighter powered by an inverted-Vee, air-cooled engine of the type Walter Sagitta or Isotta Fraschini Delta. It would have been completely manufactured in metal, with retractable landing gear and four 7.92-mm Madsen machine guns. There was also to be a fighter-bomber version, with inverted gull-wing and ventral bomb-rack.

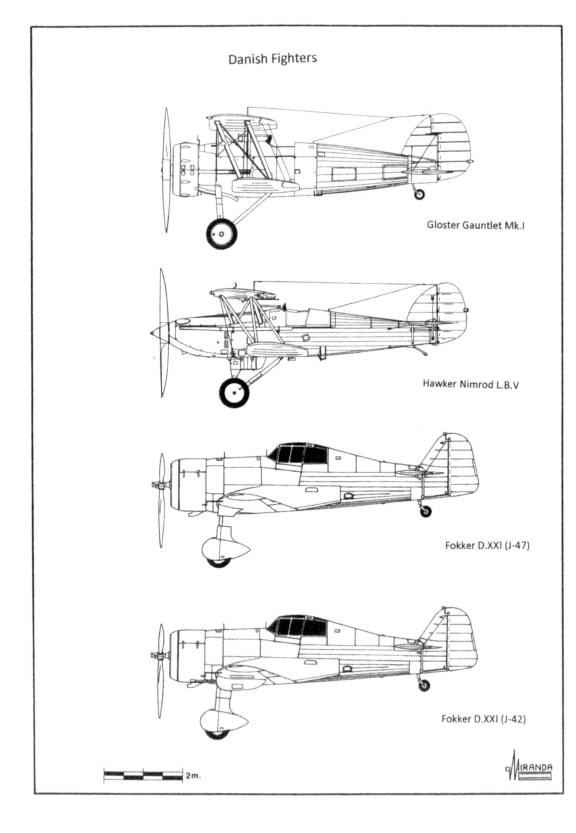

Danish Fighters

Gloster Gauntlet Mk.I

Hawker Nimrod L.B.V

Fokker D.XXI (J-47)

Fokker D.XXI (J-42)

2m.

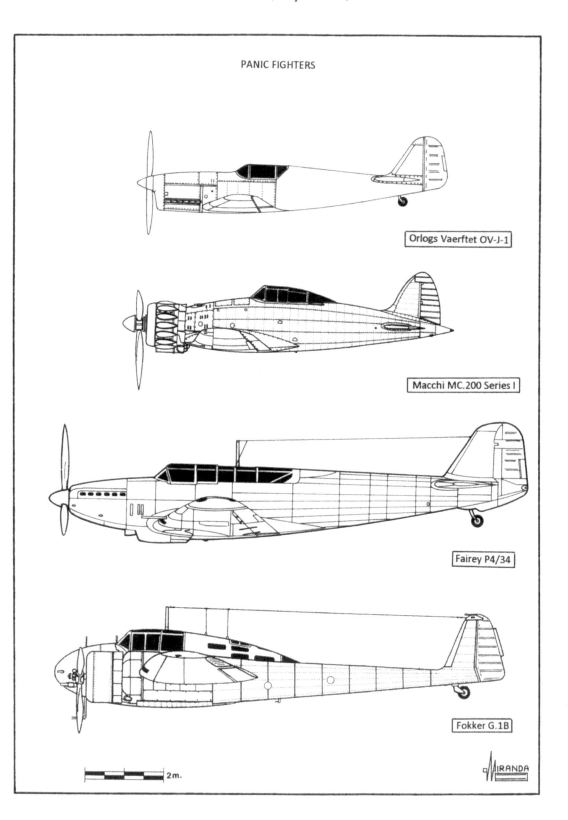

PANIC FIGHTERS

Orlogs Vaerftet OV-J-1

Macchi MC.200 Series I

Fairey P4/34

Fokker G.1B

2m.

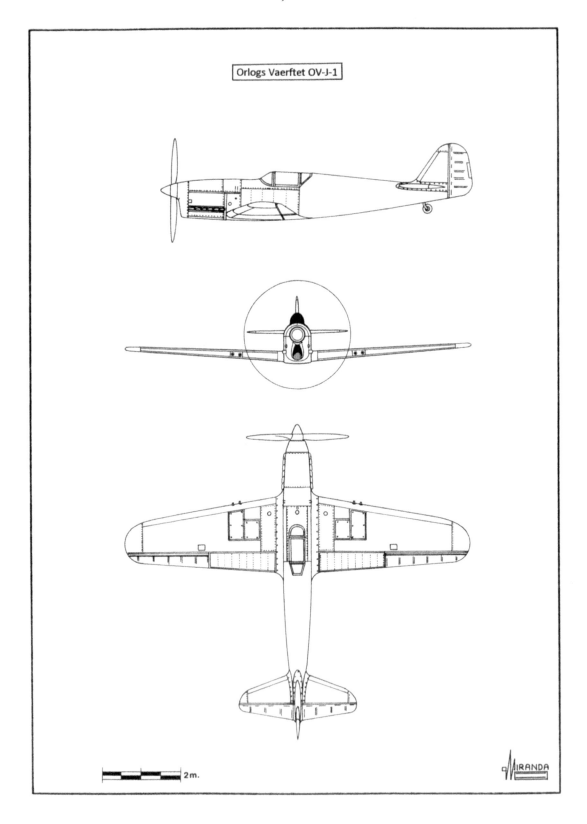

Orlogs Vaerftet OV-J-1

2 m.

5

Norway
(9 April–7 June 1940)

To support the invasion of Norway, Operation *Wesertag*, the Luftwaffe used seventy Messerschmitt Bf 110 C-1s, thirty Bf 109 E-1s, forty Junkers Ju 87 R-1s, forty-seven Ju 88s, 691 Ju 52/3ms, six Ju 52/3m floatplanes, twelve Ju 90s, 243 Heinkel He 111s, twenty-two He 59s, fourteen He 115Bs, twelve Hs 126s, twenty-four Dornier Do 17Ps, and six Focke-Wulf Fw 200s.

The Norwegian air defence consisted only of four Gloster Gladiators Mk I and five Mk II biplane fighters, equipped with skis and two-bladed wooden propellers, four Armstrong Whitworth Scimitars, and one Hawker Fury. Only seven of the Gladiators, based at Oslo-Fornebu and Kjeller airfields, were in combat condition. The other aircraft were all undergoing maintenance and could not be made operational in time.

On the first day of combat, the Gladiators shot down two Bf 110s of 1./ZG 76 and one Ju 52/3m of II/KG zbV1, losing two aircraft in air combat and six destroyed on the ground.

The Norwegian 'panic fighter' was the Curtiss Hawk 75 A-6 *Norske Modellene*. In July 1939, the Ministry of Defence—the *Forsvarsdepartementet*—purchased twelve aircraft with 1,200-hp Pratt & Whitney R-1830-SC3-G engines, then twelve more after the invasion of Poland.

On 9 April 1940, nineteen Curtiss were delivered; seven had been assembled in Kjeller airbase, but none of them were armed and could not take off without start-skis. Four aircraft were destroyed on the same day by Heinkel He 111 H-4 of the KG.4 and KG.26. The rest were captured without ever having come to fly.

In May, the Norwegians were assisted by two RAF squadrons: 263rd Sqn (equipped with Gloster Gladiator Mk I and initially based in Narvik-Bardufoss) and 46th Sqn (with Hawker Hurricane Mk I, based in Skånland).

The Royal Navy also participated in the defence of Norway with two squadrons of Sea Gladiator fighters and one of Blackburn Skua dive bombers (based on the aircraft carriers HMS *Ark Royal* and HMS *Glorious*), which destroyed four He 111s, five He 115s, and one Do 18 over Namsos. On 13 June, eight Skuas were shot down in combat against the Bf 110 C-1 of the I./ZG 76 and the Bf 109 E-1 of the II./JG 77.

The RAF did not have air superiority. The pressure of the Luftwaffe forced them to leave their bases, operating from frozen lakes in poor maintenance conditions and finally losing all their planes during the retreat. Between 9 April and 7 June 1940, the Germans lost 260 planes in Norway: nineteen in combat, eight by ground fire, and the rest in accidents.

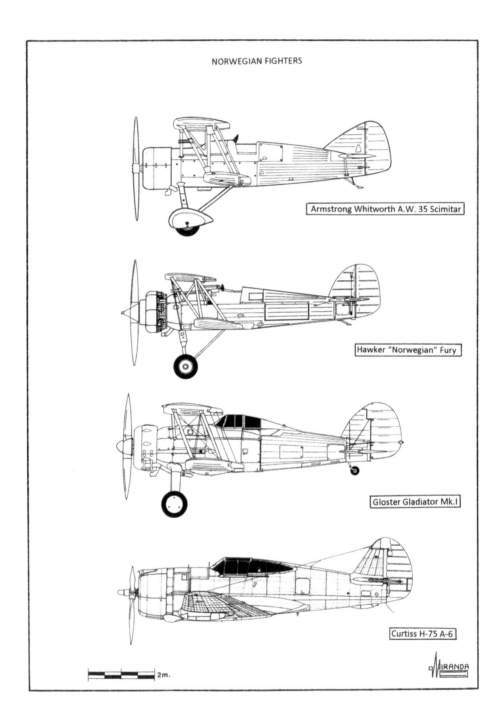

NORWEGIAN FIGHTERS

Armstrong Whitworth A.W. 35 Scimitar

Hawker "Norwegian" Fury

Gloster Gladiator Mk.I

Curtiss H-75 A-6

2 m.

6

Netherlands
(10–14 May 1940)

In the mid-1930s, a design team from Fokker, under the direction of Erich Schatzki, concluded that it would not be effective to build a monoplane fighter with retractable undercarriage using the 600–700-hp engines available at that time.

Calculations indicated that disadvantages in increased weight and mechanical problems would not justify the 3 per cent increase in overall speed that would have been obtained by hiding the landing gear in the wings. In 1935, Fokker took the decision to build the D.XXI fighter, with a fixed undercarriage streamlined to the greatest possible. During flight tests carried out in February 1936 with the FD-322 prototype, it was proved that the drag generated by the landing gear was only 10 per cent of the drag generated by the entire airframe.

The failure of the British prototypes—with which the firms Vickers, Folland, and Bristol tried to comply with the terms of the F5/34 specification, and the success of the Nakajima Ki.27 fighters in Khalkhin Gol—confirmed Fokker's calculations. The Dutch Government did not expect a war with Germany and chose to manufacture the D.XXI—designed to be exported to countries with limited resources—instead of a more advanced fighter for national defence; the projected Fokker D.XXI H (23 May 1936) would have been powered by a 910-hp Hispano-Suiza HS.12Y-45 'Vee' engine with retractable landing gear, one 20-mm HS.9 cannon firing through the propeller hub, and four wing-mounted 7.9-mm FN/Browning M-36 machine guns.

The Fokker D.XXII fighter project was considered at the end of 1937, either with a 1,050-hp Rolls-Royce Merlin II (*Ontwerp* 151, 12 January 1938) or with a 1,375-hp Bristol Hercules radial engine (*Ontwerp* 150, 27 September 1939). The *Ontwerp* 152 was a variant powered by a 1,090-hp German Daimler-Benz DB 600 H engine designed for the Swiss Government.

The D.XXII would be equipped with retractable undercarriage like that of the *Ontwerp* 150 and armed with four M-36 machine guns in the wings and two more on the nose. These machine guns were moved to the sides of the fuselage in the *Ontwerp* 151. The

Ontwerp 152 would have a 7.9-mm MG 17 firing through the propeller hub and four more in the wings.

Again, calculations showed that the *Ontwerp* 151 would have been faster than the Hawker Hurricane Mk I and a suitable opponent for the Messerschmitt Bf 109 E. On 19 June 1939, Fokker proposed the D.XXIV version. It basically was a D.XXI with a retractable undercarriage and either a 1,060-hp Bristol *Taurus* or a 905-hp Bristol *Perseus* radial engine.

During the night of 9–10 May 1940, the Germans began their Operation *Fall Gelb* (assault to the West) that would not stop until Dunkirk. During the invasion of the Netherlands, the Luftwaffe used 180 Messerschmitt Bf 109 Es, sixty-two Bf 110 Cs, 196 Heinkel He 111 Ps, thirty-four Junkers Ju 88s, twenty-eight Ju 87s, eighteen Henschel Hs 126s, nine Henschel Hs 123s, twenty-eight Heinkel He 115s, twelve Heinkel He 59s, fifteen Dornier Do 17 Ps, and 430 Ju 52/3m.

The Dutch Air Force (*Luchtvaartafdeling*) had twenty-eight single-engined Fokker D.XXI fighters based at Schiphol, de Kooy, and Ypenburg; twenty-three Fokker G.1A heavy fighters based in Bergen and six G.1B based in Waalhaven (the latter were unarmed and they were used for training); six obsolete Fokker D.XVII biplane fighters; nine Fokker T.V medium bombers; eleven Douglas 8A-3N attack bombers; fifteen Fokker C.X light bombers; sixty-one Fokker C.V reconnaissance aircraft; and sixteen Koolhoven FK.51 trainers.

The climb rate of the D.XXI was insufficient to intercept the Do 17 P reconnaissance aircraft flying at 7,000–9,000 m and lacked the firepower to shoot down the He 111 in a single attack. It could dodge the Bf 109, thanks to their greater manoeuvrability, but it was not fast enough to reach the Bf 110. Eleven aircraft were shot down in a dogfight in just five days, five strafed, eight destroyed by the Dutch themselves to prevent their capture, and four captured. In return, they managed to shoot down sixteen German planes.

The Fokker G.1A was between 40 and 70 kph slower than the Bf 109 and Bf 110, and it was less manoeuvrable because of its excessive weight. Its powerful armament of eight FN/Browning M-36s could easily destroy any German bomber, but the G.1A often carried only 100 rounds of 7.9-mm ammunition for each machine gun to prevent crashes caused by the weight in the nose. The first Luftwaffe attack managed to destroy eleven planes taken by surprise on the ground; five more were shot down in combat, and two in accidents in the four following days.

On 13 May, three G.1B were hastily armed with four M-36s and joined the combat. The G.1s shot downed four He 111s, six Ju 52s, one Bf 110, one Bf 109, one Ju 87, and one Do 215. In total, the Luftwaffe lost 220 Ju 52/3ms, twenty-eight He 111s, eighteen Ju 88s, six Ju 87s, eight Bf 110s, twenty-nine Bf 109s, six Hs 126s, and two Hs 123s. They destroyed ninety-four Dutch aircraft. From 1935, the Koolhoven firm had tried to compete with Fokker using radical aerodynamic solutions.

In November 1936, it presented the mock-up of an advanced fighter at the *Salon de l'Aviation* in Paris. It had slot spoilers (instead of conventional ailerons), retractable landing gear, and in-line engine, mounted behind the cockpit, driving contraprops via an extension shaft. A prototype was built in 1938 with conventional ailerons and a 9-m wingspan, solely to test the operation of the power system. It took its first flight on 30

June, powered by an 860-hp Lorraine 12H Pétrel, suffering insurmountable problems with the Duplex reduction gear and the engine cooling system. The prototype was destroyed on 10 May 1940 during the bombing of the Koolhoven factory.

The production version, called Koolhoven FK.55—with a 9.6-m wingspan, 9.25-m overall length, and 16-sq. m wing surface—would have had an estimated maximum speed of 520 kph (powered by one 1,200-hp Lorraine *Sterna*) and a 2,100-kg gross weight. It would have had a 20-mm Oerlikon cannon firing through the hub propellers and two 7.7-mm machine guns in the wings.

At the beginning of 1938, the engineer Van der Eyk designed the FK.58, a more conventional fighter able to fly at 500 kph powered by a Daimler-Benz DB 600. However, the Munich Agreement cancelled the availability of German engines, and Koolhoven was forced to start the production of the FK.58 using Gnome-Rhône 14 N-39 radial engines that allowed a maximum speed of 475 kph only.

Historical circumstances converted the FK.58 into the 'panic fighter' that everyone wanted in 1939. On January, the French acquired the eighteen aircraft that had been manufactured, four of them with 1,080-hp Hispano-Suiza 14 Aa radial engines and four with 7.62-mm FN/Browning machine guns. On 22 July, the Dutch Government commissioned the production of a new series of twenty-six aircraft with 1,060-hp Bristol *Taurus* III radial engines, but the British cancelled their export (2 March 1940) using them to propel the Beaufort bombers. Ten more units that had been manufactured by SABCA in Belgium were destroyed by the Luftwaffe on 10 May.

Yugoslavia commissioned the manufacturing in France of forty aircraft and Finland of another forty-six, but the rapid development of the *Blitzkrieg* ended all these plans.

The lack of indigenous aircraft engines was the main limitation of the Dutch aeronautical industry. When Fokker started the design of the successor of the D.XXI at the end of 1937, he made it taking into account that, in any future European war, it would be difficult to access the powerful 1,000-hp engines that were already being manufactured in Germany, France, and Great Britain.

It was decided that the Fokker D.XXIII would be powered by two 500–700-hp engines, making it possible to increase the CAP range using only one of them. A twin tail booms airframe, with a short wingspan and tandem engines, was then chosen to obtain a fast aircraft. This configuration neutralised the gyroscopic coupling of the propellers and the power plant's torque effect, giving the D.XXIII superior manoeuvrability compared to the Bf 110 and Potez 63 conventional twin-engine fighters. The D.XXIII could indistinctly use air-cooled engines of the types Walter Sagitta I.S.R. (528 hp), Isotta-Fraschini Delta (700 hp), or Gnome-Rhône 14 M-4 (700 hp), or liquid-cooled Rolls-Royce Kestrel V (755 hp), Hispano-Suiza HS.12 Xcrs (690 hp), or Junkers Jumo 210 Ga (745 hp).

The project *Ontwerp* 156 was also considered. It was a version of the D.XXIII propelled by two 1,030-hp Rolls-Royce Merlin *II*, which would have been the fastest fighter of its time.

The D.XXIII prototype flew for the first time in May 1937, surpassing the 500-kph and 9,000-m ceiling, propelled by two Walter Sagitta. Hit by a bomb on 10 May 1940, it never flew again.

The construction system of the airframe was the same than that of the D.XXI, but the idea was to use a wing entirely built of metal for the production version. It was armed with two 7.9-mm (synchronised) machine guns in the fuselage and two 13.2-mm FN/Browning heavy machine guns in the tail booms.

In opposition to the 'low tech' policy of Fokker, the De Schelde firm decided to enter the market of the fighters in 1938 with the S.21, a sophisticated twin tail booms design built entirely of metal, spanning 8.5 m, and incorporating a number of innovatory features. It would have been powered by a 1,050-hp DB 600 Ga, twelve-cylinder inverted-Vee German engine driving a three-bladed VDM, controllable-pitch, pusher propeller.

The armament would have consisted of one rear-firing 7.9-mm MG 17 machine gun through the propeller hub for deterrent purposes, four 7.9-mm FN/Browning forward-firing machine guns, and one flexibly mounted 20-mm *Solothurn Tankbüsche* S18-350 anti-tank cannon. During a low-level attack, an automatic stabilising system controlling the ailerons and elevator, the pilot just had to operate the rudder to aim the cannon, which could be set in two positions: horizontal and 25 degrees downwards. The pilot used a retractable periscope to aim the MG 17. The propeller could be detached using explosive bolts when the pilot had to bail out.

The S.21 was expected to have excellent manoeuvrability and flight stability due to the use of fixed-wing slots and the position of the engine, which was installed over the CG. It was decided to change the engine to a 1,360-hp DB 601 Aa, with a turbocharger, in March 1940, to improve performance at high altitude. The prototype c/n 58 was captured by the *Wehrmacht* in May. The production version, with DB 601 Aa, would have had an estimated maximum speed of 590 kph and a 10,000-m ceiling.

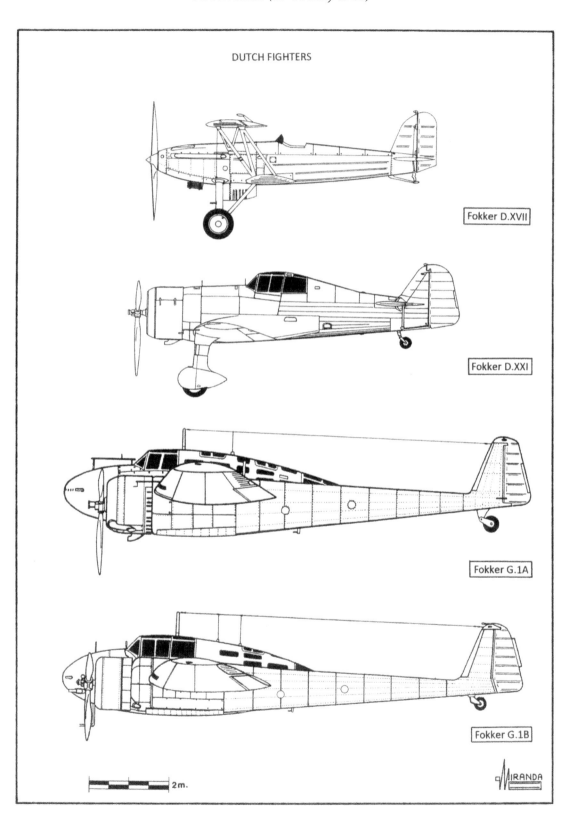

DUTCH FIGHTERS

Fokker D.XVII

Fokker D.XXI

Fokker G.1A

Fokker G.1B

2 m.

MIRANDA

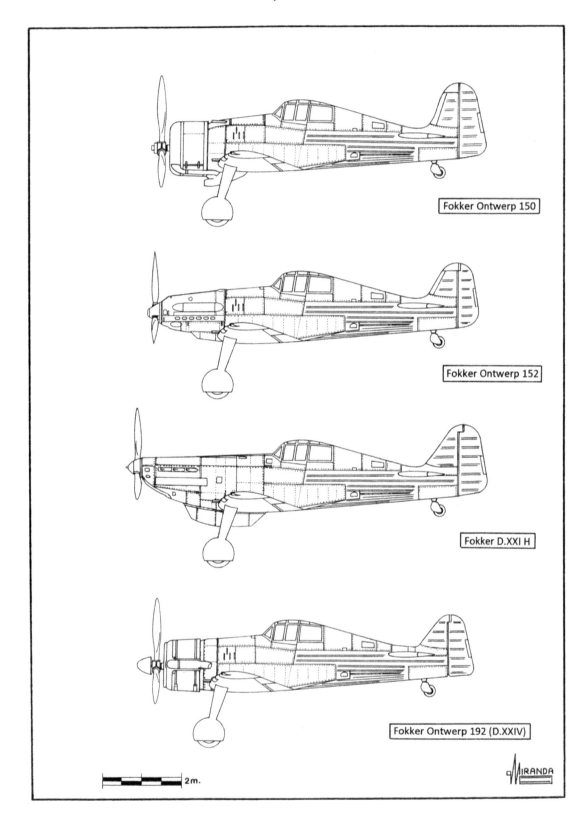

Fokker Ontwerp 150

Fokker Ontwerp 152

Fokker D.XXI H

Fokker Ontwerp 192 (D.XXIV)

2m.

MIRANDA

Fokker Ontwerp 151

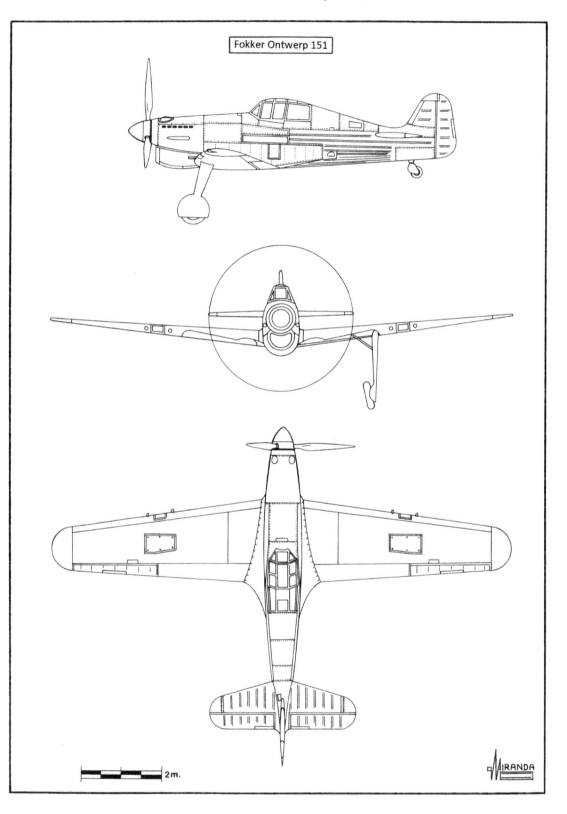

2m.

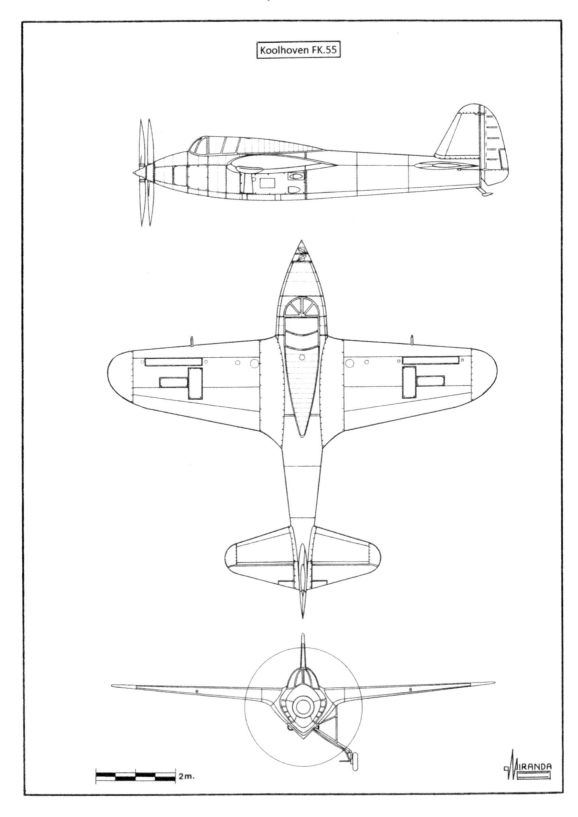

Koolhoven FK.55

2m.

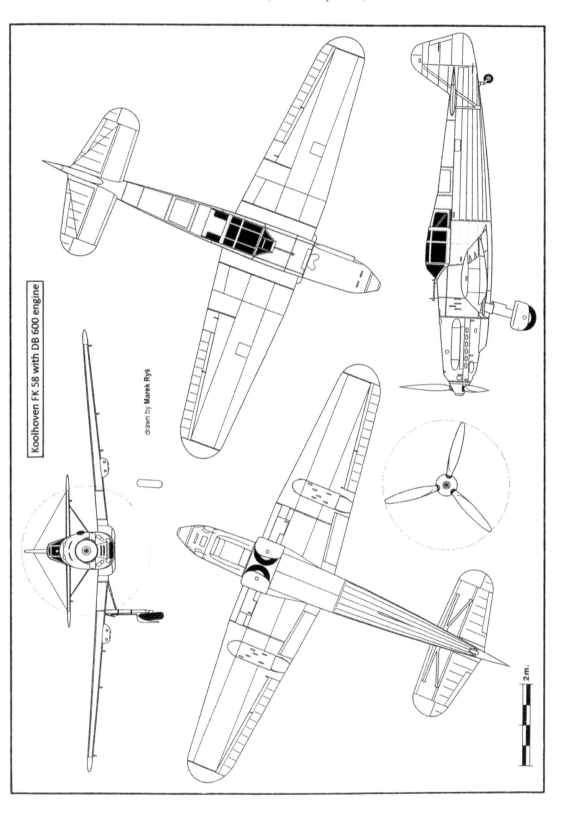

Koolhoven FK 58 with DB 600 engine

drawn by **Marek Ryś**

2 m.

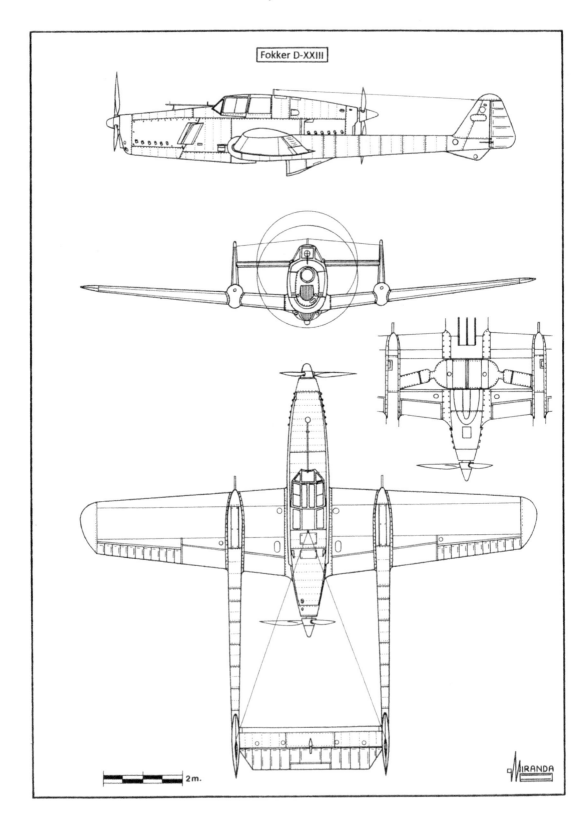

Fokker D-XXIII

2m.

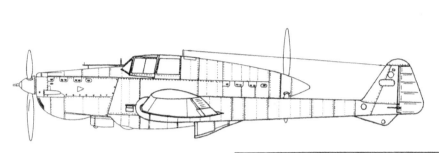

Fokker D-XXIII with Hispano-Suiza HS 12Xbrs

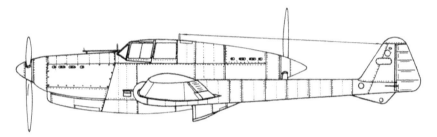

Fokker D-XXIII with Rolls-Royce Kestrel XV-I

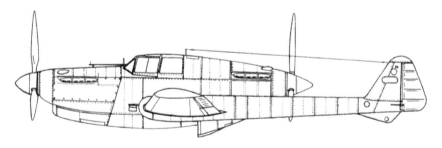

Fokker D-XXIII with Rolls-Royce Merlin II

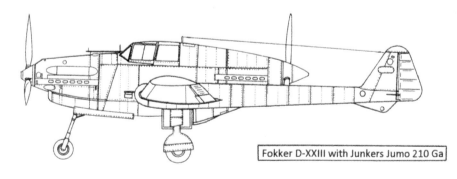

Fokker D-XXIII with Junkers Jumo 210 Ga

2 m.

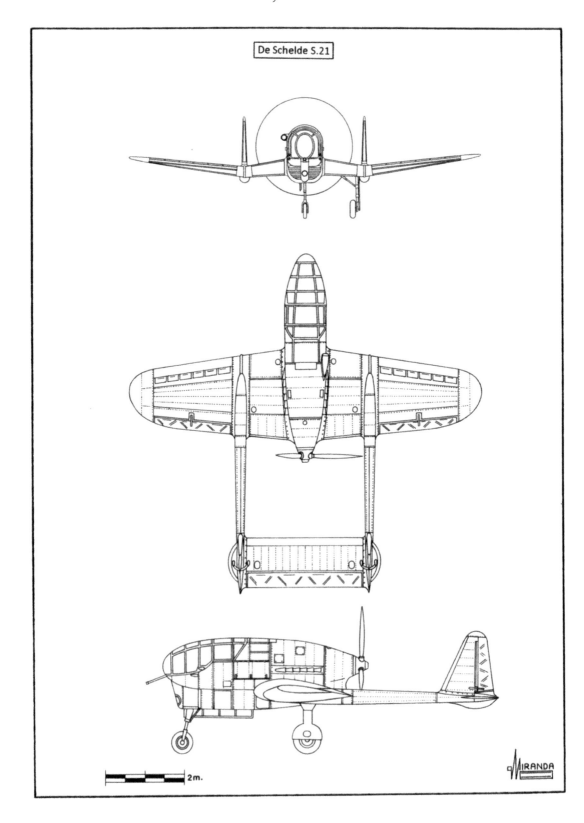

De Schelde S.21

2 m.

7

Belgium
(10 to 28 May 1940)

In the attack on Belgium, during Operation *Fall Gelb*, the Luftwaffe used 1,326 aircraft—202 Messerschmitt Bf 109 E-1 and E-3 fighters, ninety-three Bf 110 C-1 heavy fighters, forty-five Henschel Hs 123 A dive bombers, 151 Junkers Ju 87 B-1 dive bombers, fifty-five Dornier Do 17 Z-1 and Z-2 medium bombers, eight Do 17 P reconnaissance aircraft, 216 Heinkel He 111 P-1 heavy bombers, eighty-four Junkers Ju 88 A fast bombers, 430 Ju 52/3m transport aircraft, and forty-two DFS 230 A assault gliders.

On 10 May, *l'Aéronautique Militaire Belge* had 219 aircraft for the defence of the country, mostly biplanes. The main force of fighters was formed by eleven Hawker Hurricane Mk Is, fifteen Gloster Gladiator Mk Is, and twenty-three Fiat CR.42s, plus fifty-eight Fairey Firefly IIM, Fairey Fox VIc, and Fox VII aircraft that could be used as 'emergency fighters'. The force of bombers consisted of thirteen Fairey Battles and nine Fairey Fox VIIIs. Reconnaissance missions were performed by nineteen Renard R.31s and thirty-nine Fairey Fox III and VIs. Another twenty Fairey Fox IIIs were used in Army cooperation. The German attack took *l'Aéronautique Militaire* by surprise, as they lost 45 per cent of their aircraft and most of its Hurricanes and Gladiators during the first day of combats.

The Schaffen Air Base was bombed by the Do 17 Z of the KG.77, while the Bf 110 of the ZG 26 performed strafing, flying at just 15 m, managing to destroy nine Hurricanes, seven Fairey Fox VIcs, and one Gladiator. The KG.77 also destroyed eleven Koolhoven FK.56 trainers and most of the Fox III in Gossoncourt airfield.

In Nivelles and Knokke-Zoute, the Ju 87 of the 4./StG2 destroyed three Fiat CR.42s and fourteen Fairey Fireflys. In Belsele, the He 111 of the KG.27 destroyed a Fairey Battle. A new attack of the KG.77 destroyed four Fox IIIs in Neerhespen, and the Ju 87 of 1./StG2 destroyed fourteen Fiat CR.42s and four Fox VIcs in Brustem. In air combat, two Gladiators were shot down by the Bf 109 of the II./JG27, three Fairey Fox VIcs by the Bf 109 of I./JG21, a Fiat CR.42 by the Bf 109 of the I./ JG1, and a Renard R.31 by the Flak.

On the 11th, four Gladiators were shot down by the Bf 109 of I./JG21, seven were destroyed by strafing of the I./JG1 in Beauvechain, and three more were lost in Le Culot by the JG 27, together with the last Hurricanes. The auxiliary airfields of Vissenaken, Neerhespen, and Jeneffe were attacked by the Henschel of the II./LG2, with seven Fox VIcs being destroyed. Six Fairey Battles were shot down by the Bf 109 of I./JG27, one Heinkel He 111, and the Flak. A Renard R.31 was shot down by a Henschel.

On the 12th, a Fox was shot down by mistake by French fighters Morane of the GC III/2. The next day, two more were shot down by the Flak, and a third was strafed in the Belgrade airfield. On the 14th, one of the surviving Fiat was shot down by a Bf 109 of the III./JG3. A Firefly, a Fox, and two Battles were also shot down by the Flak. The next day, the Flak destroyed four Fox, a Renard R.31, and two Battles.

On the 16th, a Fox and a Renard were destroyed on ground. On the next day, *l'Aéronautique Militaire* only had seven Foxs, fourteen Renards, and one Battle serviceable. On the 18th, all the Foxs and Battles were destroyed in Aalter by the He 111 of I/KG 54 and the Flak downed another Renard. On the 19th, a Fiat was shot down in Chartres-France; on the 22th, a Renard was shot down by Flak; on the 23th, a Fox and a Renard by the Flak; and on the 25th, another Fox by the Flak.

On the next day, all the surviving Fiat and Firefly fighters retreated to French territory with the intention of continuing the fight there with the long-awaited Brewster B-339 fighters. On February 1940, forty of these 'panic fighters' had been acquired by the Belgian Government to replace the Fairey Foxs of Escadrilles 5/III/2 and 6/III/2 based in Nivelles, but they did not arrive in time to fight and were integrated in the RAF.

In 1936, the engineer Alfred Renard designed the R.36 fighter, a metallic low-wing monoplane, powered by a Hispano-Suiza HS.12Y crs engine and armed with a 20-mm cannon and four machine guns. With a maximum speed of 500 kph, it was one of the most advanced fighters of the time, but the Belgian Government showed little interest in its construction, opting for the acquisition of the Hawker Hurricane. The prototype flew first on 5 November 1937 and was destroyed in accident on 17 January 1939. There were speculations of sabotage.

The series of prototypes continued with the R.38, powered by a Rolls-Royce Merlin II that flew on 18 July 1939. The R.37 was designed as an attack aircraft powered by a Gnome-Rhône 14N1 radial engine, the prototype was captured before its first flight on May 1940 and the R.38 fled to France.

The R.40 was a high-altitude interceptor equipped with a cabin that could be ejected. The pressurisation technology developed for the Renard R.35 stratospheric airliner had been used for its design. The prototype, propelled by a Merlin XII, had equivalent performances to those of the Spitfire Mk I and was destroyed in Tournai-France during a bombing of the Luftwaffe. There were also plans to build the R.42, another high-altitude interceptor, matching two R.40 in a double fuselage configuration with four Hotchkiss 13.2-mm machine guns in the wings.

A fighter-bomber version was foreseen with four 20-mm Oerlikon FF cannons and 500-kg bombs under the central section of the wing. In March 1939, the Belgian Government acquired twenty Hurricane Mk Is with a Rolls-Royce Merlin II engine driving one Watts wooden propeller, to replace the Fairey Firefly IIMs of the II Groupe de Chasse.

On the day of the German attack, only fifteen aircraft had been delivered to *l'Aéronautique Militaire*. By then, the Belgians had begun (under licence) the construction of eighty more aircraft in the factories of Fairey-Gosselies and SABCA-Evere, but only three Hurricanes had been completed by 10 May 1940. The aircraft manufactured in Belgium lacked armour plates and were armed with four 12.65-mm FN/Browning machine guns.

During the Phoney War, a British Hurricane of the 43rd Sqn, with Rotol airscrew, and two of the 87th Sqn were interned according to the rules of neutrality taken by the Belgian Government.

BELGIAN FIGHTERS

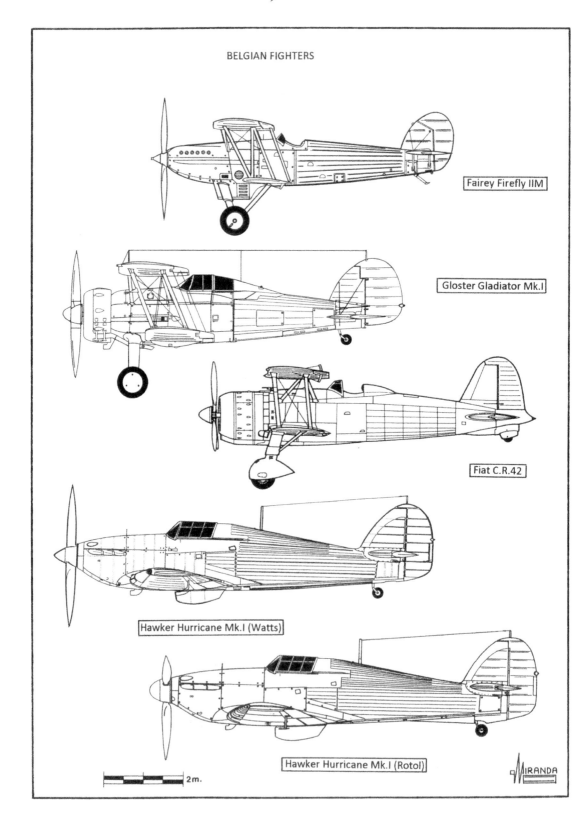

Fairey Firefly IIM

Gloster Gladiator Mk.I

Fiat C.R.42

Hawker Hurricane Mk.I (Watts)

Hawker Hurricane Mk.I (Rotol)

2m.

MIRANDA

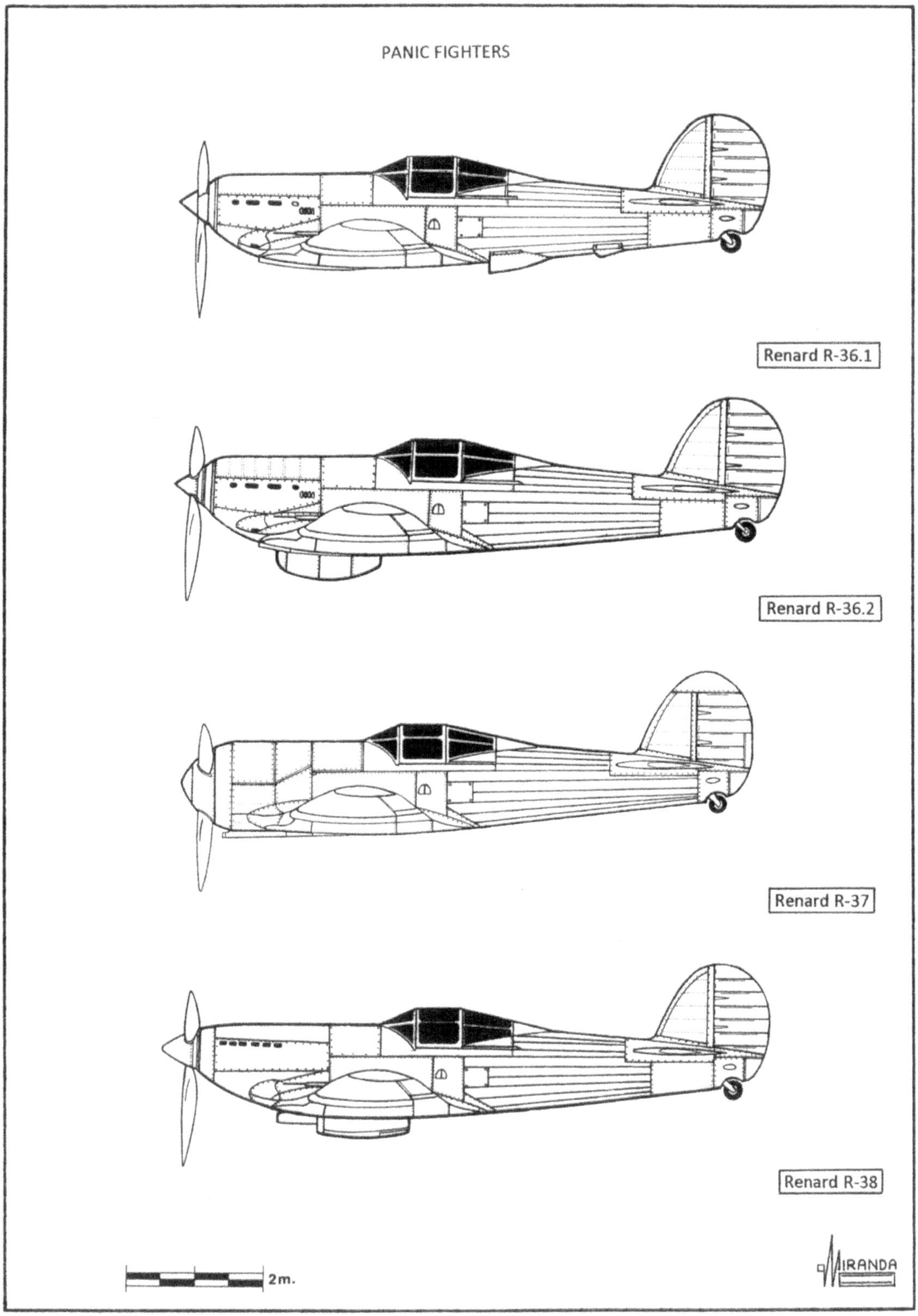

PANIC FIGHTERS

Renard R-36.1

Renard R-36.2

Renard R-37

Renard R-38

2m.

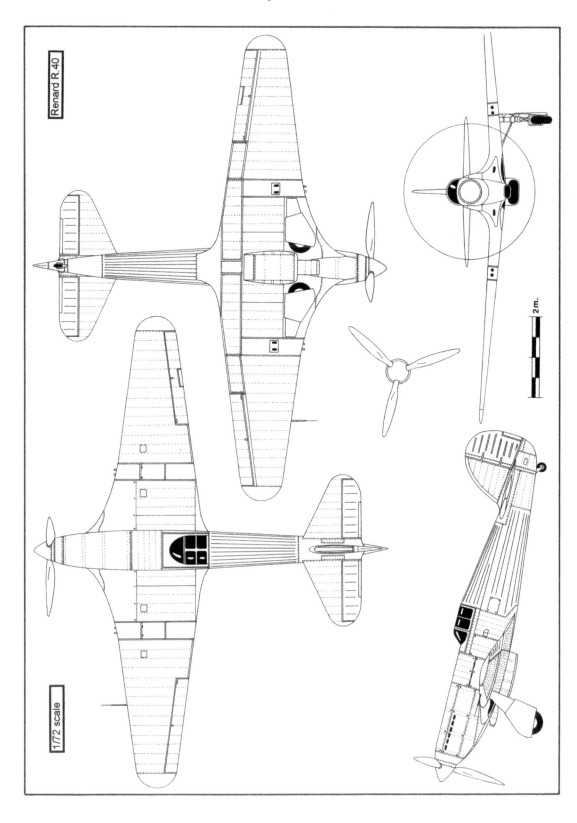

Renard R.40

1/72 scale

2 m.

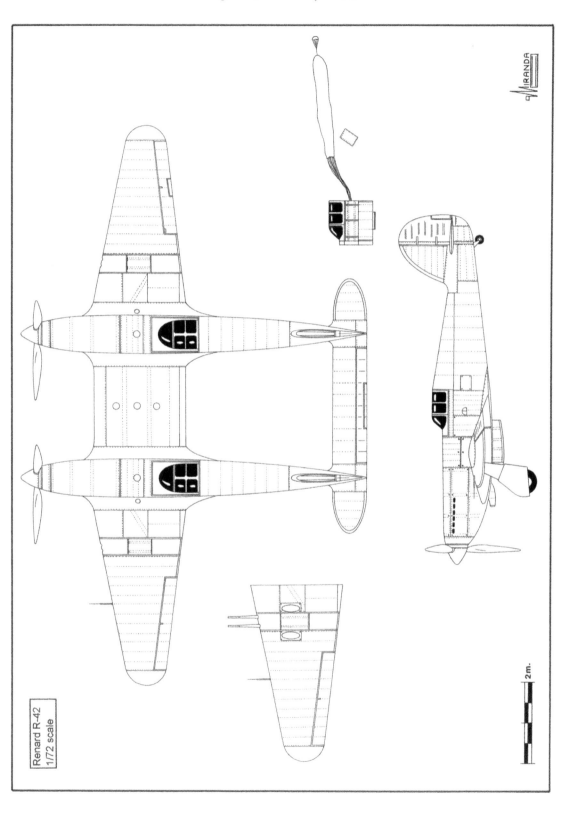

Renard R-42
1/72 scale

2m.

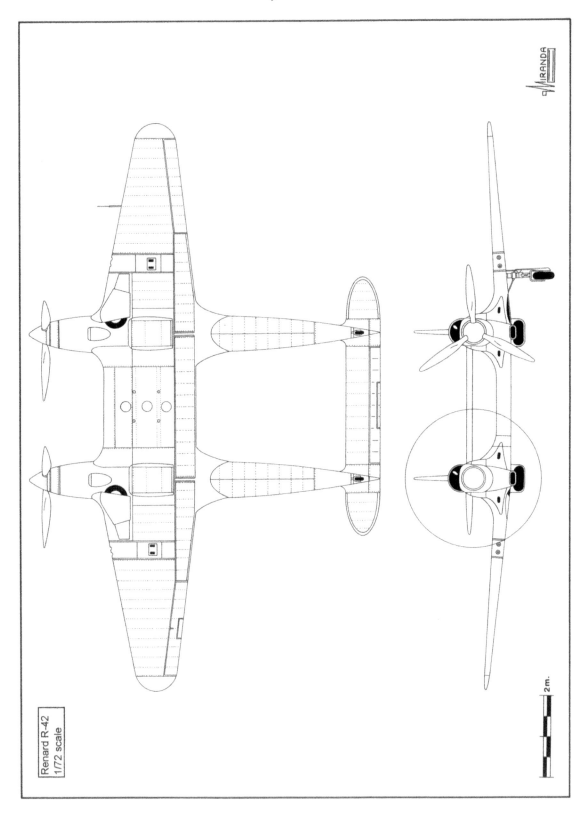

Renard R-42
1/72 scale

2 m.

8

France
(10 May to 25 June 1940)

The best fighter in the world in 1937 was French. The Morane-Saulnier M.S.405 was a single-engined, single-seat, low-wing monoplane with a retractable undercarriage and a closed cockpit.

The production model M.S.406 C.1 of 1939 was armed with a 20-mm gun (a secret weapon at that time) firing through the propeller hub, capable of shooting any German bombers in service. It also possessed enough speed and manoeuvrability to face the Bf 109 B, C, and D of the Luftwaffe using its MAC machine guns.

During the Phoney War (3 September 1939 to 10 May 1940), the M.S.406 made 10,119 combat missions, destroying eighty-one German aircraft. The appearance of the Bf 109 E over the French skies on 21 September 1939 amounted to a technological advantage that gave the aerial superiority to Germans at the critical moment of the *Blitzkrieg* offensive in May 1940.

The French answer was an improved version of the M.S.406—the M.S.410; this was externally different from the M.S.406 by having four guns in the wings, a fixed cooler, increased armour, a more inclined windshield (to house the GH 38 gunsight), a Ratier 1607 electric propeller, and Bronzavia propulsive exhaust pipes. However, it did not arrive on time, and only five 406s were transformed before the defeat.

In 1935, the firm Morane-Saulnier decided to develop a two-seat trainer to facilitate the transition of the pilots from the Dewoitine D.510 to the M.S.405 with a retractable landing gear. The first prototype, called M.S.430-01, flew at 360 kph in March 1937, powered by a 390-hp Salmson 9Ag radial engine. In June 1939, *l'Armée de l'Air* ordered the production of sixty units under the name M.S.435 P2 (*Perfectionnement biplace*), powered by a 550-hp Gnome-Rhône GR 9 Kdrs radial engine, but the acceleration of the production of the M.S.406 and M.S.410 fighters and the acquisition of the North American 57 and 64 trainers in the USA led to the cancellation of the M.S.435.

Foreseeing the possibility of a serious delay in the production of the Hispano-Suiza HS.12 Y-31 engine, the firm considered the construction of M.S.408 C.1 single-seat light fighter, powered by a radial engine GR 9 Kdrs or a Hispano-Suiza 14 Aa-10 armed with only wing-mounted MAC 34A machine guns. The prototype M.S.408-01, with a 10.71-m wingspan, was built using many parts of the M.S.430 and a Salmson 9 Ag engine, but the increasing availability of the 12Y-31 dismissed its serial production.

On 15 June 1936, *l'Armée de l'Air* high command published the Chasseur Monoplace C.1 specification, calling for a single-seat fighter capable of flying at 500 kph at an altitude of 4,000 m, reaching a 8,000-m ceiling in under fifteen minutes. Intended to replace the Morane-Saulnier M.S.406, the new fighter would be powered by a 935-hp Hispano-Suiza HS.12Y-45, twelve-cylinder 'Vee' liquid-cooled engine and armed with one cannon and two machine guns.

Upon learning of the performances of the Messerschmitt Bf 109 B-1 that the Germans had started to manufacture in the fall of 1936, the C.1 specification was amended as Program Technique A23 (12 January 1937), calling for a 520-kph maximum speed and armament increase to one 20-mm Hispano-Suiza HS.404 cannon and four 7.5-mm MAC 34 M39 belt-feed machine guns. Four prototypes were produced to fulfil the requirement—the Morane-Saulnier M.S.450, the SNACAO 200, the Arsenal VG 33, and the Dewoitine D.520.

By January 1938, French intelligence services estimated the Luftwaffe strength at 2,850 modern aircraft, including 850 fighters. In response, the *Ministère de l'Air* issued the Plan V (15 March 1938) to increase the inventory of the *Armée de l'Air* to 2,617 aircraft, including 1,081 fighters, to equip thirty-two *Groupes de Chasse* and sixteen *Escadrilles Régionales*. However, on 1 April 1939, *l'Armée de l'Air* had only 104 M.S.405/406s, one Bloch MB.151, and forty-two Curtiss H.75As; none of these fighters reached the 500 kph.

The M.S.450 prototype was an aerodynamically improved version of the M.S.406. It could fly at 560 kph propelled by a 1,100-hp HS.12 Y-51 engine, but the *Ministère de l'Air* did not want to interrupt the manufacturing of the M.S.410 and dismissed its production.

The CAO.200 reached 550 kph with the same engine than the M.S.406, but its production was also dismissed due to a longitudinal instability revealed during test flights in August 1939. During the Battle of France, the prototype participated in the Villacoublay defence, armed with a HS.404, managing to shoot down a Heinkel He 111 on 15 June 1940.

The Arsenal VG 30 was designed as a light fighter to fulfil the Chasseur Monoplace C.1 (3 June 1937) specification that called for a small fighter propelled by one 690-hp Hispano-Suiza HS.12 X crs engine and armed with one 20-mm HS.9 cannon and two 7.5-mm MAC 34A drum-feed machine guns, from the obsolete Dewoitine D.510 fighters. Anticipating the possibility of a long attrition war, the VG 30 was built in wood/plywood, not to compete with the conventional fighters in the use of strategic materials. It could be manufactured in a third of the time of an M.S.406 for 630,000 F, at 75 per cent of the price of a Bloch MB.152.

On October 1938, the VG 30-01 prototype reached a maximum speed that was 30 kph higher than that of the M.S.406, propelled by a less powerful 180-hp engine. It was estimated that it could fly at 560 kph with the engine of the M.S.406 and the VG 33 prototype (armed with one HS.404 and four MAC 34 M39s) was built with that purpose.

Fifteen days after the declaration of war on Germany, the SNCA du Nord received a commission for the manufacture of 220 units of the VG 33, later expanded to 500.

Deliveries to *l'Armée de l'Air* were to start at the beginning of 1940, but there were problems with the import of spruce from Canada and Romania and only seven planes entered combat between 18 and 25 June 1940, carrying out thirty-six missions with the GC I/55. The VG 33 outperformed the Bf 109 E-1 in manoeuvrability and firepower and was almost as fast with a less powerful 240-hp engine. On 20 January 1940, the VG 34-01 prototype reached 590 kph, powered by one HS.12 Y-45.

In February, the VG 35-01 flew powered by a 1,100-hp HS.12 Y-51 engine and the decision was taken to start the production of the VG 32, propelled by the American engine Allison V-1710 C-15, but only a prototype was eventually built before the German attack. In May, the VG 36-01 flew with a 1,100-hp HS.12 Y-51. The VG 39-01 flew during the same month, propelled by a 1,200-hp HS.12 Z reaching the 625 kph.

The first aircraft to fulfil the specifications of the Programme Technique A23 was the prototype Dewoitine D.520-01, exceeding the 520-kph speed on December 1938 and being declared winner of the contest. In June 1939, the *Ministère de l'Air* made an order of 600 planes (later expanded to 710) that were to be delivered to *l'Armée de l'Air* from the beginning of January 1940. Unfortunately for the French, the deliveries were delayed by problems with the engine cooling, the freezing of the MAC 34 M 39 machine guns, and the pneumatic firing system.

The day of the German attack (10 May 1940), only 228 D.520 had been manufactured, seventy-five of which had been accepted by the *Centre de Réception des Avions de Série* (CRAS), with fifty making their operational conversion into the GC I/3. When the armistice came (25 June 1940), 437 D.520 had been manufactured, of which 112 were in the CRAS for armament installation and 105 had been destroyed by different causes, fifty-three of them in combat.

The D.520 was the only French fighter that faced the Bf 109 E-3 in conditions of equality. However, the scant experience of its pilots with the new model and the accidents caused by the HE 20 × 110-mm ammunition of the HS.404 cannon led to premature explosions within the barrel when firing the second burst. Tests carried out with a Bf 109 captured at the end of 1939 revealed that the D.520 matched its climb rate between 4,000 and 6,000 m (with 190 hp less power), beating the German aircraft in diving, structural strength, manoeuvrability, and firepower.

To avoid competing against Morane-Saulnier for the Hispano-Suiza engines, the Marcel Bloch firm chose the Gnome-Rhône Série 14 radial engines to propel its fighters between 1937 and 1942. Its first design, the Bloch MB.150, was a loser in the Chasseur Monoplace C.1 contest of 1934. However, the publication of Plan V (15 March 1938) allowed the firm to obtain a contract for the manufacture of 140 units of the improved MB.151 model, powered by a 920-hp Gnome-Rhône 14N-35.

During the Spanish Civil War, the radial engine fighters proved that they needed 30 per cent extra power to fight on equal terms with the in-line engine fighters. The MB. 151 had 180 hp less than the Messerschmitt Bf 109 E, was 105 kph slower due to the poor aerodynamic design of the engine cowling, and was only armed with four 7.5-mm MAC 34A drum-feed machine guns, with 300 rounds each.

On July 1939, after some tests carried out in the *Centre d'Expériences* at Rheims, the MB.151 was considered unsuited for first-line duties. *L'Armée de l'Air et l'Aéronavale*

(French naval aviation) mainly used it as advanced trainer at the *Centres d'Instruction de Chasse*. It was eventually used in combat; four were destroyed and one of them rammed a Fiat CR.42 of the *Regia Aeronautica*.

They tried to correct all these deficiencies with the MB.152, using a 1,100-hp fourteen-cylinder air-cooled Gnome-Rhône 14N-49, with a new 85-cm diameter cowling, inspired by that of the Curtiss H.75A, driving a variable-pitch Chauvière 371 propeller. Its armament consisted of two HS.404 cannon and two MAC 34A machine guns installed on the wings. The gunsight reflector was a Baille-Lemaire GH 38.

The new fighter was 88 kph slower than the Bf 109 E-1 in level flight and 50 kph slower in dive but surpassed the German aircraft in firepower and structural strength. Forced to prematurely entering service, the MB.152 suffered several accidents. The engine caught fire in inverted flight due to of a bad design of the carburettor. The deficient pneumatically actuated firing system operated the weapons with delay and did not have enough pressure to operate the cannons at an altitude above 7,000 m.

After the Molotov–Ribbentrop Pact (23 August 1939), the French communists received orders to delay the weapon's production through a programme of strikes and coordinated sabotages. The most affected were the Farman and Renault factories that manufactured the only bomber capable of reaching Berlin and the tanks that could surpass those of the Germans. However, the biggest damage was the chaos created in the manufacture and distribution of aircraft components.

When the Allies declared war on Germany (3 September 1939), out of the 123 Bloch fighters that have been built, ninety-five did not have propellers and half of them had not yet received weapons, radio equipment, or gunsights. At the beginning of 1940, delays in the delivery of the Messier landing gear forced the manufacture suspension of fifty-nine MB.152 fighters. Fearing that the machine guns would fall into the hands of communists, *l'Armée de l'Air* was in charge of the installation, but the process was slow and required numerous modifications.

The MB.152 came from factory temporarily equipped with wooden propellers, 14N-25 engines with the old cowling of 100-cm diameter and OPL R-39 gunsights. Faced with a shortage of Chauvière 371 propellers, many were sent to combat with Gnome-Rhône 2590 propellers (with adjustable pitch in ground only) or armed only with machine guns, due to the delays in the delivery of the HS.404 cannons.

The replacement of the waste pneumatic firing system by Deltour-Jay electro-pneumatic devices, which ensured a more rapid trigger response, caused further delays at the beginning of 1940. On 10 March 1940, there still were fifty Bloch MB.152 fighters without armament and propellers in the *Entrepôt 301* centre. When the German attack came thirty days later, 140 MB.151s, 363 MB.152s, four MB.155s, and one MB.153 with Twin Wasp engine had been accepted by *l'Armée de l'Air*, but only eighty-three of them, considered *bons de guerre* (combat-ready), had been delivered to the *Groupes de Chasse*. During the Battle of France, the Bloch fighters shot downed 146 German aircraft, including forty-five Bf 109 fighters. Eighty MB.152s and four MB.151s were destroyed for different causes.

Worse still was the availability of the bombers, whose priority was lower than that of the fighters. The delivery of the Amiot 350, Bloch MB.174, and Breguet 693 *bons de guerre* to the *Groupes de Bombardement* suffered from inadequate supplies of the Alkan and Gardy bomb racks. Many LeO 45 did not receive the Gnome-Rhône 2590 propellers in time, being destroyed on land without any opportunity to combat.

As a consequence of the disorganisation caused by the sabotages, on Armistice Day (25 June 1940), *l'Armée de l'Air* had 2,348 planes, many more than on the invasion day, even counting losses. Most fell intact in the hands of the Germans.

On 10 May 1940, *l'Armée de l'Air* had five *Escadrilles de Chasse de Nuit* with forty-seven Potez 631 night fighters. These aircraft were operating in sectors of the front that were 15 km wide and 20 km deep, helped by searchlights and sound locators, with one control centre positioning the aircraft by using direction finding (D/F) equipment. Depending on conditions of visibility, a night fighter pilot could see an unilluminated bomber from between 400 and 600 m, and between 1,000 and 6,000 when illuminated by searchlights. During the Battle of France, the Potez 63 managed to shoot down three Heinkel He 111s and one Dornier Do 17.

The failure of the MB.151 and the delays in the delivery of the MB.152 forced *l'Armée de l'Air* to maintain various types of obsolete fighters in service. The Dewoitine D.510, which constituted 70 per cent of the French fighter force during the Munich Agreement, still equipped five *Groupes de Chasse* and two *Escadrilles* of the *Aéronavale* (141 aircraft) at the time of the Poland invasion. At the beginning of 1940, two *Patrouilles de Défense* were still active with forty aircraft piloted by Poles.

On September 1939, one *Escadrille* of the *Armée de l'Air* equipped with Dewoitine D.371 fighters was based in Bizerte-Tunis, and the *Aéronavale* still used thirteen D.373 and D.376 aircraft. When the war started, three *Groupes de Chasse*, still equipped with Loire 46 fighters, were making the transition to the M.S.406. By May 1940, twenty-three aircraft were left in various training schools and sixteen in reserve.

Some old biplanes of the Blériot-SPAD 510 type were returned to service in the *Groupe Aérien Régional de Chasse* at Le Havre-Octeville and in the *Centre d'Instruction à la Chasse* at Montpellier, being gradually replaced by the Bloch MB.151.

The force of fighters of the Air Component of the British Expeditionary Force (BEF) were integrated by two squadrons of biplane fighters Gloster Gladiator Mk I (thirty aircraft) and two squadrons of Hawker Hurricane Mk I; they lost most of their aircraft in the first week of combats. The rest were destroyed during the bombardment of the Vitry-en-Artois airfield.

The Advanced Air Striking Force also had two squadrons of Hurricane Mk I in Belgium, later joined by seven more. During the Battle of France, seventy-five Hurricanes were destroyed in combat, another 120 had to be abandoned to the enemy, due to lack of spares, and only sixty-six returned to England. The RAF also lost nine Defiant Mk I fighters in the Netherlands and sixty-seven Spitfire Mk I in Dunkirk.

The 'Panic Effect' caused by the Munich Agreement forced the French Government to carry out large massive purchases of foreign aircraft, initiating talks with the USSR for the acquisition of Polikarpov I-16 fighters, an operation that was cancelled after a treaty of non-aggression between Germany and the Soviet Union, known as the Molotov–Ribbentrop Pact. They placed orders for 200 Curtiss H.75As and 100 Curtiss H.81s (P-40) fighters to the USA and acquired forty Koolhoven FK.58 fighters to the Netherlands together with the licence to manufacture them in Nevers-France. One Spitfire Mk I was also purchased to Great Britain to study the compatibility of its engine with the D.520.

On March 1940, *l'Armée de l'Air* had eighteen serviceable Koolhoven. During the Battle of France, they were used to equip four *Patrouilles de Défense* piloted by Poles. On 25 June, ten of them had survived the combats.

The Curtiss H.81 did not arrive in time to prevent the fall of France. They were transferred to the RAF, but the H.75A performed well, fighting on equal terms with the Messerschmitt Bf 109 D during the Phoney War and eluding the attacks of the Bf 109 E during the Battle of France; this was thanks to its greater manoeuvrability, but its armament of four machine guns proved to be insufficient to destroy German bombers.

Between both world wars, the size and weight of the fighters was progressively augmented in parallel with the increasing power of the available engines. Against that general trend, there was a minority of aeronautical designers defending the small-sized fighters, known as 'Jockey Fighters' at that time. This type of aircraft, if well designed, could generally compete in performance with the conventional fighters, using a less powerful engine with an important save in fuel, manpower, and strategic materials. They were also easier to maintain and store, and their reduced size and weight helped to increase agility in combat, making it more difficult to be seen by the rear gunners in the bombers or by the pilots in the escort fighters; their destruction required a higher consumption of ammunition.

At the beginning of the Second World War, the conventional fighters used to have 10–12 m of wingspan, operational weight of 2,500–3,500 kg, and a maximum speed of 450–500 km/h. The light fighters of the time could be divided in two categories: 'Jockey Fighters', with less than 10 m wingspan, maximum weight of 1,800–2,500 kg, and the same speed than the conventional fighters; or 'Midget Fighters', with less than 10 m wingspan, maximum weight of 600–1,800 kg, and a maximum speed of 350–400 km/h.

Potez 230

The Potez 230 inherited the most advanced elliptical wing of the time, built with an integral torque box from its ancestor (Les Mureaux 190 light fighter), developed during the 1930s. The philosophy of design of the Potez 230 was based on the Chasseur Monoplace C1 specification (3 June 1937), calling for one high-performance small aircraft that could use some technical elements left aside by first line fighters.

Thus, the surplus of Hispano-Suiza HS.12 Xcrs engines, HS.9 cannons and MAC 34A machine guns coming from the obsolete Dewoitine D.510 fighters could go back to combat without overloading the French war production of HS.12 Y-45, HS.404, and MAC 34 M39 intended for the Dewoitine D.520. Had the new equipment be available in enough quantity, it would also had been used by the Potez 230 as it was compatible to both of them.

A prototype was built in the Potez CAMS factory of Sartrouville in 1939. During a series of tests performed in the Villacoublay test centre in March 1940, it reached the speed of 560 km/h being equipped with an HS.12 Xcrs of just 680 hp (the Dewoitine D.520 reached 525 km/h and the Bf 109 E-1, 575 km/h with much more powerful engines). It was expected that the Potez 230 could fly at 622 km/h after the installation of one of the new HS.12 Y-45 of 910 hp, but it was captured by German forces in June and translated to a technical research centre of the Luftwaffe to study the wing construction system.

Technical Data

Engine: one 680-hp Hispano-Suiza HS.12 Xcrs twelve-cylinder 'Vee' liquid-cooled, driving a three-bladed Ratier airscrew with pneumatic variable-pitch.
Armament: one 20-mm engine-mounted HS.9 cannon and four 7.5-mm MAC 34A machine guns mounted under the wings.
Wingspan: 8.74 m.
Length: 7.57 m.
Height: 2.18 m.
Wing area: 10.97 sq. m.
Maximum weight: 1,800 kg.
Maximum speed: 560 kph.

Roussel R.30

The Roussel R.30 was conceived as a private venture 'Jockey Fighter' in answer to the Programme Technique A23 (12 January 1937) that required a light fighter able to fly at 520 km/h. Construction of the prototype began at Courbevoie, flying for the first time equipped with a 690-hp Gnome-Rhône 14 M7 engine in April 1939.

In August 1939, it was transferred to the *Centre d'Essais du Matériel Aérien* (CEMA) for official trials; as a result of these, it was recommended to install a more powerful engine to better use its excellent flying performances. During the Battle of France, the aircraft was armed with two 20-mm Oerlikon FFS cannons mounted in the wings, and some tests were performed for the installation of a bomb rack under the fuselage.

In combat, the R.30 could have destroyed any Luftwaffe bomber thanks to its high firepower of 2 kg/second, 2.8 times that of the Bf 109 E-1. In ground attack mode, it would have had more possibilities to survive the Flak than the unfortunate Breguet 693 of the GBA 54 due to its high speed and small size. The only prototype was destroyed in Bordeaux-Mérignac airbase during a He111 bomb raid.

Technical Data

Engine: one 690-hp Gnome-Rhône 14 M7 of fourteen-cylinder, air-cooled radial driving a Ratier 1527 airscrew with electrically adjusted pitch.
Armament: two 20-mm Oerlikon FFS cannons and one 250-kg GP bomb.
Wingspan: 7.75 m.
Length: 6.15 m.

Height: 2.10 m.
Wing surface: 10 sq. m.
Maximum weight: 1,766 kg.
Maximum speed: 520 kph at 6,000 m.

Bloch MB.700

The Bloch MB.700 was also designed as an answer to the Programme Technique A23. This small interceptor differentiated from the Roussel in that it was built from wood. This fact made its mass production easier as it did not require strategic materials that could be used for the Dewoitine D.520 conventional fighter. Outwardly, it looked like an 83 per cent scaled-down version of the conventional fighter Bloch MB.152. The main advantage of the MB.700's reduced size was that while equipped with an engine with 75 per cent of the power of an MB.152, it flew 80 kph faster, while still carrying the same armament, and was a more difficult target in a dogfight.

In 1939, a prototype was built in the Blériot Aéronautique of Suresnes, flying for the first time by mid-April 1940. During the flight tests made on 13 May, it reached a maximum speed of just 380 kph, instead of the expected 580 km/h. As a consequence, the Mercier engine cowling and clear canopy were modified, and external plates were installed in the main undercarriage.

The aircraft was destroyed shortly afterwards by the German troops in Buc airfield. There was a plan for a shipboard variant named MB. 720 with a tail hook and the armament reduced to four MAC 1934 M 39 machine guns.

Technical Data

Engine: one 700-hp Gnome-Rhône 14 M6 fourteen-cylinder, air-cooled radial engine driving a Gnome-Rhône variable-pitch airscrew.
Armament: two 20-mm Hispano-Suiza HS.404 cannons and two 7.5-mm MAC 1934 M39 belt-feed machine guns mounted in the wings.
Wingspan: 8.9 m.
Length: 7.34 m.
Height: 3.4 m.
Wing surface: 12.4 sq. m.
Maximum weight: 2,000 kg.
Maximum speed: 550 kph.

Caudron CR.714

On 12 July 1934, the *Service Technique de l'Aéronautique* laid down the *Programme Technique de Chasseur Léger C.1*, a specification for a lightweight interceptor with a maximum speed of 400 kph and armed with four machine guns. The original specification was amended on 22 August, dividing it in two categories: one for aircraft powered by 800–1,000-hp engines, armed with a cannon and two machine guns, and another for 450–500-hp engines and two cannons. On 17 December 1934, the maximum speed rose to 450 kph, and on 16 November 1935 to 500 kph. The winner of the first category was the Morane-Saulnier M.S.405, winning the production of the 860-hp Hispano-Suiza HS.12 Y engines.

In the second category were competing small manufacturers and designers of racer aircraft experienced in obtaining the maximum speed with minimum power, often using self-made engines. The success achieved by the Caudron racers encouraged designer Marcel Riffard to build the C.710 and C.713 prototypes, two wooden, cannon-armed, light fighters capable of flying to 455–470 kph powered by a 450-hp Renault 12 R.01 engine. In December 1937, *l'Armée de l'Air* dismissed its serial construction in favour of the Arsenal VG 30, which was much faster and had a better climb rate.

In November 1938, to meet the requirements of Plan V, *l'Armée de l'Air* ordered the production of 200 units of the CR.714 model, an aerodynamically improved version, with a 450-hp Renault 12 R.03, twelve-cylinder, air-cooled, inverted-Vee engine and four MAC 1934 M39 machine guns. The order was later reduced to only twenty aircraft when all the spruce stocks were assigned to the massive construction programme of the Arsenal VG 33.

In January 1940, the CR.714 were handed over to *l'Armée de l'Air* who used them as advanced trainers at *l'École de Chasse et d'Instruction Polonaise*. The G.C. I/145 was formed during the Battle of France with M.S.406 and CR.714 fighters piloted by Poles who claimed the destruction of four Bf 109 and four Do 17. The formula was perfected with the CR.760 and CR.770 prototypes, powered by 730–800-hp engines and armed with six MAC, but both were destroyed to prevent their capture by the Germans.

Bugatti 110 C.1

On September 1937, Louis de Monge designed the Bugatti Model 100, a *Monoplace de Course* (single-seat racer) to beat the Germans on their own soil in the Deutsch Cup Race of 1938. Underpowered with one 450-hp Bugatti T50 B engine, it was necessary to use one ultra-sleek highly streamlined airframe with forward swept wings, variable geometry automatic flaps, 120-degree V-tail, and retractable landing gear.

To save weight, the engine crankcases were made of magnesium and the airframe mostly of wood with sandwiched layers of balsa and tulipwood. Looking to restore national pride after the exhibition made by the Messerschmitt Bf 109 V13 on November 1937, the *Ministère de l'Air* offered to finance the construction of two special planes to break the world speed records of 634 kph over 100 km and 709 kph over 3 km.

The first was called Bugatti Model 100P (*Poussée*-boosted), with two 525-hp Bugatti 50P, eight-cylinder, straight liquid-cooled engines; two drive shafts; one gearbox reduction; two counter-rotating Ratier S.O.B. airscrews; an 8.23-m wingspan; and a 650-kph estimated maximum speed. The second was Model 110P with two 50P engines boosted to 550 hp; clipped wings with 6.7-m wingspan; and a 750-kph estimated maximum speed. The contract, signed in August 1938 for 6,900,000 F, included two Type 50P spare engines and a bonus of 1,800,000 F if the two records were broken.

In 1939, Germany accepted the 'Propaganda War', flying the Heinkel He 100 V8 at 746.606 kph on 30 March and the Messerschmitt Me 209 V1 at 755.138 kph on 29 April. The French prototype Dewoitine D.551 tried to overcome that mark on 22 November but could only reach 701.5 kph powered by one HS.12 Y boosted to 1,300 hp.

At the end of 1939, the French preferred to concentrate its efforts on the production of 'panic fighters'. Anticipating the possibility of a long attrition war, the *Ministére de l'Air* promoted the construction from wood/plywood of the Arsenal VG 33 and commissioned the design of the Bugatti 110 C.1 (a third-generation fighter of the M.S.460 and D.520T class) with increased wingspan and propelled by one 1,600-hp HS.12 Z or one 1,500-hp Bugatti T67 sixteen-cylinder 'Vee' liquid-cooled engine. Production would be made at the new Bugatti factory in Bordeaux.

The construction of the Model 100P suffered delays caused by the complexity of the transmission, cooling and automatic flaps control systems. On 10 May 1940, the prototype was just nearing completion and was hidden to prevent access to their secrets by the Germans.

Author's Note

A service aircraft would have needed larger air intakes for the radiators and less complex cooling and flaps systems. The magnesium engine crankcases would have been very vulnerable to the incendiary ammunition and the tulipwood, with a breaking strength of 70 MPa, too fragile to stand the tensile strength during a dogfight.

In my opinion, the Bugatti 110 C.1 should have been armed with six 7.5-mm MAC 34 M39 machine guns in the wings (similar to the D.520T installation) and one HS.404 cannon. I believe that the fighter version would have a unique power shaft in starboard position and a flat windscreen to avoid the optical distortion when using the GH 38 gunsight.

Given the decentralisation policy of aeronautical production, started by the French Government in the last years of the 1930s, it seems reasonable to assume that the Bugatti military version would have been propelled by an engine of the same firm; I have been working on the scale drawings of the T67 V16 engine as published at bugattiaircraft.com.

As per my estimations, the installation of the T67 in the Model 100P airframe requires the following modifications: the undercarriage wide track should have been increased to 3.3 m, wingspan to 8.68 m, tailplane to 1.46 m, overall length to 8.33 m, height to 2.16 m, and propeller disc diameter to 1.89 m. Based on all these assumptions, I will try to draw the look that the mythical aircraft might have had.

CAPRA R.300

The midget fighters usually are a good defensive solution when a country feels threatened and needs to quickly increase its production of combat aircraft. The CAPRA RR.20 was a small racer aircraft designed by Roger Robert in 1938 to compete in the Coupe Deutsch 1939 race. After the declaration of war, the project was modified to be used as a fighter-trainer under the name R.30 or as the R.300 Midget Fighter.

Entirely built in metal, the R.30 would be powered by a 360-hp *Bèarn* 6C-1, six-cylinder in-line air-cooled engine, with which it was expected to reach 539 kph maximum speed and 9,500 m service ceiling. The wings, spanning 7.5 m with sq. m surface, would serve as housing for the hyper-sustentation system, the Messier landing gear, and the armament, possibly two MAC 34A machine guns for the R.300 version. Not a single unit was built.

Payen Fighters

Between 1932 and 1942, Nicolas Payen designed a series of wooden canard-delta aircraft with a radical tandem-wing configuration.

In 1933, he built the Pa 100 *Flèche Volante* with small wings called *machutes* and a 67-degree swept delta tailplane, to compete in the Third Coupe Deutsch. The *machutes* had mobile wingtips that acted as ailerons and electrically operated metallic flaps. The landing gear consisted of one centreline main leg retracting backwards and two outrigger auxiliary wheels retracting into the tailplane.

The engine should have been one 180-hp *Regnier* R6 (six-cylinder and straight air-cooled) driving a fixed pitch wooden airscrew, but it was not possible to get one in time to participate in the competition, so Payen had to adapt his project to the only engine available: a 380-hp Gnome-Rhône 7Kd *Titan Major* (seven-cylinder and radial air-cooled) weighting 270 kg, which was totally unsuited for a racing aircraft. It was necessary to install a fixed undercarriage in a more advanced position to compensate the extra weight, and a tail skid. The wingtips ailerons were also changed by others—safer and of a conventional type.

The refurbished plane was named Pa 101 *Avion-Flèche*; it had a 4.26-m wingspan, a 5.75-m length, a 2.2-m height, a 6.86-sq. m wing surface, a 750-kg maximum weight, and an estimated maximum speed of 400 kph. It flew for the first time on 17 April 1935, being damaged in an accident just eight days later.

The Pa 101 airframe served as the basis for a new racer project—Pa 110 CD (Coupe Deutsch). Designed in 1935, it differed from the previous model by its conventional landing gear, which retracted backwards into the fuselage sides. It was hoped that it might be able to fly at 490 kph powered by one 200–240-hp Hirth 508D, eight-cylinder, inverted-Vee, air-cooled engine, but the project was cancelled due to lack of funding.

When the Spanish Civil War began, the Republican Government had great difficulties in acquiring combat aircraft abroad due to the international blockade. In the summer of 1936, Nicolas Payen offered the Spanish communists to build the Pa 110 C.1, the military version of the racer, through the Luxembourgian banker Rosenthal.

The power system designed for the fighter was made up of two 220-hp Renault 6Q-01, six-cylinder, straight air-cooled engines installed in tandem face-to-face. Both engines were connected to the contra-rotating propellers power shaft by means of a Cotal-Baudot gearbox that allowed the electrical disconnection of any engine by means of a clutch.

It was going to have an armament of two 7.5-mm Darne machine guns installed under the *machutes* and one 20-mm HS.9 cannon, firing through the propeller hub, but the French Government banned its export to Spain and it had to be replaced by one 23-mm Danish Madsen cannon. The Pa 110 C.1 would have an estimated maximum speed of 460 kph flying with one engine, and 550 kph with both engines. The estimated range was of 850 km.

The arrival of the Soviet fighters Polikarpov to Spain in October meant the cancellation of the project, which was redesigned as Pa 112 C.1 to adapt it to the Chasseur Monoplace C.1 specification published by the *Ministère de l'Air* on 3 June 1937.

The Renault 6Q were replaced by two 200–205-hp Salmson 9ND, nine-cylinder, radial air-cooled (surplus) engines commonly used by the Bloch MB.81 of *l'Armée de l'Air* and by the Besson B. 411 of *l'Aéronavale*. Proposed armament was either a 20-mm HS.9 or an Oerlikon FFS cannon and two 7.5-mm MAC 34 M39 belt-feed machine guns installed in the interior of the *machutes*, or two MAC 34A drum-feed installed under the *machutes*.

A mock-up using the airframe of the Pa 101 was built in 1938. After being examined by technicians of *l'Armée de l'Air*, the project was rejected at the beginning of 1939 because of the great complexity of the power system. Payen offered to build the Pa 300 instead—a fighter capable to surpass the 520 kph of the Programme Technique A23 if they provided him with an HS.12 Y-45 engine. However, the military, who had done most of his career flying in biplanes, found the *flèche* aerodynamic solution to be too radical and preferred to build the Arsenal VG 33.

To fight these prejudices, Payen built the technological demonstrator Pa 22/2 *Fléchair*, which was captured by the Germans in 1940 while performing aerodynamic tests in the ONERA wind tunnel of Chalais-Meudon. Under the new administration, the prototype was modified with the installation of a 180-hp *Regnier* R6B-01 engine and a new open cockpit with the windscreen of one Arsenal VG 33. It made its first flight on 18 October 1941 and was destroyed during an Allied bombing in April 1944.

The Phoney War ended with the invasion of Belgium and the Netherlands and the German attack against France, using 860 fighters Bf 109Es, 350 Bf 110s, 1,120 medium bombers, 342 dive bombers, and 591 reconnaissance aircraft.

L'Armée de l'Air had only thirty-seven Bloch MB.151s, ninety-three Bloch MB.152s, ninety-eight Curtiss H.75As, 278 Morane-Saulnier M.S.406s, and sixty-seven Potez 631 fighters *bons de guerre*, supported by thirty Gloster Gladiators and forty-eight Hurricanes British fighters. During the Battle of France, 1,279 German, 872 French, and 944 British aircraft were destroyed by different causes.

One of the main reasons for the success of the *Blitzkrieg* against the French and British Armies, in May 1940, was the aerial superiority obtained when the Messerschmitt Bf 109 E-3 entered service with the Luftwaffe. It happened at the right time, when the main French fighter Morane-Saulnier M.S.406 was replaced by the second-generation fighters

Dewoitine D.520 and Arsenal VG 33. During the Phoney War, *l'Armée de l'Air* tried to fill the gap with the Bloch MB.152 and Curtiss H.75A fighters, helped by the British Hawker Hurricane Mk I. However, the Messerschmitt would prove superior.

This seems to be the origin of the commonly accepted paradigm about the assumed inferiority of the French technology. It is not common knowledge that France already had operational naval radar in 1934, and that at the beginning of June 1940, the anti-aircraft artillery defending Paris was controlled by the most advanced radar in the world, able to operate in wavelengths from 80 to 16 cm against the 3.5 to 1.5 m of the British or the 2.4 m to 53 cm of the German radar.

The French scientists were also ahead of their German equivalents in the field of nuclear fission. By early 1940, the CNRS controlled the highest reserve in the world of uranium (8 tons coming from the Belgian Congo) and 200 kg of heavy water from the Norwegian enterprise *Norsk Hydro*.

The French tanks of 1940 had better armour and armament than the Germans. The *Marine Française* (the French combat fleet) was superior to the *Kriegsmarine* in firepower with the *Béarn* carrier and six squadrons of Loire-Nieuport LN.401/411 dive bombers that technically surpassed the German Ju 87.

The destructiveness of the air-to-air weapons installed in the French fighters was slightly higher that their German equivalents, although the quality of the aiming devices OPL 31, RX 39, and GH 38 used by *l'Armée de l'Air* was somehow inferior to the Zeiss *Revi* C/12 reflector gunsight of the Luftwaffe. The following text compares the armament used by the French and German fighters during the Battle of France

MAC 34 (7.5 mm)

Designed and built by *Manufacture d'Armes in Chatellerault* (MAC) during the year 1934, it was the standard machine gun used by the French fighters during the Phoney War and the Battle of France. The commonest model was the MAC 34A (for *Aile*, the French word for wing), which was gas-operated, electro-pneumatically loaded, and fed from a helical pan 'drum' magazine containing 300 rounds.

The MAC 34 was installed under the wings of the Morane-Saulnier M.S.406 and Potez 631 fighters in aerodynamic fairings with the drum magazine housed within the wing. The joining system was of the cardan type and could be regulated for convergence at an affective range of 250 m. The mechanism was very sensitive to cold temperatures and might occasionally cause a great firing dispersion.

The belt-feed MAC 34 M39 (with 500–675 rounds) was developed to solve this problem and reduce drag. It could be installed within the wing of the M.S.410, Dewoitine D.520, Arsenal VG-33, and Bloch MB.155, which all constituted the second generation of French fighters of the war. There was a variant developed for the M.S.406 exportation version that could be integrated with the engine (firing through the propeller hub) and replaced the HS.9 cannon. It was a version of the MAC 34A that was fed with a 500-round drum.

Another variant with flexible mounting, named MAC 34T (for *tourelle*, or turret in French), was used in bombers and multiplace fighters. The MAC 34 had a high rate of fire because of the short length of its barrel. Consequently, the muzzle velocity and destruction capacity were reduced up to a point of being considered an inefficient weapon against the He 111, Do 17, and Ju 88 bombers. The MAC 34 fired the short cartridge modified in 1929 with armour-piercing (AP), armour-piercing/incendiary (API), and armour-piercing tracer (APT) ammunition. In the M.S.406 and MB.152, the three types of ammunition were sequentially stored in the drums and belts: 40 per cent of AP, 40 per cent of API, and 20 per cent of APT.

In the Dewoitine D.520, two machine guns were loaded with AP and the other two with API (a hollowed AP that was then filled with phosphor). The incendiary power of the API was big and its penetration capacity almost non-existent. Additionally, its ballistic features differed from the AP type in the different weight between both bullets. The API was thermally unstable. The heating system of the D.520 weapons had to get disconnected after several cases of spontaneous ignition of the phosphor at temperatures between 40 and 45 degrees C.

Rheinmetall-Borsig MG 17 (7.92 mm)

Designed to be installed over the engine of the German fighters, it should fire through the propeller disk by means of a synchronisation device. Therefore, its rate of fire was lower than that of the MAC 34, a shortage that was partially compensated by the greater capacity of destruction of the projectile, and its higher effective range, due to the use of a long barrel.

It was a recoil operated type weapon designed and built in 1934 by the Rheinmetall-Borsig firm. It used an electro-pneumatic loading system, with belt feeding, and fired ammunition of the armour piercing (50 per cent), armour piercing/incendiary (40 per cent), and high explosive/incendiary (10 per cent).

The latter, when exploding by impact, informed the pilot that his target had been hit and was used to replace the conventional tracers. The Luftwaffe technical staff thought that the tracers were not convenient during dogfighting as they might alert the enemy pilot of the firing aimed to him.

The Messerschmitt Bf 109 E-1 carried two MG 17 over the engine with 1,000 rounds per gun and another two in the wings with 420 rounds per gun, having a total weight of fire of 0.72 kg/second. This disadvantageously compared to the 2 kg/second of the Morane-Saulnier M.S.406 and the 1.46 kg/second of the Hawker Hurricane Mk I.

To balance this situation the Bf 109 E-3 (with a firepower of 2.66 kg/second) entered service at the beginning of the autumn of 1939, replacing the MG 17 of the wings with two MG FF cannons.

The Messerschmitt Bf 110 heavy fighters of the C series also took part in the Battle of France. They were equipped with four MG 17 machine guns with 1,000 rounds per gun and two 20-mm MG FF cannons with 180 rounds per gun located in the nose.

Ikaria MG FF (20 mm)

During the 1920s, the Swiss firm SEMAG committed itself to the design of the 20-mm gun Becker used during the WWI by some German bombers. During the first years of the 1930s, the research was continued by the Swiss firm Oerlikon who, in 1933, started to commercialise three basic models using cartridges of progressive length and power. They were the Oerlikon FFF type (72-mm case length), the Oerlikon FFL type (100-mm case length) and the Oerlikon FFS type (110-mm case length).

The FFS was acquired by *l'Armèe de l'Air* to serve as a base for its own Hispano-Suiza HS.7 and HS.9 designs which were both modified for aircraft engine mounting. The FFL was acquired by the Imperial Japanese Navy (IJN) in 1939 and manufactured under licence from 1941 onwards, as 99-2 Type, to be used in the *Zero-Sen* fighters. The FFF was chosen by the German, Polish, and Romanian Air Forces to equip the Bf 109 E-2/E-3, Bf 110C, PZL P-24 C/F/G, and IAR 80 fighters.

The Luftwaffe version was extensively modified to adapt the original design to the German production techniques, being mass manufactured by the *Ikaria Werke Berlin* as MG FF (*Maschinen Gewehr Flügel Fest*, meaning 'machine gun wing installation') from 1935 onwards. It was the lightest short-barrelled weapon in its class with just 28 kg. Yet it had a lower effective range and power of penetration than the contemporary French and Swiss designs.

These shortages were partially compensated by a higher rate of fire and the introduction of the MG FFM (*Modifizierung*, meaning 'modification'), which could fire the HE ammunitions *Minengeschoss*.

It is unclear if the MG FFM was ever used during the Battle of France. Some authors state that the Bf 109 E-2 was armed with four MG 17 machine guns and a 20-mm cannon located behind the engine, firing through the axis of the hub propeller. As per this version of facts, the 'M' meant 'motor'.

The Bf 109 E-2 passed through some operational tests with discouraging results because of the strong vibrations that the cannon produced in the engine crankcase during firing. Apparently, the decision to mount the two cannons in the wings of the Bf 109 E-3 went against the initial German project that preferred the French *moteur-canon* device. This system was eventually adopted as a matter of urgency after the failure of the Bf 109 E-2 to alleviate the big difference in firepower between the Bf 109 E-1 and the Morane and Hurricane fighters.

The MG FF fired 20-mm ammunition of the twenty 80RB type that could be HE (134 g), HEI (115 g), or *M-Geschoss* (92 g). When installed in the Bf 109 E and Bf 110 C fighters of, it used a sixty-round drum while the Do 17Z night fighters used a fifteen–forty-five-round drum, which could be manually replaced in combat. The Luftwaffe always considered the MG FF a transition weapon to fill the gap until the excellent MG 151 was available.

Oerlikon FFS (20 mm)

A small amount of these guns, together with their manufacturing licence, was acquired by France in 1933. The FFS was not suitable for aircraft engine mounting because of the too-advanced position of the recovery cylinder/yoke unit and had to be modified as Hispano-Suiza HS.7. The French developed the SPAD S.XII in 1916 for the destruction of balloons. It was armed with a single-shot SAMC (APX) 37-mm cannon mounted between the V8 cylinder blocks of the 200-hp Hispano-Suiza 8c engine.

The *moteur-canon* was not very successful due to its slow reloading capacity and excessive recoil shock, and the SPAD S.XII was abandoned, but the French retained the idea until the arrival of the right time. This came in 1932 with the 690-hp liquid-cooled engine Hispano-Suiza HS.12 Xbrs of twelve cylinders in a 60-degree 'Vee' configuration.

This was the right engine to combine with one 20-mm Oerlikon FFS cannon, manufactured under licence as Hispano-Suiza HS.7-mounted between the two-cylinder banks. The crankcase was strengthened and the reduction gear modified to bring the hollow propeller shaft in line with the gun barrel.

The ammunition was the same than that of the Swiss gun, contained in a sixty-round drum. The HS.7 was heavier due to the fixation system to the engine and had a rate of fire of just 350 rpm (compared to the 470 rpm of the Oerlikon) to protect the engine from any destructive vibration. This engine was then known as Hispano-Suiza 12 Xcrs ('c' for *canon*, meaning 'cannon') and had reduced its power to 680 hp as a consequence of the modifications made in the gearbox. The new *moteur-canon* was installed in the Dewoitine D.510 fighter and in the Loire-Nieuport LN.401/411 dive bombers of *l'Aeronavale*, which fought the panzers on 15 May 1940.

The Germans tried to use the *moteur-canon* system with their Bf 109 V4, C-2, and E-2 fighters, trying different combinations of Jumo 210 and Daimler Benz 601 engines with MG 17 machine guns and MG FF cannons. However, they found insoluble problems of cooling and crankcase destructive vibrations. On October 1940, they finally adapted an MG FF cannon behind the DB 601N engine of the Bf 109 F-0, but the device suffered structural damages during tests. The problem could not be solved until the MG 151/20 gun was available and could be installed in the Bf 109 F-2 in March 1941.

Hispano-Suiza HS.9 (20 mm)

In 1935, a 900-hp improved version of the HS.12 Xcrs engine appeared, known as Hispano-Suiza HS.12 Ycrs. The integrated cannon was also an improved version of the HS.7, although it was somehow lighter and with a 420-round-per-minute rate of fire but maintaining the same muzzle velocity and destructive power than the Oerlikon. It fired the same type of HE, HET, and AP ammunition as the Oerlikon, stored in a sixty-round drum.

The HE type model 1936 was identified by a yellow band, the HET of 1939 with a yellow and blue band, and the AP was overall painted in black. The HE had a 1937 model 17/19 B impact fuse and the HET also had a self-destruction system. The *moteur-canon* was very successful in the market, being acquired by the Czech Air Force to equip their Avia B-534, B-536, and B-135 fighters and by the Yugoslavian Air Force for their Ikarus IK-2 and Rogožarski IK-3. It was also used by *l'Armèe de l'Air* to power the Morane-Saulnier M.S.405.

Hispano-Suiza HS.404 (20 mm)

After the experience in combat against the fast and well-armoured He 111 and Do 17 German bombers obtained during the Spanish Civil War, the engine designer Mark Birkigt decided to develop the HS.404 with higher performance. It was gas-operated with a 166-per-cent higher rate of fire and a muzzle velocity of 880 m/second compared to the 820 m/second of the HS.9. The new weapon entered service in 1939 and could be installed either in the HS.12 Y-31 engines of the M.S.406 or in the HS.12 Y-45 of the Dewoitine D.520, MB.155, and Arsenal VG 33 fighters.

The HS.404 fired 20 × 110-mm ammunition (that was not interchangeable with the 20 × 110-mm RB cartridges of the H.S .9) stored in a 60 rounds drum. There were six different types: HE model 1938 or 1939 (130 g) with a 17/19B 1938 model fuse identified by a yellow band, HET identified by a yellow and a blue-grey band, AP (165 g) black projectile with a red band, APT with black nose and metal-grey-metal-red bands, AP/HE with red-yellow-green bands, and HEI with red-yellow-blue bands.

This type of ammunition had not been sufficiently tested and caused several accidents during combat. The Dewoitines D.520 of the GCI/3 were specially affected, experiencing premature explosions within the barrel when firing the second burst. Between 5 and 8 June 1940, the M.S.406 of the GCI/6, GCII/2 and GCIII/7 were used in ground attack task against the German tanks with AP and APT ammunition.

The manufacturing of the HS.404 was slow and costly. At the beginning of the war, only 928 units had been delivered to *l'Armée de l'Air*, and in March 1940, there were 2,319 units available.

The HS.404 was a formidable weapon when integrated in a Hispano-Suiza engine or installed in the nose of the twin-engined Potez 631 fighters. However, it was less resilient when installed in the wings of the Bloch fighters, causing different problems of vibration, stoppage, freezing, and dispersion of firing.

The HS.404 was acquired by the RAF and manufactured under licence in the United Kingdom as Hispano-Suiza Mk I, Mk II, and Mk V, and as Hispano AN/M2 in the USA. A version over flexible mounting was also manufactured to be used by the rear gunners of the French medium bombers LeO 451 and Amiot 354.

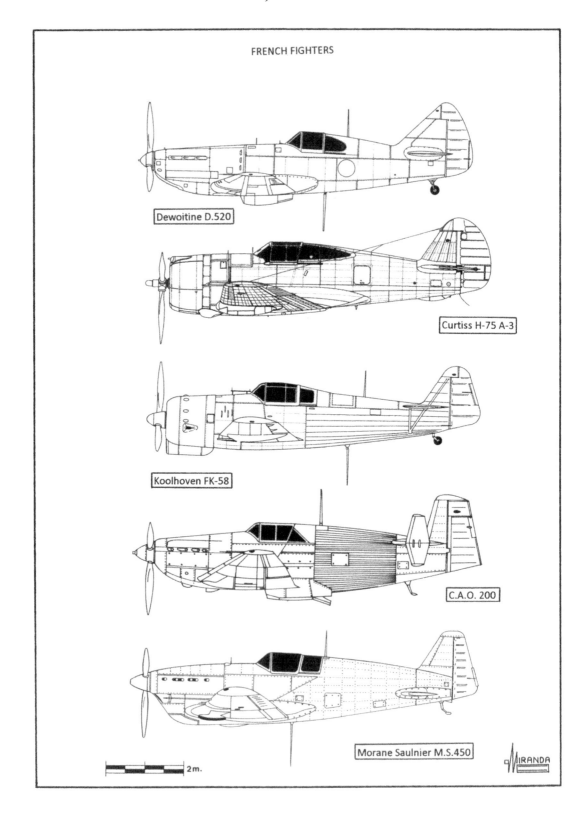

FRENCH FIGHTERS

Dewoitine D.520

Curtiss H-75 A-3

Koolhoven FK-58

C.A.O. 200

Morane Saulnier M.S.450

2m.

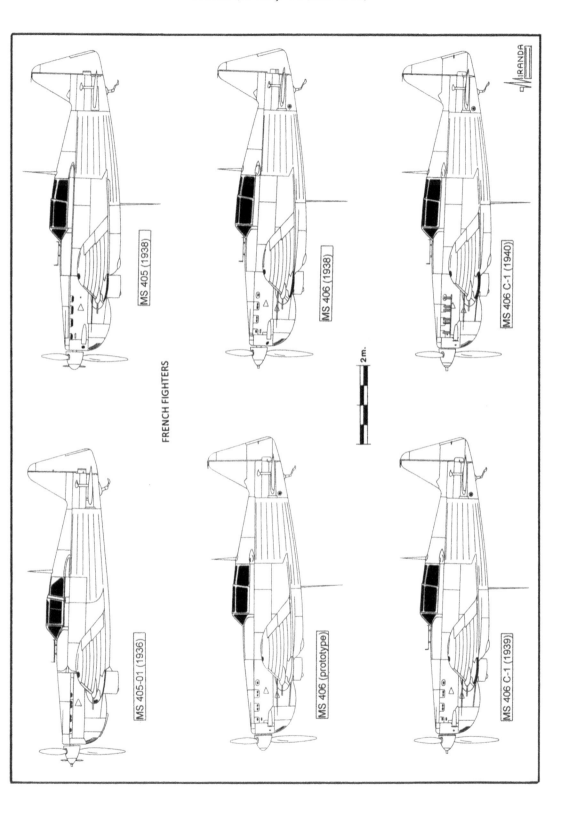

FRENCH FIGHTERS

MS 405 (1938)

MS 406 (1938)

MS 406 C-1 (1940)

MS 405-01 (1936)

MS 406 (prototype)

MS 406 C-1 (1939)

2 m.

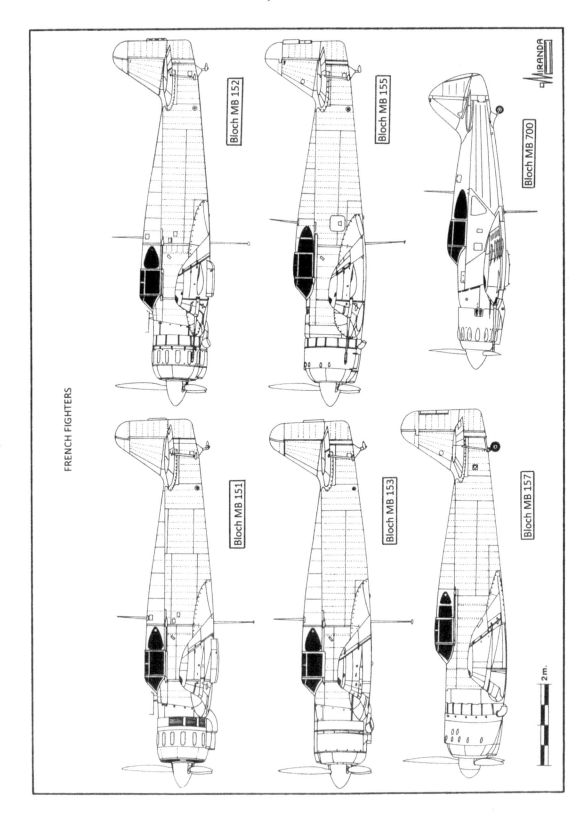

FRENCH FIGHTERS

Bloch MB 152

Bloch MB 155

Bloch MB 700

Bloch MB 151

Bloch MB 153

Bloch MB 157

2 m.

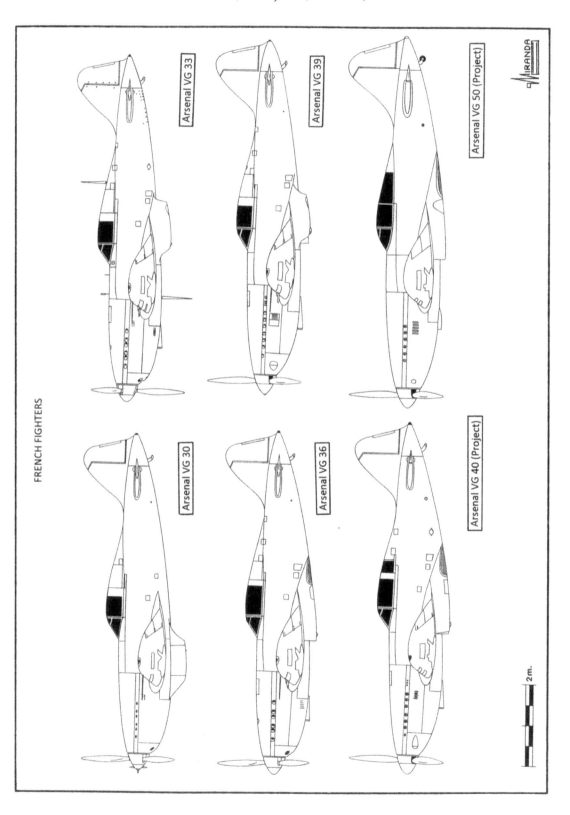

FRENCH FIGHTERS

Arsenal VG 33

Arsenal VG 39

Arsenal VG 50 (Project)

Arsenal VG 30

Arsenal VG 36

Arsenal VG 40 (Project)

2 m.

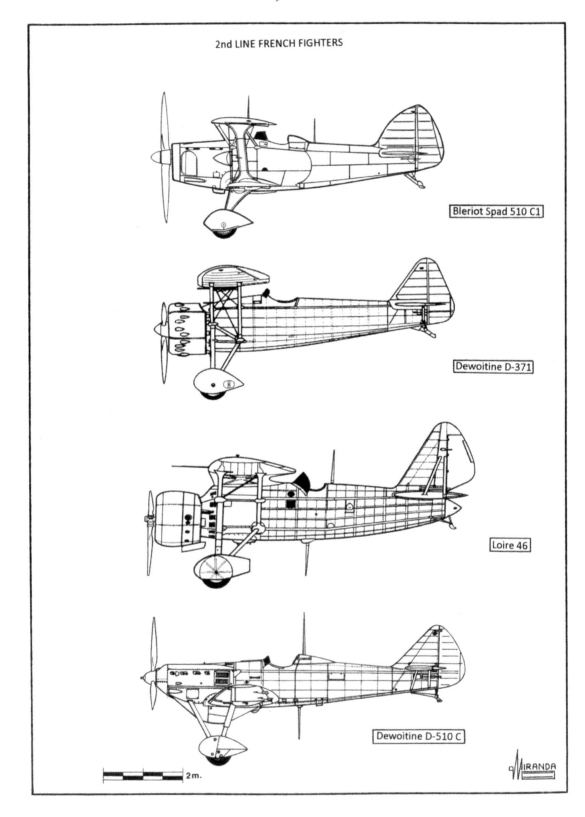

2nd LINE FRENCH FIGHTERS

Bleriot Spad 510 C1

Dewoitine D-371

Loire 46

Dewoitine D-510 C

2 m.

2nd LINE FRENCH FIGHTERS

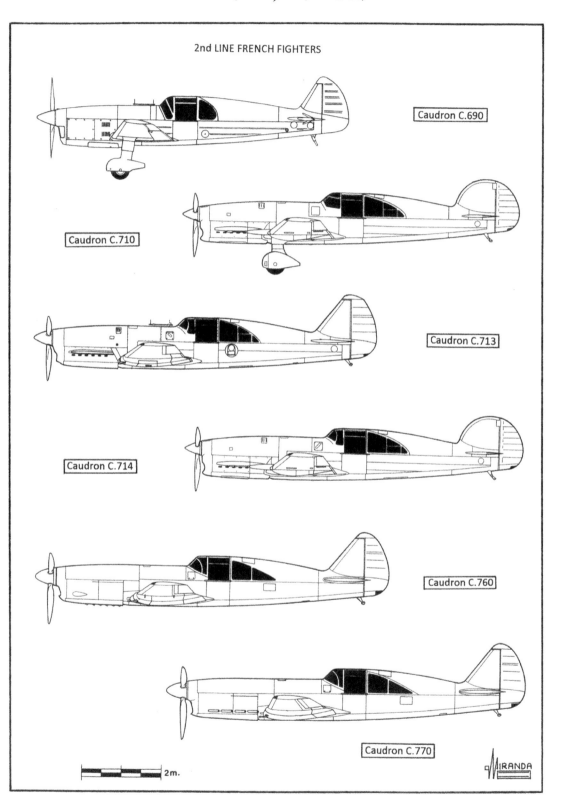

Caudron C.690

Caudron C.710

Caudron C.713

Caudron C.714

Caudron C.760

Caudron C.770

2m.

MIRANDA

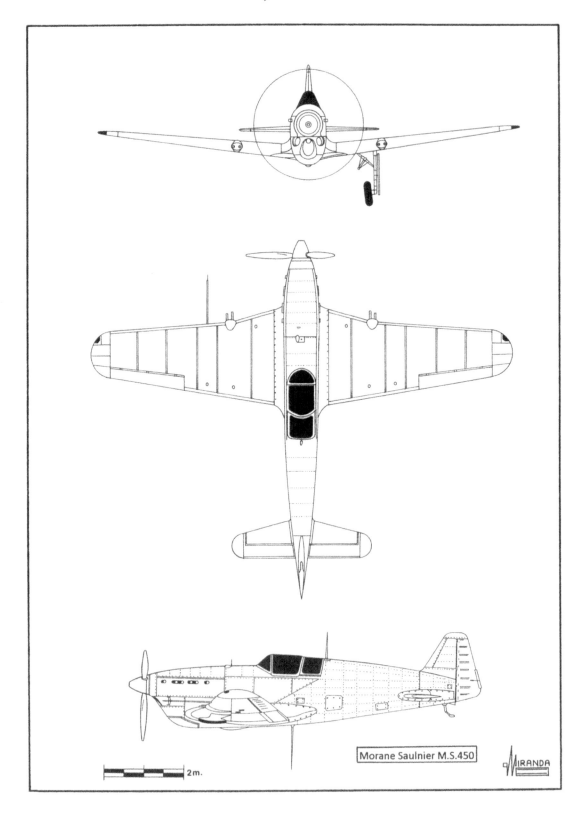

Morane Saulnier M.S.450

2 m.

C.A.O. 200

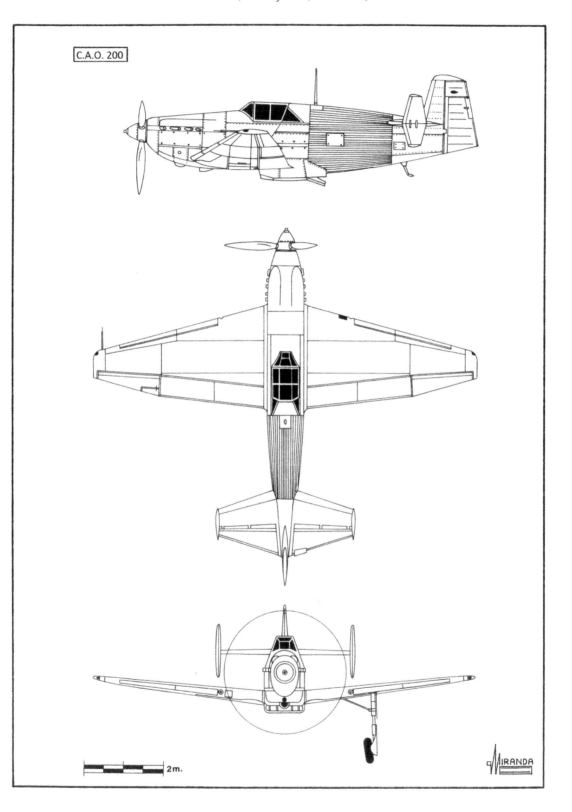

2m.

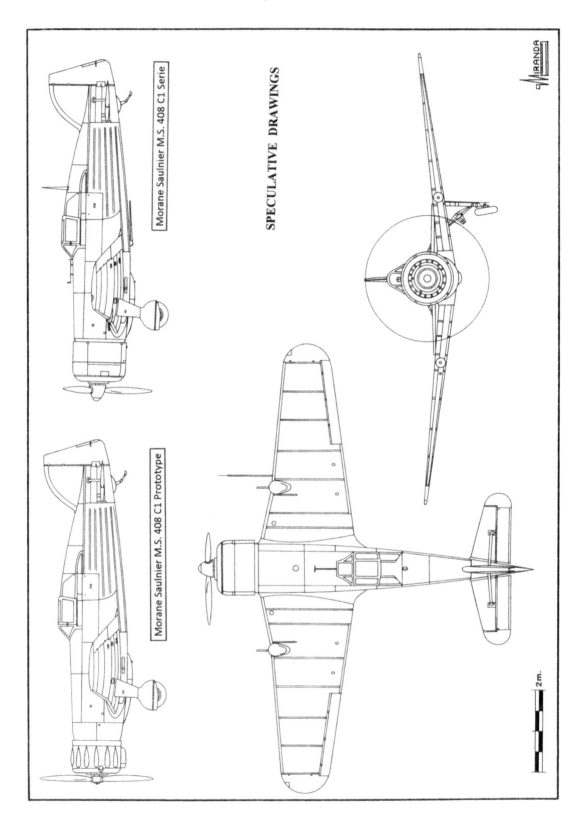

SPECULATIVE DRAWINGS

Morane Saulnier M.S. 408 C1 Serie

Morane Saulnier M.S. 408 C1 Prototype

2 m.

C.A.P.R.A. R.30

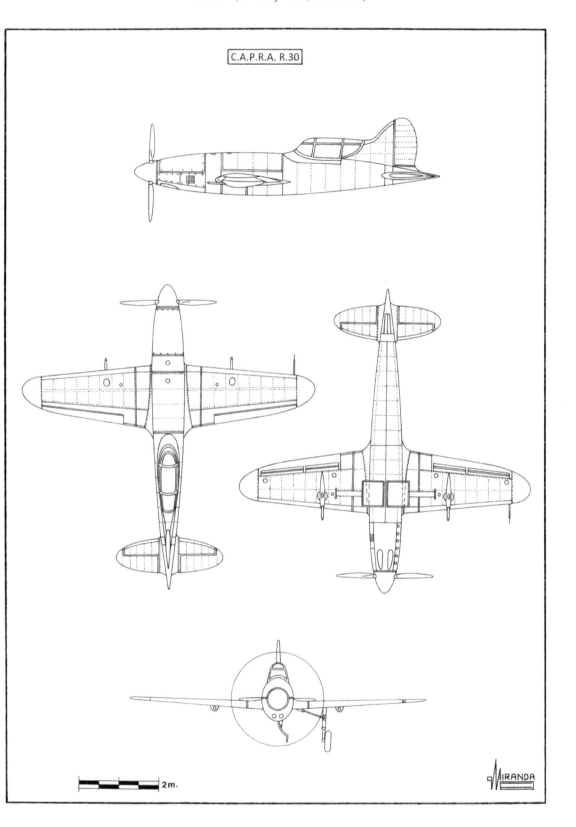

2m.

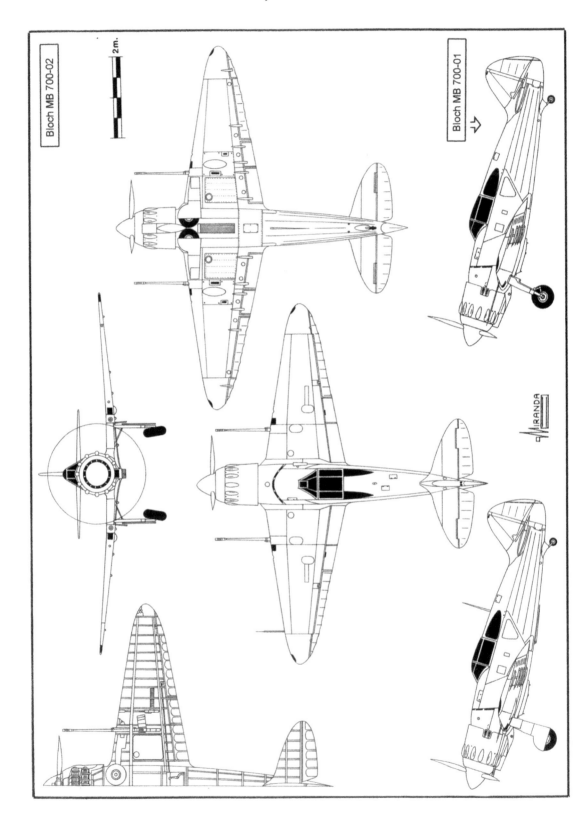

Bloch MB 700-02

Bloch MB 700-01

2 m.

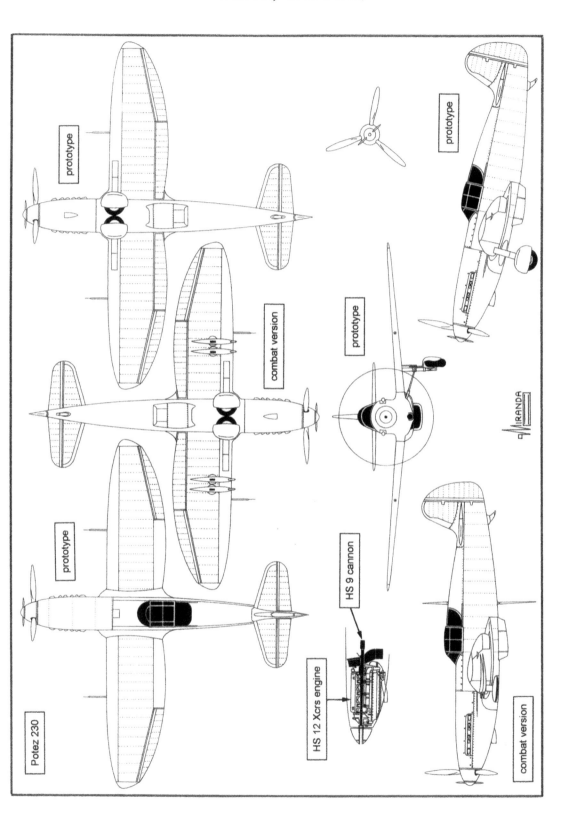

prototype

prototype

combat version

prototype

prototype

HS 9 cannon

HS 12 Xcrs engine

Potez 230

combat version

MIRANDA

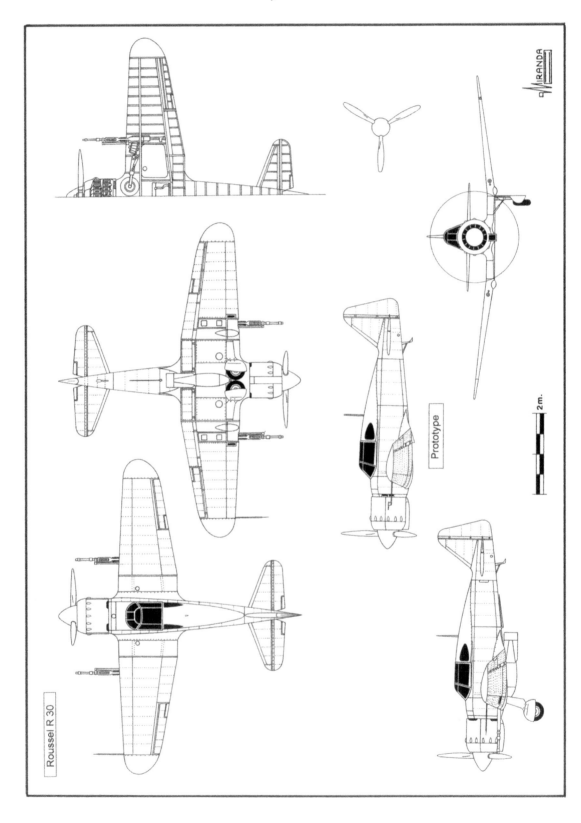

Prototype

Roussel R 30

2 m.

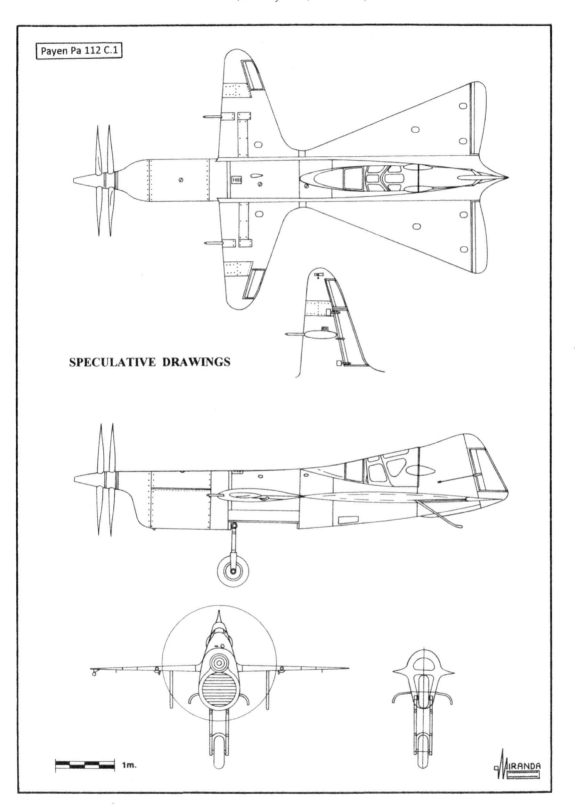

Payen Pa 112 C.1

SPECULATIVE DRAWINGS

1m.

Payen Pa 112 C.1

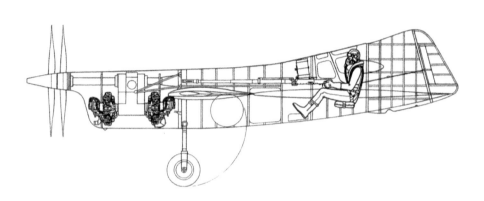

SPECULATIVE DRAWINGS

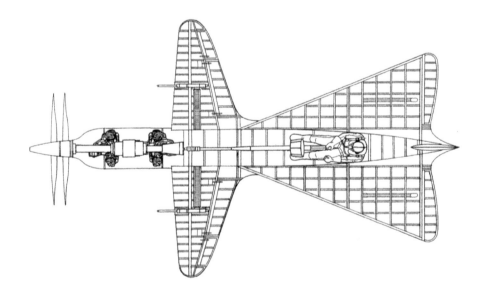

1m.

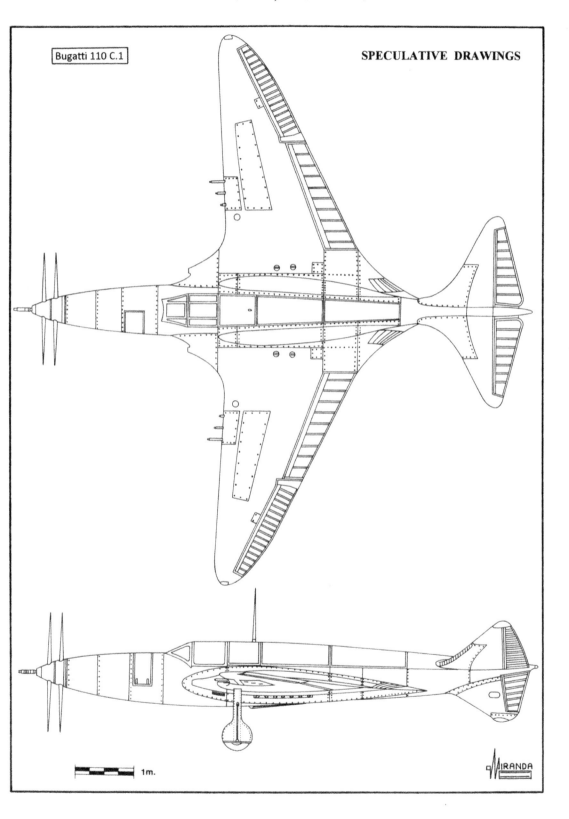

Bugatti 110 C.1

SPECULATIVE DRAWINGS

1m.

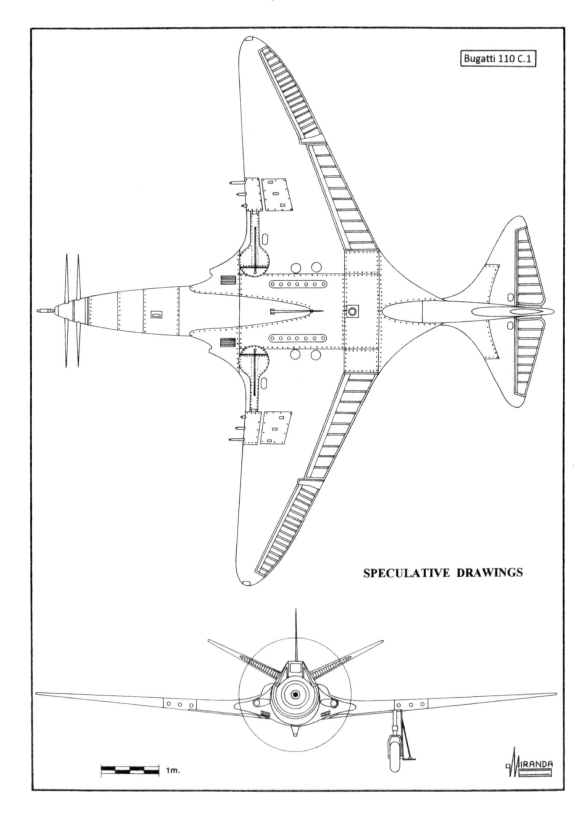

Bugatti 110 C.1

SPECULATIVE DRAWINGS

1m.

MIRANDA

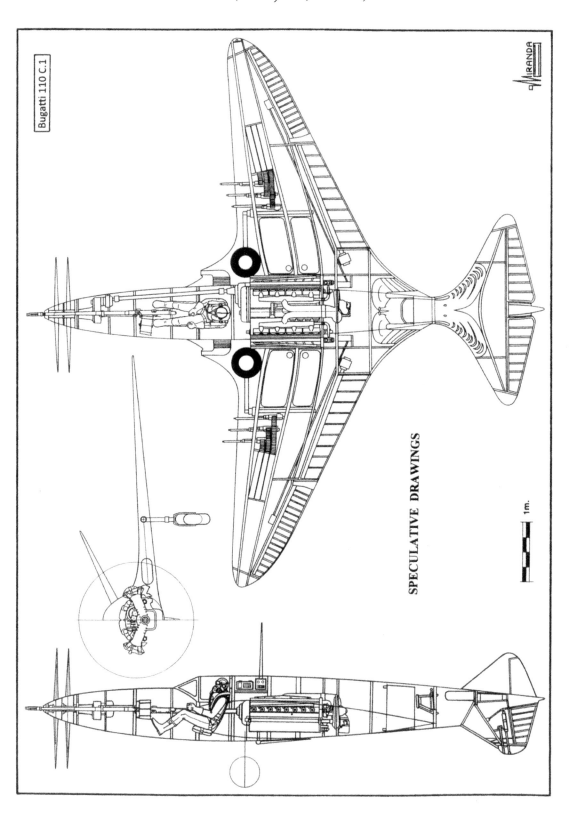

Bugatti 110 C.1

SPECULATIVE DRAWINGS

1 m.

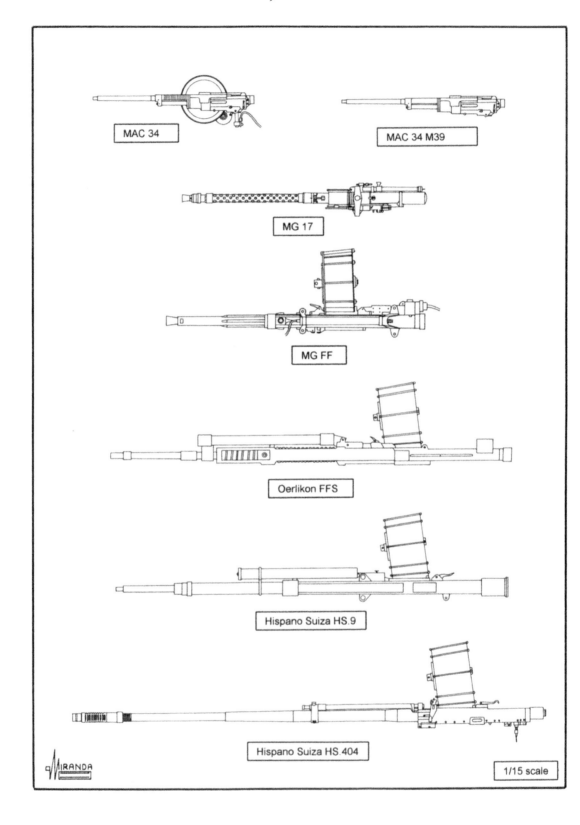

MAC 34

MAC 34 M39

MG 17

MG FF

Oerlikon FFS

Hispano Suiza HS.9

Hispano Suiza HS.404

MIRANDA

1/15 scale

9

Great Britain
(10 July 1940–15 March 1945)

By the time of the Munich Crisis, it was unclear to the British authorities if the production of the new monoplane Hawker Hurricane and Supermarine Spitfire fighters could be accelerated sufficiently to equip the 123 Squadrons that the Fighter Command required for the defence of the British Islands.

In October 1938, F. G. Miles, designer of the Miles Master advanced trainer, proposed the construction of a single-seat fighter that could supplement the Hurricanes and Spitfires already in production without competing with them for the Merlin engines or in the use of strategic materials. The project, called Miles M.20/1 'Munich Fighter', could be built entirely of wood/plywood using the retractable landing gear and several parts of the Miles Master trainer.

It would be propelled by one 885-hp liquid-cooled V-12 Rolls-Royce Peregrine engine, driving a two-bladed airscrew and would be armed with two 20-mm Hispano-Suiza HS.404 cannons. A wooden mock-up was built at the end of 1938, but no orders were placed because production of the Peregrine was reserved for the Westland Whirlwind twin-engined fighter.

Miles persisted with the M.20/2 project, adapted to the Specification F.19/40, calling for a fighter armed with eight 0.303-inch Browning Mk II machine guns and propelled by one 1,300-hp Rolls-Royce Merlin XX 'power egg' interchangeable with the Bristol Beaufighter and the Avro Lancaster aircraft. The M.20/2 had a fixed landing gear, thus removing the need of hydraulic circuits and enabling the construction in a quarter of the time of a Hurricane and a tenth of the time of a Spitfire. During the flying tests carried out on 14 September 1940, the prototype AX 834 showed a top speed exceeding that of the Hurricane Mk I and manoeuvrability equivalent to that of the Spitfire Mk I. The stabilisation of the German offensive and the increase in production of the conventional fighters rendered its mass production worthless and the project was left aside in April 1941.

The projected fighter Percival P.33 AB, based on the aerodynamic configuration of the Mew Gull racer that competed for the Merlin XX engine, was also cancelled. It would have been a 556-kph fighter armed with four Brownings, with a 12.24-m wingspan, a 9.2-m overall length, and a 2,848-kg maximum weight.

During the critical days of 1940, the 'Panic Effect' boosted numerous interim solutions to increase the number of fighters available; A. A. Bage, the Percival chief designer, proposed to build a version of the Mew Gull armed with two 0.303-inch Vickers Mk II machine guns. The projected light fighter, called Percival P.32 AA, would have a 7.62-m wingspan, a 6.57-m overall length, and a 1,087-kg maximum weight. However, it was rejected in favour of the Miles M.24, the single-seat version of the Miles Master armed with eight Brownings, capable of flying at 370 kph, and with handling characteristics similar to those of the Hurricane.

During the Battle of Britain, some Tiger Moth training biplanes were equipped with bombs of up to 110 kg, and the Percival Proctor prototype P5998 radio-trainer was also converted into anti-invasion light bomber with sixteen 20-lb bombs under the wings.

As a result of a study conducted by the Air Ministry between 1933 and 1934, it was established that at the high speeds reached by the monoplane fighter, in future combats, the target should be destroyed with a burst of just two seconds. To achieve this effect with the standard Colt-Browning Model 1934 machine gun, a fighter should be armed with at least eight of these weapons.

This study considered impossible a combat between two fighters flying at 500 kph, and it was not foreseen that the Germans could develop one capable of flying to England. Consequently, the RAF concentrated its efforts in the interception of bombers, developing rigid flight training techniques that were terribly ineffective in 1939.

During the Spanish Civil War, international observers found that the Soviet fighters armed with four PV-1 machine guns usually failed in their attempts to intercept the last generation of German bombers that acquired a reputation of invulnerability, helped by the Nazi propaganda and the hysterics of the French press.

In France, the Hurricanes of the BEF proved how difficult it was to shoot down a Heinkel He 111 with 270-kg armour in 1940. The British pilots often exhausted their 2,600 ammunition rounds without obtaining visible results while the Heinkels returned to their bases with more than 100 impacts of 7.7-mm ammo and were repaired in a few days. These experiences influenced the design of the cannon armed Hurricane Mk II and Spitfire Mk V.

The British had acquired the manufacturing rights of the 20-mm Hispano-Suiza HS.404 cannon with explosive shells, but its installation on the wings of fighters was problematic. The weapon had been designed as an integral part of the Hispano-Suiza HS.12 Y-31 engine and lacked structural strength to act independently. The adaptation was difficult; during the Battle of Britain, some Spitfires Mk I of the 19th Sqn were experimentally equipped with two Hispano Mk I, suffering numerous stoppage problems. The RAF avoided its usage until the appearing of the Mk II in the summer of 1941.

Several methods were considered to mitigate this situation, including air-to-air bombing and rockets vertically fired from the rear fuselage of the Hurricanes. Another idea was the ramming, inspired in the Soviet *Taran* tactics developed in Spain and Khalkhin Gol that assured the destruction of an enemy bomber by collision. In the summer of 1940, the British pilots were forced to resort to ramming in some extreme combats, destroying four Bf 109, two Do 17, one Ju 88, one Bf 110, one Fiat CR.42, and one He 111.

The ramming sometimes happened accidentally due to miscalculation of distances by the attacking aircraft or because the pilot had been injured or killed by the defensive fire of the attacked aircraft. At other times, it was a desperate measure consequence of the malfunction of arms in a conventional attack made from behind. The impact used to occur at low speed—between 40 and 80 kph—because both aircraft were flying in the same direction, with the propeller of the attacking plane acting as a circular saw on the tail surfaces of the attacked plane. The rammer usually suffered damages in the propeller, engine bearings, and engine cowling; the survival rate of the pilot used to exceed 50 per cent with a good chance of making a glide landing.

When ramming large aircraft, it was more effective to target the fuselage section between wing and tailplane to sever control cables, but the side attack manoeuvre required a very precise calculation of relative speeds that only very expert pilots could perform. The impact, between 300 and 450 kph, used to boot a wing of the attacking aircraft that fell into an uncontrollable flat spin; the pilot was violently thrown in the opposite direction to the damaged wing, getting wounded or shocked and with survival possibilities below 25 per cent because the fuselage airframe tended to deform, rendering the opening of the cockpit very difficult.

The most effective ramming, and also the most extreme solution, was the head-on-attack, a manoeuvre that Japanese pilots termed *Tai-atari* (body crashing) in which both aircraft crashed at a joint speed close to 1,000 kph with decelerations of up to 100 *g*. No one could survive an impact like this, with the rammer embedded into the nose of the bomber and both aircraft falling while intertwined. Any aircraft could be used for this task if it had enough ceiling and speed to reach the target. The main problem was the survival of the pilot after a collision in a time when the ejector seats did not exist.

On May 1939, the British inventor Mr. I. Shamah proposed the transformation of a standard fighter into a specialised rammer to the firm Phillips and Powis (later known as Miles). The modification included the replacement of the engine by a surplus Rolls-Royce Kestrel and the guns by an armoured wing-leading edge, the installation of steel rammers in the propeller hub and wingtip, and one downwards ejector seat located over a ventral hatchway. The idea was considered in 1940, due to the shortage of experienced pilots that mastered the technique of the deflection shooting. Out of the 2,330 fighter pilots who fought against the Luftwaffe between July and November, only 900 managed the destruction of an enemy aircraft, almost always by surprise and firing from closer than 200 m.

By 1943, the increasing speed reached by the fighters created many difficulties for bailing out as the air pressure acting over the pilot tended to return him to the cockpit or impact against the tail surfaces. In the Spitfire Mk 21, the plan was to install the 'swinging arm', a Martin-Baker invention, to help the pilots overcome the air pressure at high speeds. The upper part of the fuselage detached itself to form an articulated arm that extracted the pilot from the cockpit by means of two hooks inserted in the parachute harness. The arm was actioned by powerful springs and by the air drag, rotating around a hinge located at the base of the tailfin, launching the pilot backwards over the tail surfaces. The project was started in 1944, although it was finally decided to use the seat fitted with an explosive catapult as it was lighter and required fewer modifications in the airframe.

After the fall of France, the German Army High Command (OKH) planned the invasion of the British Islands by landing over forty divisions. After collecting 2,400 barges, 471 tugs, and 155 transports from the invaded countries, the planners were informed that the *Kriegsmarine* had suffered great losses in Norway, that it had only three cruisers and four destroyers to escort the improvised invasion fleet, and that at the other side of the English Channel, which was mined, the Royal Navy had eight cruisers, fifty-four destroyers, and 700 small coastal motor gun boats, corvettes, and minesweepers.

In the face of the hesitations of the OKH, the *Oberkommando der Luftwaffe* (OKL)— poorly informed about the British radar system, the number of aircraft of the Fighter Command, and the ability of British industry—decided to start an attrition campaign over the territory between London and the south coast of England. Its objective was the annihilation of the RAF fighter force, which had already lost 195 Hurricanes and sixty-seven Spitfires in France, so it could not oppose an airborne invasion. The Luftwaffe, conceived as a tactical air force specialised in supporting the operations of the *Wehrmacht*, was not prepared for this kind of strategic war as it lacked four-engine heavy bombers.

During the fighting in Poland, the Germans had lost 285 aircraft, 260 in Norway, 317 in the Netherlands, 432 in Belgium, and 1,279 in France. One third of the total were Junkers Ju 52 transport aircraft that could had been used in the invasion project. Outside combat operations, the 'usual' attrition rate of the Luftwaffe was eighty-five aircraft destroyed and ninety-six damaged every month, a third of them in accidents.

By the end of July 1940, the Germans had 769 medium bombers, 656 single-engine fighters, 168 twin-engine fighters, 316 dive bombers, and 100 reconnaissance serviceable aircraft in France. The Fighter Command only had 650 fighters at that time, but the British aeronautical industry had already accelerated production so that on 13 August, the day of the German offensive, it already had 1,381 fighters.

At the end of August, the German intelligence services estimated that 800 British fighters had been destroyed, with an attrition rate of 100 aircraft per week. They believed that by the end of September, Fighter Command would have been neutralised, but in fact, it still had 750 fighters capable of fighting at that time. In its attempt to achieve air superiority, the Luftwaffe lost 1,887 aircraft. The price of British survival were 1,023 aircraft of Fighter Command, 376 of Bomber Command, and 148 of Coastal Command.

France only had the Maginot Line for its defence, but the British Islands were protected by eight barriers that the Germans did not manage to cross—the English Channel; the Royal Navy; the Chain Home with twenty-one radar stations; Anti-Aircraft Command with 350,000 personnel, 1,340 heavy guns, and 370 low level guns; Balloon Command with 40,000 personnel and 1,400 balloons; the Royal Observer Corps with 30,000 personnel; the Fighter Control System force multiplier; and the Hurricanes, Spitfires, Defiants, and Blenheims of Fighter Command. After the Battle of France, the Germans neglected the manufacture of aircraft and the training of pilots, believing the war was over. On the other hand, the British in their desperate isolation doubled the production of the previous year by building 15,000 aircraft in 1940.

They also strove to improve the performance of the fighters in combat operations by introducing numerous modifications on existing models. New self-sealing fuel tanks, armoured windscreens, constant speed airscrews, and special carburettors for the Merlin engines to not lose power in inverted flight and IFF equipment were installed. The harmonisation of guns was reduced to 200 m to increase the hitting power, and the Browning Mk II machine guns were hurried into service with Ball and de Wilde incendiary and tracer rounds. Some 100 octane gasoline was also imported from the USA.

During tests carried out in May 1940 with a captured Messerschmitt Bf 109 E, it was found that in realistic combat conditions, its manoeuvrability was inferior to that of the Spitfire, although experienced pilots could make more closed turns by forcing the slats to the limit. During the Battle of Britain, the Bf 109 used to fly at great heights trying to surprise the British fighters while climbing to intercept the bombers. After a fast diving attack, they regained altitude to avoid a dogfight below 6,000 m.

Despite being more manoeuvrable than the Spitfire, the Hurricane Mk I had half the chance of survival in a confrontation with the Bf 109 E. Depending on the flight altitude, the Hurricane was between 15 and 48 kph slower than the German BF 109 E and a difference of speed of more than 20 kph was considered lethal in 1940. To reduce the number of loses, Fighter Command banned flights over sea and Fighter Control tried to lead the Hurricanes only against the bombers, although it was very difficult to distinguish them from fighters with the radar of the time.

On 20 October 1942, the *Reichsluftfahrtministerium*'s Technical Department published a specification for a *Schnellbomber* (fast bomber) with a 1,000-kg payload, a penetration depth of 1,046 km (one-third of the operational range), and a top speed of 700 km/h, later increased to 1,000 km/h, at operational altitude.

On January 1943, the American bombers based in England started their daylight incursions over the Reich. Simultaneously, the RAF started to use the H2S cartographic radar that greatly improved the accurateness of night bombing. The German defences, despite their sophisticated early warning network, could not stop them.

The British launched 600 tons of bombs over Berlin on 1 March. The German retaliation meant the loss of fifty-seven bombers for the Luftwaffe, with the mediocre result of 100 tons launched at London's outskirts. After the failure of the Messerschmitt Me 210, the Germans did not have anything to compete against the Mosquito.

During a conference in Karinhall on 18 March, Göring warned the representatives of the aeronautical industry that he would not approve any new project until the requirement in the 1942 specification was met. The German industry, badly damaged by the bombing and the planification errors, was not able to create the *Schnellbomber* required by the Luftwaffe.

At the beginning of 1944, in retaliation for the bombing of German cities, the OKL began the strategic bombing campaign *Unternehmen Steinbock* against some British towns. The offensive was a costly failure; night after night, the German bombers were located and hunted down by sixteen squadrons of de Havilland Mosquito Mk VIII and Bristol Beaufighter Mk VI night fighters equipped with the Mk VIII airborne interception radar, resulting in the shooting down of 121 Dornier Do 217s, 270 Junkers Ju 88s, thirty-five Junkers Ju 188s, twenty-five Focke-Wulf Fw 190 A-4/U8s, twenty-seven Messerschmitt Me 410s, and forty-six Heinkel He 177s. On the other side, only eight British fighters were lost. The Battle of Britain was not the only moment of panic experienced by the RAF, however. Between June and September 1944, they had to cope with 11,700 flying bombs.

In May 1943, Allied intelligence services discovered the existence of a German catapult-launched missile that was being developed at Peenemünde-West test centre. In August, an air-launched prototype of pilotless aircraft of the Karlshagen research centre crashed on Bornholm-Denmark and some pictures, taken by the Resistance, came into the hands of the Allies.

In September, the photographic reconnaissance carried out by Mustang Mk III, Mosquito PR IV, and Spitfire PR XI located 133 'ski-shaped buildings' with axis pointing directly towards London. They were launch ramps built for the new cruise missiles V-1 manufactured by the firm Fieseler, under the designation Fi 103, using welded sheet steel and plywood with a 280 man-hour and 1,500-Reichmark cost. They were powered by an Argus As 014 pulsejet that worked with 625 litres of *Br-Stoff* (75-octane non-refined petrol) generating between 245 and 366 kp, enough to transport to London a warhead containing 830 kg of high-explosive Amatol-39 A.

The Askania gyroscopic autopilot was a mechanical guidance system that could not be interfered by the Allies electronic countermeasures. A vane anemometer installed in the nose calculated the distance covered, cutting off the fuel flow when the V-1 was on the target. The autopilot of the flying bombs, designed to attack targets the size of a city, was not accurate enough to achieve impacts on Normandy beachheads, or in the ports in southern England from where the supplies were sent to the armies of the Allies.

Yet the British did not know that and during the weeks preceding the 'D-Day', they launched a desperate offensive against the V-1 launch sites and storage buildings built between Cherbourg and Calais. Using all available aircraft, capable of carrying bombs or rockets, they were able to destroy 25 per cent of the facilities, delaying the release of the first missiles until a week after the Normandy landings.

The British defences had been continually reinforced since 1940. In June 1944, they consisted of 100 radar stations, some 2,000 barrage balloons, and 2,729 anti-aircraft guns shooting proximity-fuse shells. Many batteries located between Dover and Hastings were equipped with a predictor fire-control radar system.

To face the 'robot offensive', the defences of Operation Diver was formed by four lines: long range fighters, operated from the southeast of England to near the French coast; the anti-aircraft artillery located in the south coast of England; the area between the coast and London, covered by high performance interceptors; and the urban areas protected by balloons barrages.

The aerodynamic drag of the V-1 airframe was higher than anticipated due to low standards of manufacturing, decreasing from projected 900 kph to the real 640 kph. Fortunately for the Allies, this made the new missile susceptible to be intercepted by conventional fighters.

In the outward perimeter operated the Mustang Mk III of 129, 306 (Polish), and 313 (Polish) Squadrons and the Mosquitoes FB Mk VI of the 418th Canadian Squadron. By night, Mosquito NF Mk VIIs of 29 and 465 (Australian) Squadrons, the NF. Mk XII of the 488th Sqn (New Zealander), the NF. Mk XIII of Squadrons 96, 264 and 409 (Canadian), the NF. Mk XVII of 125th Squadron, the NF. Mk XVIII of 25 and 68 Squadrons, the NF. Mk XIX of 157th Squadron, and the Northrop P-61 Black Widows of American squadrons 422nd and 425th took part in the operations.

The Spitfires Mk IX of 1, 165, 274, 453 (Australian), and 610 Squadrons, Spitfires Mk XV of 41st Squadron, Tempest Mk V of 3, 56, 80, 274, 486 (New Zealander), and 501 Squadrons, and Meteors Mk I jet fighters of 616th Squadron operated in the inner area.

The V-1 had a reduced frontal area equivalent to half of the Bf 109, an engine with the diameter of a dish, a mechanic pilot fitted in a shoe box, and a steel airframe. It was very difficult to shoot down. As they were camouflaged, it was very difficult to distinguish them from the landscape when over land. Over sea and at low altitude, the estimated height over the surface in diving attack left very little margin to the pilots. By night, the outburst of the pulsejet was visible from 24 km and gave false range measurements. Some Mosquito pilots, dazzled by the shine, shot from 100 m and one lucky P-61 survived the blast of a V-1 just 46 m from its nose.

Flying at 725 kph, a Tempest had just two seconds to dodge the debris produced by the explosion of the V-1, which had just shot from 275 m. Some pilots preferred to cross the centre of the explosion where there was less shrapnel, but the inflamed fuel affected the engine, the paint, and the fabric-covered control surfaces.

To avoid this, a Mosquito FB VI of 418th Squadron destroyed a V-1 by simply cutting the missile trajectory and putting it out of control with the trail turbulence. On the contrary, a Meteor of the 616th Squadron stroke the missile wing with the fighter wingtip, decontrolling the gyroscopes. This technique, called 'Tipping', required speed and piloting ability and was only used on seventeen occasions.

For the Spitfires, the game was even more dangerous due to its lower structural resistance. They used to start the attack with a dive to gain speed, moving on to horizontal flight at 230 m behind the missile to be able to shoot it. The calculation of relative speeds was complicated, and some pilots died when firing from too short a distance.

It was necessary to modify the fighters to make them fast enough to intercept the V-1. Some Tempest and Spitfire Mk XIVs were tuned to operate at 11 and 25 psi boost pressures; the Mustang III changed their exhaust to those of the Spitfire engine that generated less drag; the P-47 M Thunderbolts, with 2,800-hp war emergency power boosted engines, were modified, halving its armament and fuel capacity, and the armour plates were also stripped. To reduce the drag on some Spitfires, wingtips, rear view mirrors, and armoured glass windscreens were replaced by those of the photo reconnaissance versions of curved type. The camouflage paint was also removed to gain some speed. During Operation Diver, between June 1944 and March 1945, sixteen squads of interceptors used the new aviation fuel (150 grade) produced in the USA. Out of the 3,957 V-1 destroyed during the 'robot war', 1,785 were shot down by fighters.

The missiles that survived the first line of interceptors used to cross the English coast, between Bexgill and Folkestone, flying between 550 and 650 kph and at an altitude between 300 and 2,500 m. The anti-aircraft artillery managed to shoot down many of them.

During the weeks that followed D-Day, the forces of the Allies neutralised in their advance numerous V-1 launch sites built by the Germans in northern France. When the units of the *Wehrmacht* retreated eastward, the new frontiers of the Reich got progressively further from London. The V-1s launched from central Netherlands, with its maximum range of only 240 km, could no longer reach the British capital.

The Luftwaffe intended to continue its bombing offensive on 9 July 1944, launching the V-1 from the obsolete bombers Heinkel He 111 H-16 of the III./KG3. Taking off with great difficulty from the Dutch airfields of Gilze-Rijen and Venlo, the Heinkels ventured far into the North Sea to launch their missiles against English cities. These V-1s came from the east, thus taking British defenders that expected them from the south by surprise. Until the end of the war in Europe, the III./KG3 made just 300 launches, and it was dangerous work as some V-1 exploded prematurely and others beat the bomber after the launch because of turbulence.

From the strategic point of view, the low frequency of launches was useless, and the Heinkels were easy prey for the all-weather Mosquito and Black Widow interceptors that searched them over the sea, led by the radars of the Chain Home.

The simplest solution to the problem of the short-range missile was to improve the effectiveness of the pulsejet, originally designed for only twenty minutes of operation. The DFS, FKFS, AVA, and LFA Institutes took care of this study to search for different systems to improve the performance and durability of the valves.

They also proposed replacing the E-1 *Br-Stoff* fuel (75-octane non-refined petrol) by the other so-called E-2, of higher heat capacity, with which it was expected to increase the range by 7 per cent.

The capacity of the fuel tank was successively expanded to 810 and 1,025 litres, but the limit continued to be the time of operation of the pulsejet valves system. The most elegant solution would have been to replace the Argus for an expendable turbojet. The German industry was working on three different models since October 1944: the BMW P.3307, the Porsche 109-005, and the Porsche T.300, but none reached the production stage.

The extended range also increased the inaccuracy of the missile, reaching a situation in which its use would only be profitable by increasing the number and frequency of launches. The 'robot war' had been reduced to a matter of statistics and production capacity—a game that Germany could only lose.

In early 1945, the Allies electronic technology was so advanced that they could interfere with any German radio-control system. The Axis' only possibility was using suicide pilots. The successes achieved by the *kamikazes* in the Far East strengthened the position of those in favour of creating *Selbstopfermanner* (S.O.) units of self-sacrifice pilots, so the OKL authorised the conversion of several V-1 missiles into piloted bombers under the codename *Reichenberg*.

The S.O. version named *Reichenberg* IV was a single-seat suicide bomber based on the airframe of the Fieseler Fi 103 B-1, with a 5.37-m wingspan, wooden wings, and an *Amatol* 39A warhead; it was powered by an Argus As 109-014 pulsejet with 366-kp thrust at sea level and 254 kp at 3,000 m, a 640-kph maximum speed, and a 330-km range. The launch system was dangerous and ineffective. The Heinkel He 111 H-22 should take off with a large asymmetric load of 2,250 kg, which would mean the loss of both aircraft in the event of failure of the port engine.

It was suggested that one *Reichenberg* IV would be carried under one Heinkel He 177 to attack the industrial Soviet centres of Kuybyshev, Chelyabinsk, and Magnitogorsk. The accuracy of the *Reichenberg* allowed the Luftwaffe to destroy (for the first time in the war, with security and economy of means) all kinds of high valuable targets like warships, aircraft manufacturers, military HQ, munitions depots, bridges, and power stations.

It was also considered its use for political purposes, based on the idea that an attack carried out against the Buckingham Palace, the Houses of Parliament, or the White House could create the right situation for some kind of peace agreement. For the attack on Washington, the proposal was to arm a U-boat Type XXI with a *Reichenberg* IV housed in a watertight container located on the rear deck behind the conning tower.

It was hoped that the *Reichenberg* IV could use various types of interchangeable warhead to attack different kinds of targets as effectively as possible. For anti-ship usage, DFS technicians had planned to use two types of warhead: an SHL 800 hollow-charge of 785 mm in diameter (a 40 per cent scaled-down version of the SHL 3500 used by *Mistel* bombers) and a torpedo-bomb BT 1400.

The *Reichenberg* IV programme was cancelled on 15 March without being used operationally because the Luftwaffe preferred to use the *Mistel* composites for their last bombing missions. At the end of the war in Europe, the Allies discovered about 500 airframes of *Reichenberg* IV in different stages of construction in the *Pulverhoff* assembly plant. At least 175 of them were ready for combat.

Anticipating the emergence of a second generation of faster missiles, propelled by the new Argus 109-044 pulsejet with 660-hp thrust, the British designed a version of the Tempest with the monstrous 3,200-hp Rolls-Royce *Eagle* engine and the Americans built the XP-47J Superbolt, an advanced version of the Thunderbolt capable of flying to 813 kph, the highest speed recorded in level flight by any propeller aircraft during the Second World War.

Enemy at the Gates

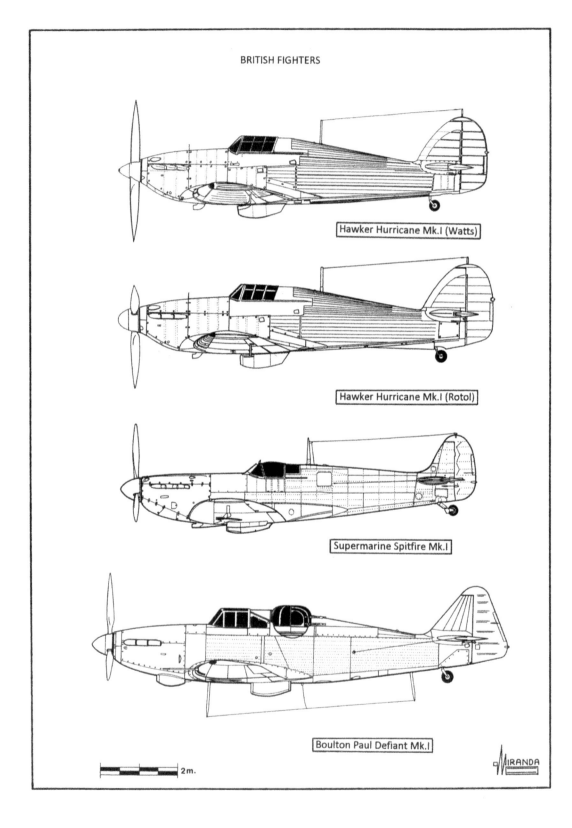

BRITISH FIGHTERS

Hawker Hurricane Mk.I (Watts)

Hawker Hurricane Mk.I (Rotol)

Supermarine Spitfire Mk.I

Boulton Paul Defiant Mk.I

2 m.

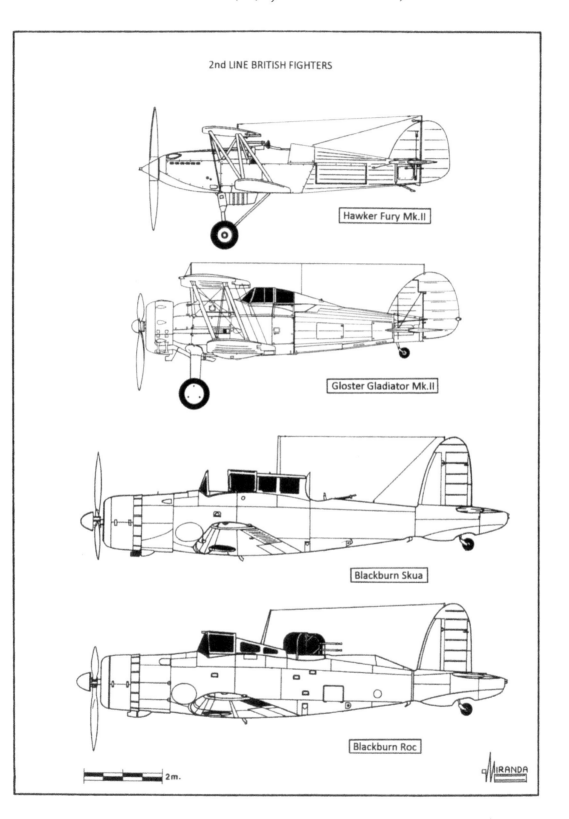

2nd LINE BRITISH FIGHTERS

Hawker Fury Mk.II

Gloster Gladiator Mk.II

Blackburn Skua

Blackburn Roc

2 m.

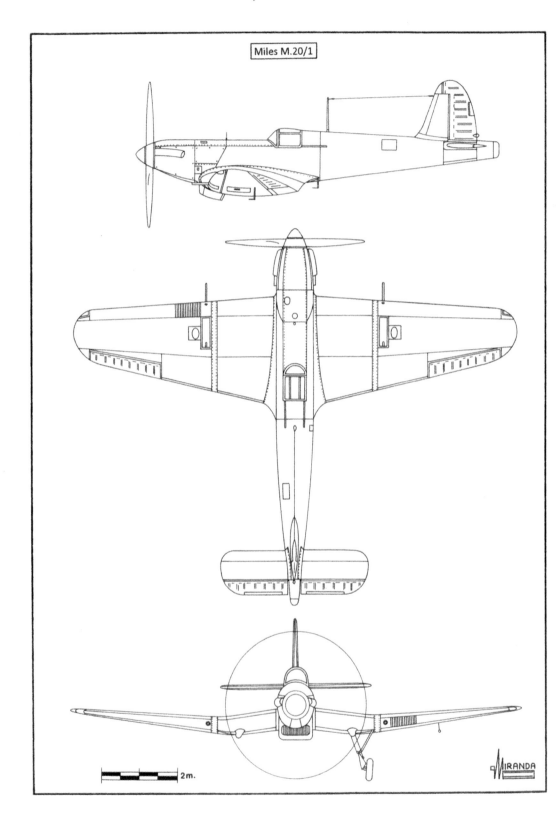

Miles M.20/1

2 m.

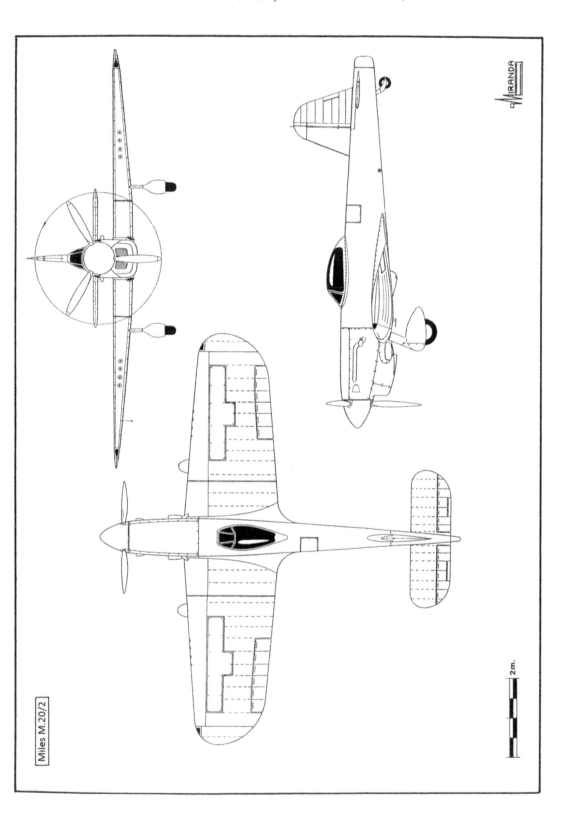

Miles M.20/2

2 m.

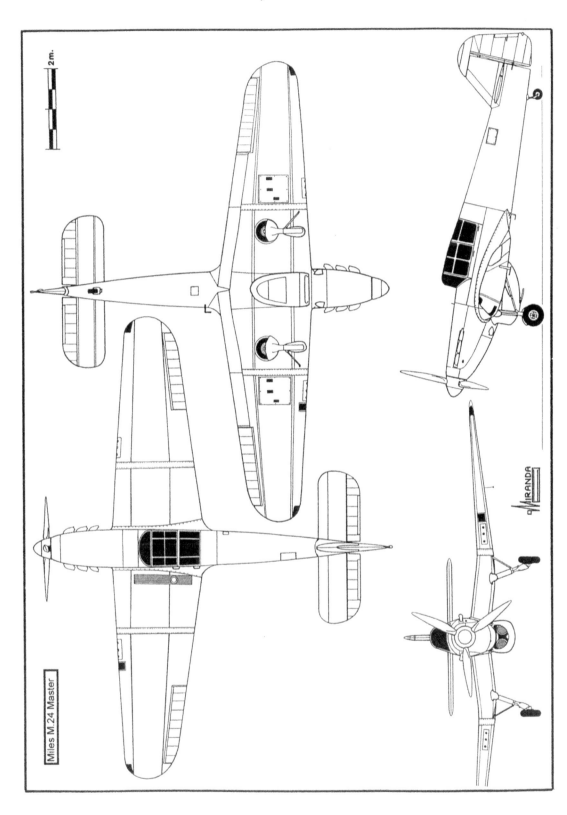

2 m.

Miles M.24 Master

MIRANDA

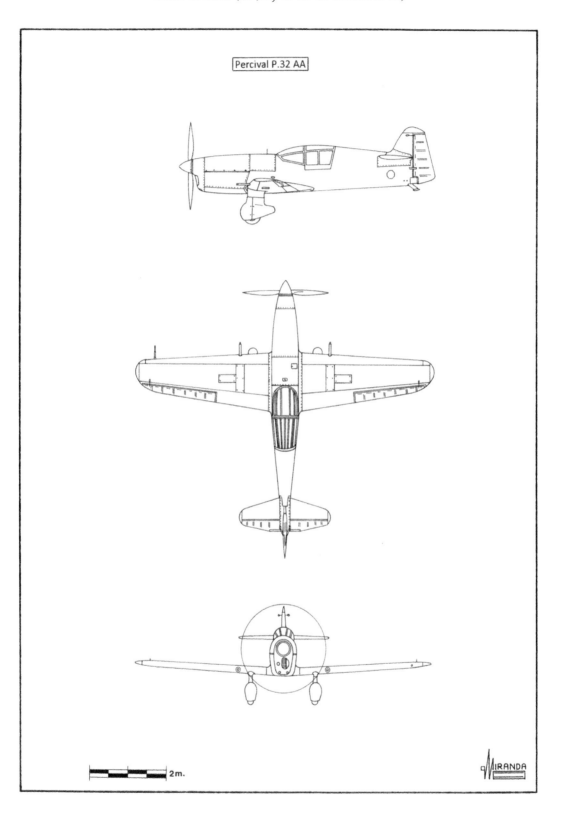

Percival P.32 AA

2m.

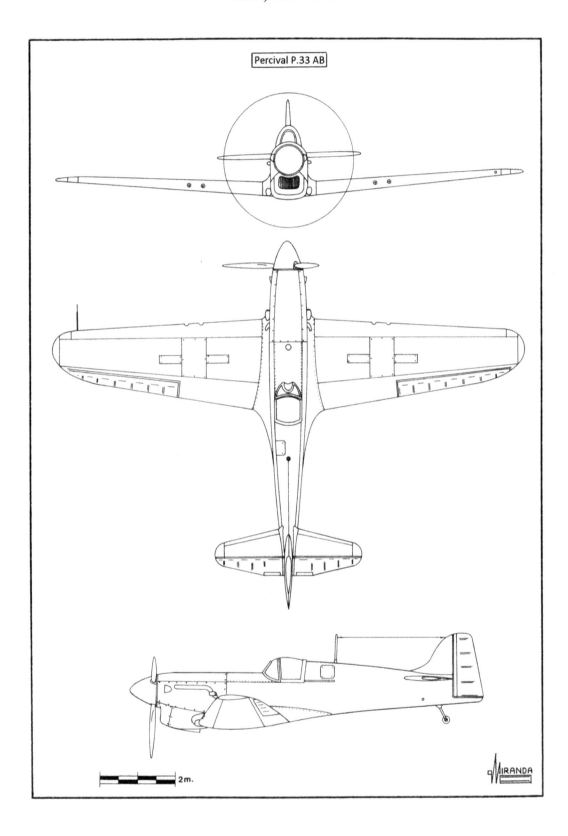

Percival P.33 AB

2 m.

MIRANDA

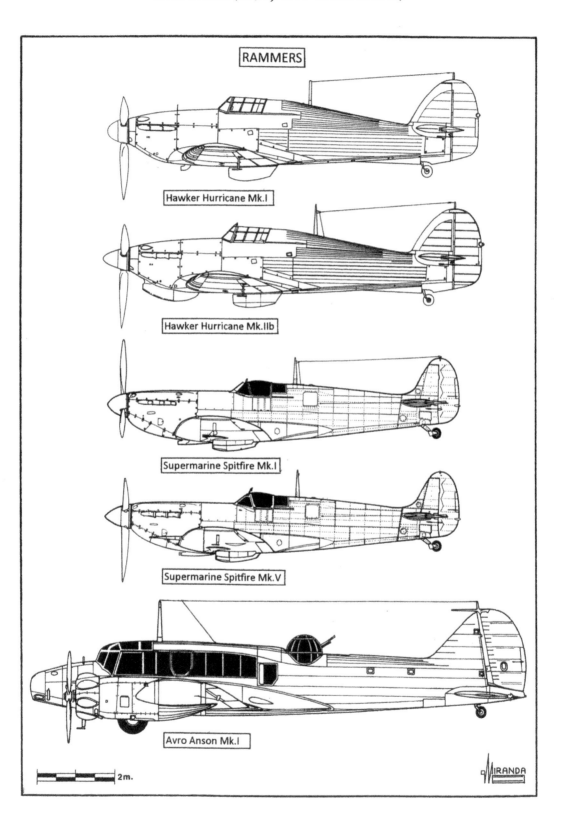

RAMMERS

Hawker Hurricane Mk.I

Hawker Hurricane Mk.IIb

Supermarine Spitfire Mk.I

Supermarine Spitfire Mk.V

Avro Anson Mk.I

2m.

MIRANDA

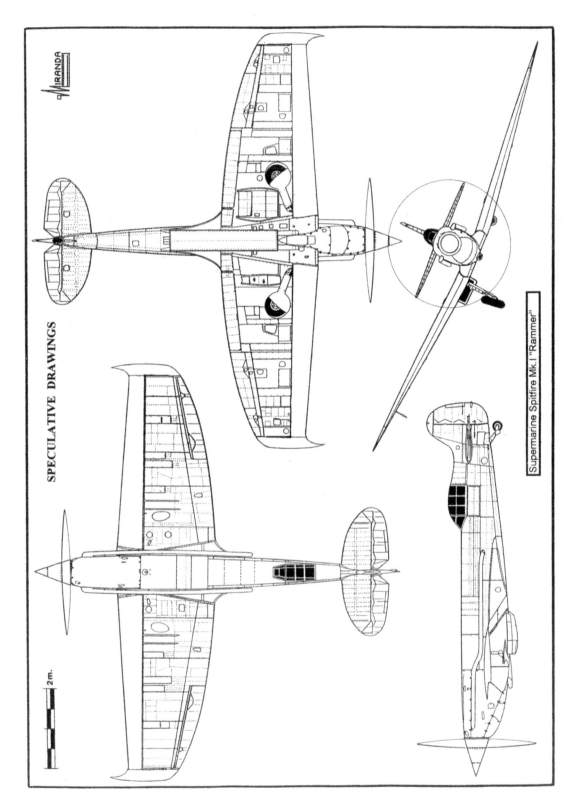

SPECULATIVE DRAWINGS

2 m.

Supermarine Spitfire Mk.I "Rammer"

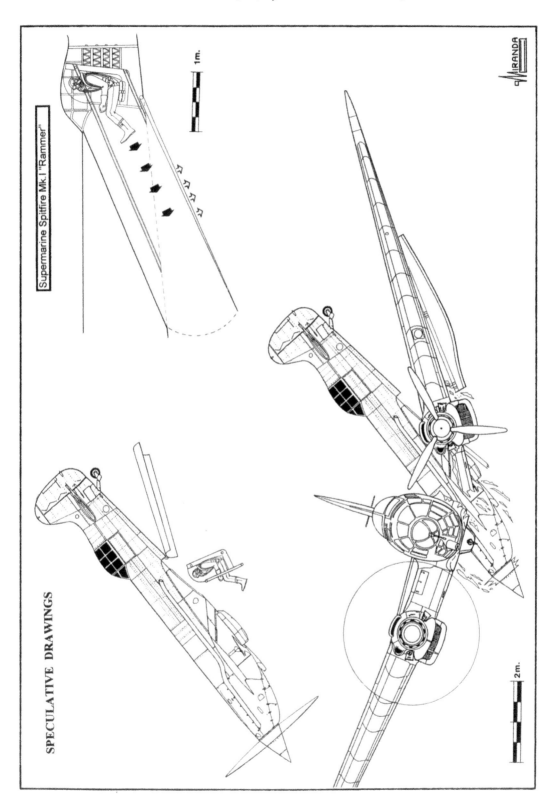

Supermarine Spitfire Mk.I "Rammer"

SPECULATIVE DRAWINGS

1 m.

2 m.

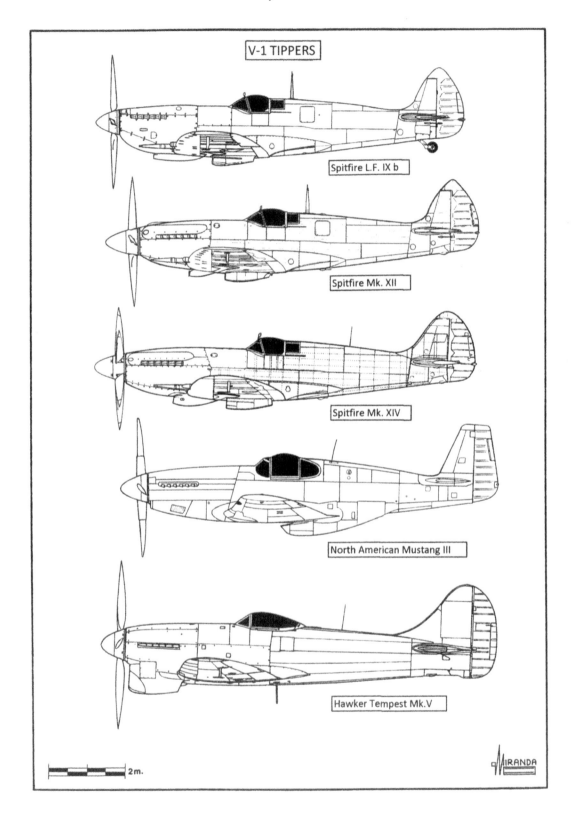

V-1 TIPPERS

Spitfire L.F. IX b

Spitfire Mk. XII

Spitfire Mk. XIV

North American Mustang III

Hawker Tempest Mk.V

2 m.

MIRANDA

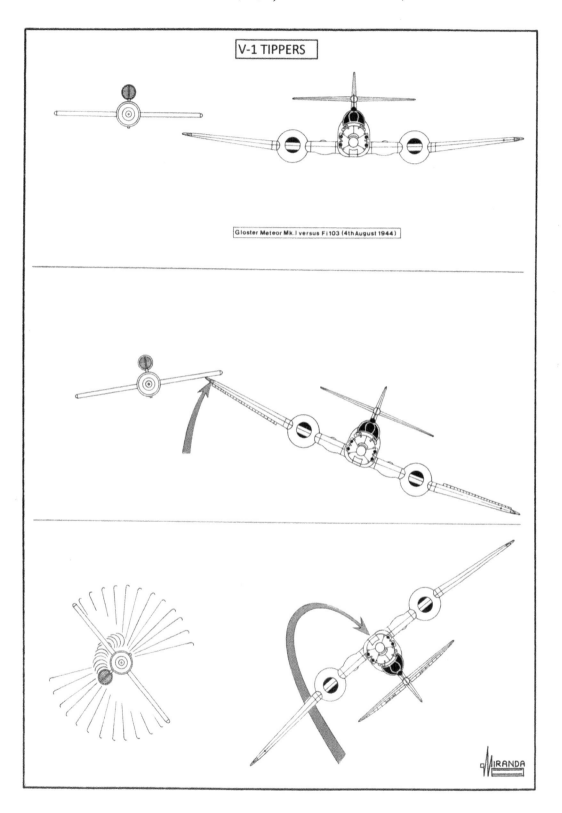

V-1 TIPPERS

Gloster Meteor Mk.I versus Fi103 (4th August 1944)

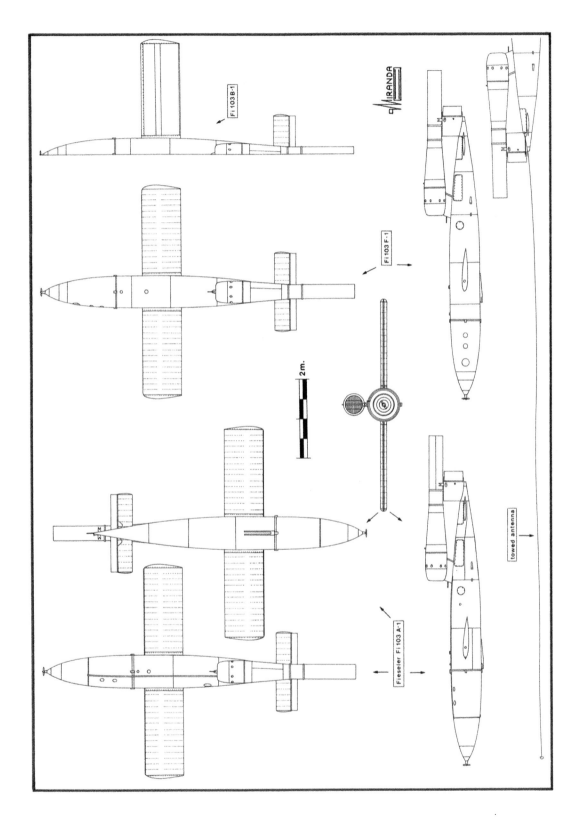

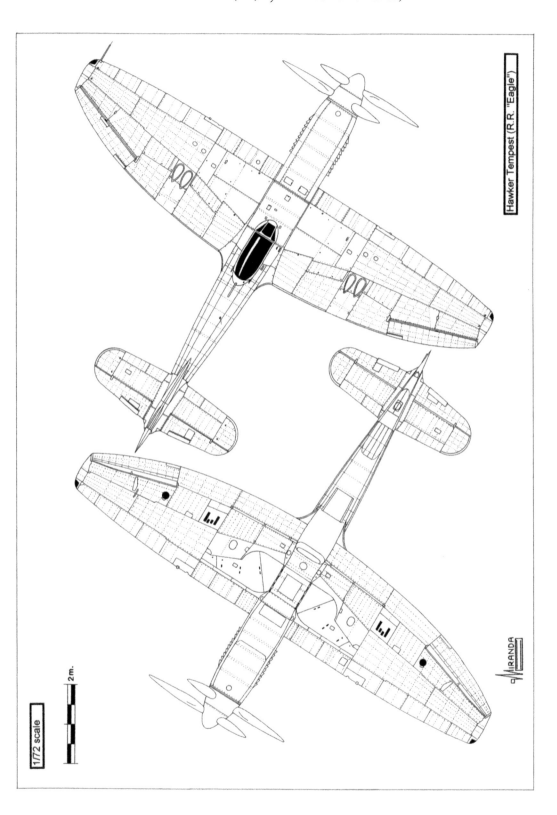

Hawker Tempest (R.R. "Eagle")

1/72 scale

2 m.

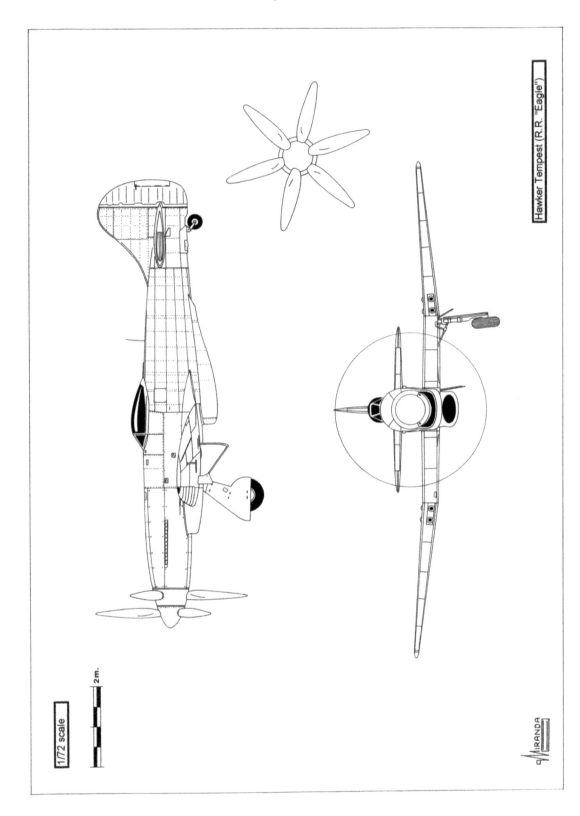

Hawker Tempest (R.R. "Eagle")

1/72 scale

2 m.

MIRANDA

Martin-Baker Swinging Arm

Drag

2m.

10

Switzerland
(16 May 1940–4 February 1945)

Following the Munich Agreement, in September 1938, Switzerland acquired ten Messerschmitt Bf 109 D-1s and eighty Bf 109 E-3 fighters. The first five D-1 aircraft were delivered by mid-December 1938 and the other five a month later. Each one was armed only with a pair of 7.45-mm MG 29 machine guns fitted in the front fuselage.

On 30 April, thirty Bf 109 E-3s were delivered, followed by fifty more units on 31 August. Also in September 1938, Switzerland acquired the manufacturing licence of the Morane-Saulnier M.S.406, together with two full aircraft. The export version, M.S.406H, kept the M.S.405 wings and the engine HS.12 Y-31. It was armed with only two drum-fed MAC 34 machine guns because the French did not want to share the technology of the 20-mm HS.404 cannon.

Between 1940 and 1942, the state factory F+W-Emmen built a series of seventy-four fighters known as D-3800. The Swiss version of the M.S.406 was powered by an 860-hp HS.12 Y-77 engine, licence-built by Adolph Saurer AG, and driving an Escher-Wyss EW V-3 controllable pitch propeller. The armament, built by *Waffenfabrik Bern*, consisted of a 20-mm Oerlikon FM-K cannon and two 7.5-mm Furrer Fl.Mg.29 belt-fed machine guns. The D-3800 came into service at the beginning of 1940, with a SE-013 R/T device and Draeger oxygen equipment.

Three days before the invasion of Poland, the Swiss Air Force was mobilised with fifty-eight Dewoitine D-27 C.1s (312 kph), ten Messerschmitt Bf 109 D-1s (470 kph), thirty Bf 109 E-3 (570 kph) fighters, and 127 observation aircraft of the type Fokker C.V and EKW C-35. When the Germans began their assault on the West on 10 May 1940, the Swiss Air Force had thirty-six D-3800s and the number of Bf 109 E-3 already amounted to seventy-eight. In May and June, Swiss airspace was violated three times by the French, ten times by the Italians, and 233 times by the Germans.

The Swiss fighters entered combat for the first time on 16 May. Between that date and 4 February 1945, they managed to shoot down one Dornier Do 17, five Heinkel He 111s, six Messerschmitt Bf 110s, two Avro Lancasters, one Boeing B-17, one Dornier Do 217, two

Consolidated B-24s, one De Havilland Mosquito, one Fiat R.S.14, two Republic P-47s, and one Junkers Ju 52/3m. They also faced 6,501 violations of airspace during which 198 aircraft were interned and fifty-six crashed.

In combat, the Bf 109 E-3 were superior in speed and manoeuvrability to the Bf 110 C of the Luftwaffe that were frequently forced to use the tactic *Abwehrkreiss* (Defence Circle). In April 1944, the Germans yielded twelve Bf 109 G-6s to the Swiss Air Force in exchange for the destruction of the electronic equipment of an interned Bf 110 G-4 night fighter.

In 1942, the EKW C-35 began to be replaced by the new EKW C-3603 (470 kph) heavy fighter. Its main purpose was to patrol the border violations of Swiss neutrality to force the intruders landing for internment. A night fighter squadron was formed in 1944.

A total of 152 C-3603s were manufactured between 1942 and 1944.

German hostility forced the Swiss to depend on fighters of their own manufacture. In 1939, Saurer began the manufacture under licence of the 1,020-hp HS.12 Y-51 French engine to improve the performances of the D-3800. Between October 1939 and December 1942, the companies Dornier Werke Altenrhein (Doflug) and SWS-Schlieren manufactured 207 units of the improved version D-3801. According to some sources, it was the Swiss version of the Morane-Saulnier M.S.412 C-1.

The new fighter was 33 kph faster and was equipped with armoured windshield and dorsal plate, a SE-012 R/T device, and Swiss Munerelle Agm 40 oxygen equipment. At the end of 1943, the Swiss Air Force had eleven *Flieger Kompagnien* equipped with D-3800 and D-3801 fighters. After the June 1940 armistice, the French continued improving the Morane fighters and their engines in Switzerland and Spain.

At the beginning of 1943, the drawings of M.S.460 C.1 (1939), M.S.540 C.1 (1941), and M.S.640 C.1 (1940) fighter projects and of the HS.12 Z-17 experimental engine were delivered to the Swiss by Morane-Saulnier personnel that collaborated with Dr Studer, chief engineer of Do-Flug, in the design of the D-3802 (640 kph)—the Swiss version of the M.S.540. Possibly also included were parts of the M.S.450 prototype for the study of their manufacturing techniques.

The D-3802 was powered by a 1,230-hp HS.12Y-89 (Saurer YS-2) driving a four-bladed Escher-Wyss EW V-8 constant-speed propeller with reverse pitch. It conserved the wing structure of the D-3801 but with the Plymax, replaced with all-aluminium-covering glycol radiators under the wings, Fowler-type flaps, and a variable-incidence tailplane. The armament consisted of one 20-mm HS.404 cannon and four 7.5-mm Fl.Mg.24 machine guns.

Four aircraft were manufactured in 1944 as prototypes of the production model D-3802A—the Swiss version of the M.S.550 with squared wingtips, bulged canopy and three HS.404 cannons. Only eleven copies were built between 1946 and 1950.

The D-3803, described as M.S.560 by some authors (with modified dorsal fuselage, all-round visibility canopy, and 1,430-hp Saurer YS-3 engine) was built as a prototype only in 1947. Its mass production was dismissed after the acquisition of 130 war-surplus P-51D Mustangs.

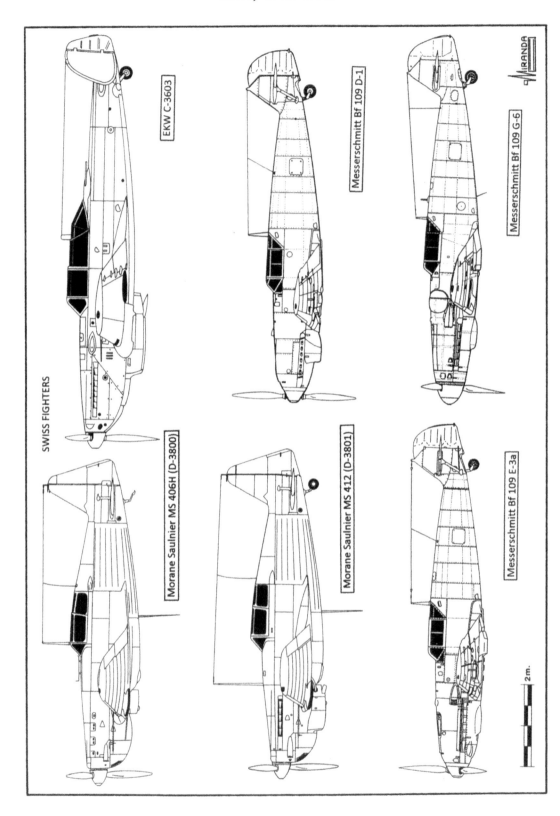

SWISS FIGHTERS

EKW C-3603

Messerschmitt Bf 109 D-1

Messerschmitt Bf 109 G-6

Morane Saulnier MS 406H (D-3800)

Morane Saulnier MS 412 (D-3801)

Messerschmitt Bf 109 E-3a

2 m.

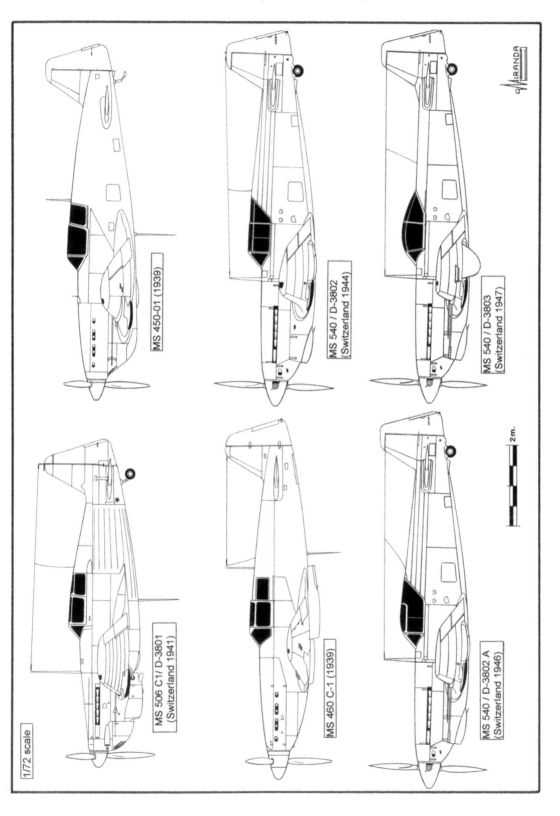

1/72 scale

MS 450-01 (1939)

MS 540 / D-3802 (Switzerland 1944)

MS 540 / D-3803 (Switzerland 1947)

MS 506 C1/ D-3801 (Switzerland 1941)

MS 460 C-1 (1939)

MS 540 / D-3802 A (Switzerland 1946)

2 m.

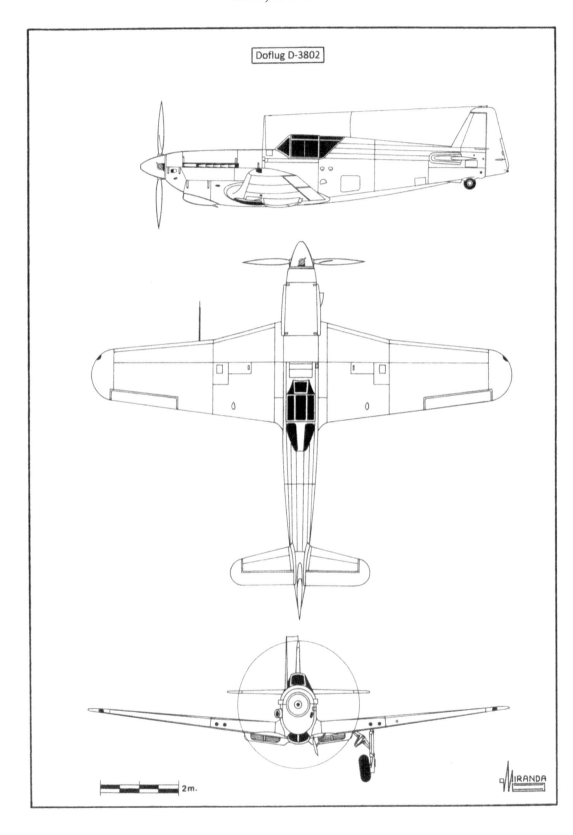

Doflug D-3802

2m.

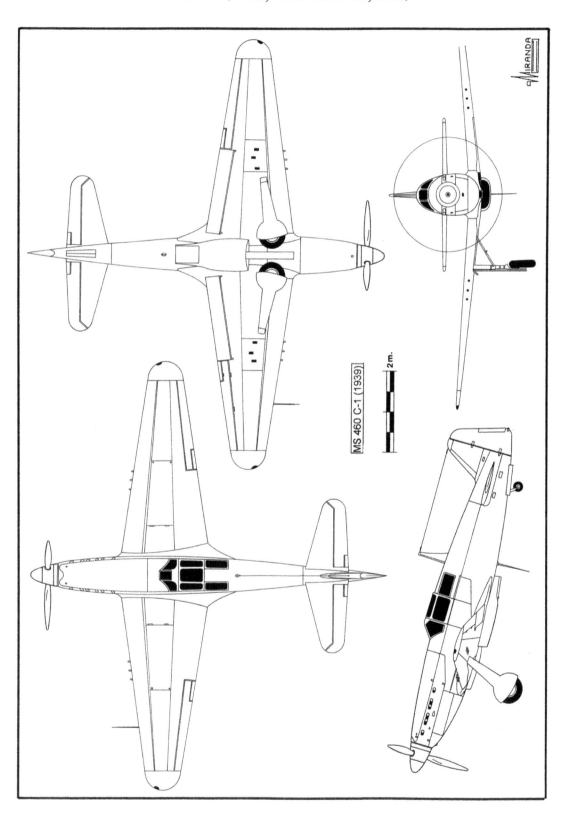

MS 460 C-1 (1939)

2 m.

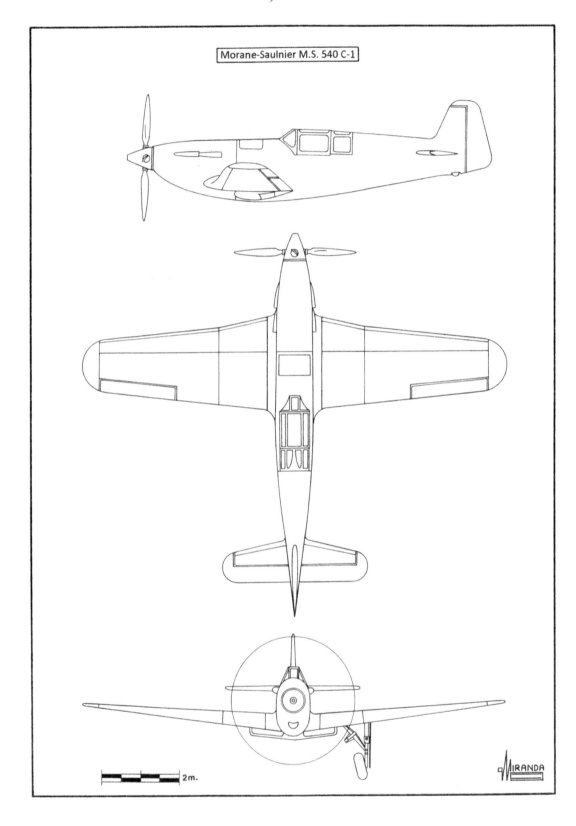

Morane-Saulnier M.S. 540 C-1

2 m.

Morane-Saulnier M.S.640

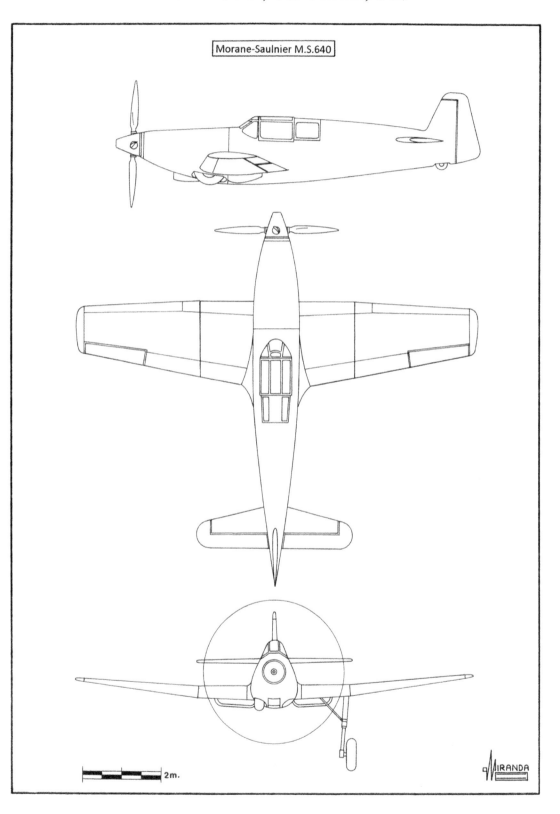

2m.

11

Romania
(6 September 1940-24 August 1944)

At the beginning of the 1920s, the aeronautical industry began to manufacture 400–500-hp engines, allowing designers to make the transition from biplane to monoplane to create a new generation of faster fighters.

Most manufacturers (Wibault, Gourdou, Morane, Nakajima, Dewoitine, and PWS) limited themselves to eliminate the lower wing to obtain a high-wing *parasol* fighter, retaining the take-off performances of biplanes. In 1928, the Polish designer Zygmunt Pulawski decided to use one strut-braced gull-wing in the PZL P.1 fighter prototype. This type of wing improved manoeuvrability during the combat turns, preventing the fighter from losing altitude thanks to the extra lift generated by the 'Vee' central section.

During the Spanish Civil War, the gull-wing made the Polikarpov I-15 superior to the Fiat CR.32. The formula was also used in the French Loire 46, the Yugoslavian Ikarus IK-2, and the PZL fighters until 1941. In 1930, the PZL P.6 won the National Air Races in the USA, but something had changed in 1932 and the Hall's Bulldog, with Pulawski wing, was overcome by the Gee Bee, with low-wing, in the Thompson Trophy race.

In January 1936, the Romanian Government acquired the manufacturing licence of the PZL P.11c fighter. The IAR firm built ninety-five units as P.11F (380 kph). In November, they also acquired the manufacturing licence for twenty-five units of the PZL P.24E (430 kph), but the model became obsolete that same month when it was learned that the Polikarpov I-16 Type 5—a low wing monoplane with retractable landing gear capable of flying at 454 kph—had entered into combat in Spain, beating the Heinkel He 51 of the Condor Legion. Three months later, the Messerschmitt Bf 109 B-1 (462 kph) entered service with the Luftwaffe.

At the end of 1936, the Pulawski fighters had reached the limit of their development; the drag generated by the bracing struts and the spatted landing gear prevented them from exceeding 430 kph. When knowing the performance of the Bf 109 B-1, IAR started the design of a low-wing version of the P.24E called IAR 80. The new fighter, powered by an IAR 14K radial engine, should use the fuselage and tail surfaces of the P.24, attached to a wing based on the Savoia-Marchetti SM.79B bomber wing (decreasing its dimensions by 50 per cent) containing a retractable Messier undercarriage.

One month later, following the annexation of the Sudetenland to the Third Reich, Romania acquired twelve Hawker Hurricane Mk IAs (518 kph) after learning that the Bf 109 B-2 (462 kph) had come into service. An even faster version, called Bf 109 E-1 (574 kph), did it in February 1939.

On 15 March 1939, Germany invaded the remainder of Czechoslovakia. Nine days later, Romania was forced to sign an economic treaty to supply oil to the Reich from the fields of Ploesti in exchange for thirty Heinkel 112E fighters. In April, the prototype of the IAR 80 flew at 510 kph. A month later, Romania signed a treaty of territorial integrity with Great Britain and France.

On 23 August 1939, the Molotov–Ribbentrop Pact was signed. Five days later, the Hawker Hurricanes Mk IA and the first He 112E were delivered to the Royal Romanian Air Force (FARR). On 1 September 1939, the Third Reich invaded Poland, followed by a Soviet attack on the 17th. At the end of that year, the FARR ordered fifty Messerschmitt Bf 109 E-3 and 100 IAR 80 fighters.

On 28 June 1940, the USSR annexed the Romanian regions of Bessarabia and northern Bukovina. Two months later, Germany and Italy forced Romania to cede northern Transylvania to Hungary and southern Dobruja to Bulgaria. On 23 November 1940, as a result of a coup, Romania signed the Axis Tripartite Pact and the FARR received the first Bf 109 E-3. Between February and May 1941, IAR delivered the first batch of seventy IAR 80 fighters. On 22 June, Romania was forced to participate in the invasion of the USSR (Operation Barbarossa) on the pretext of recovering Bessarabia.

At that time, the FARR had fifty-eight IAR 80/80As, twenty-three He 112Es, thirty Bf 109 E-3s, ten Hawker Hurricane Mk IAs, twenty PZL P.24Es, thirty-two PZL P.11Fs, and twenty-four PZL P.11cs from the Polish Air Force. In combat, the PZL fighters were superior to the Soviet I-16 during the Bessarabian campaign, being used as fighter-bombers from October 1941.

The Hurricanes were soon useless due to a lack of spares, and the He 112E, fitted with 20-mm cannons, mainly used on strafing missions, suffered heavy losses because of the absence of armour. The FARR was forced to depend more and more on the IAR 80, a fighter that equalled the Bf 109 E in climb and manoeuvrability, able to reach 500 kph with an engine of just 930 hp.

The IAR 80 of the first production batch suffered engine problems and failures of the undercarriage retraction system. They were armed with four 7.92-mm FN/Browning machine guns. The IAR 80A with six 7.92-mm FN and a 1,025-hp IAR K14 1000A engine was delivered in May 1941. The IAR 80B had larger wings, four 7.92-mm FN armaments and two 13.2-mm FN machine guns. It was delivered in June 1942, taking part in the battle of Stalingrad. The 13.2-mm FN were replaced by two 20-mm Ikaria cannons in the IAR 80C, delivered on December 1942.

The IAR 81 was built as a dive bomber, armed with six 7.92-mm FN machine guns. The fighter version, called IAR 81C, was armed with two 7.92-mm FN and two 20-mm MG 151 cannons. The 474 IAR 80/81s that had been built achieved 500 aerial victories during the Second World War. From 1942, they were gradually outclassed by the newest Soviet fighters. In 1943, all aircraft were relegated to home defence.

The IAR 14K engine could not overcome 1,025 hp, and the Germans denied the licence to manufacture the 1,700-hp BMW 801 radial engine. In early 1942, a 1,200-hp Jumo 211 in-line engine, from a Savoia-Marchetti S.M. 79B bomber, was installed in the IAR 80 c/n 111. However, during the flight tests, the aircraft experienced destructive vibration problems and the continuation of the experiments was dismissed. At the end of 1943, a DB 601 Aa from a Bf 109 E-3 was installed in the IAR 80 c/n 13, doing some test flights. On 29 June 1943, the IAR 81C c/n 326 was experimentally equipped with a 1,475-hp DB 605A engine.

On 24 August 1944, before the Soviet advance, Romania changed sides, carrying out operations of combat against the Third Reich until the end of the Second World War in Europe.

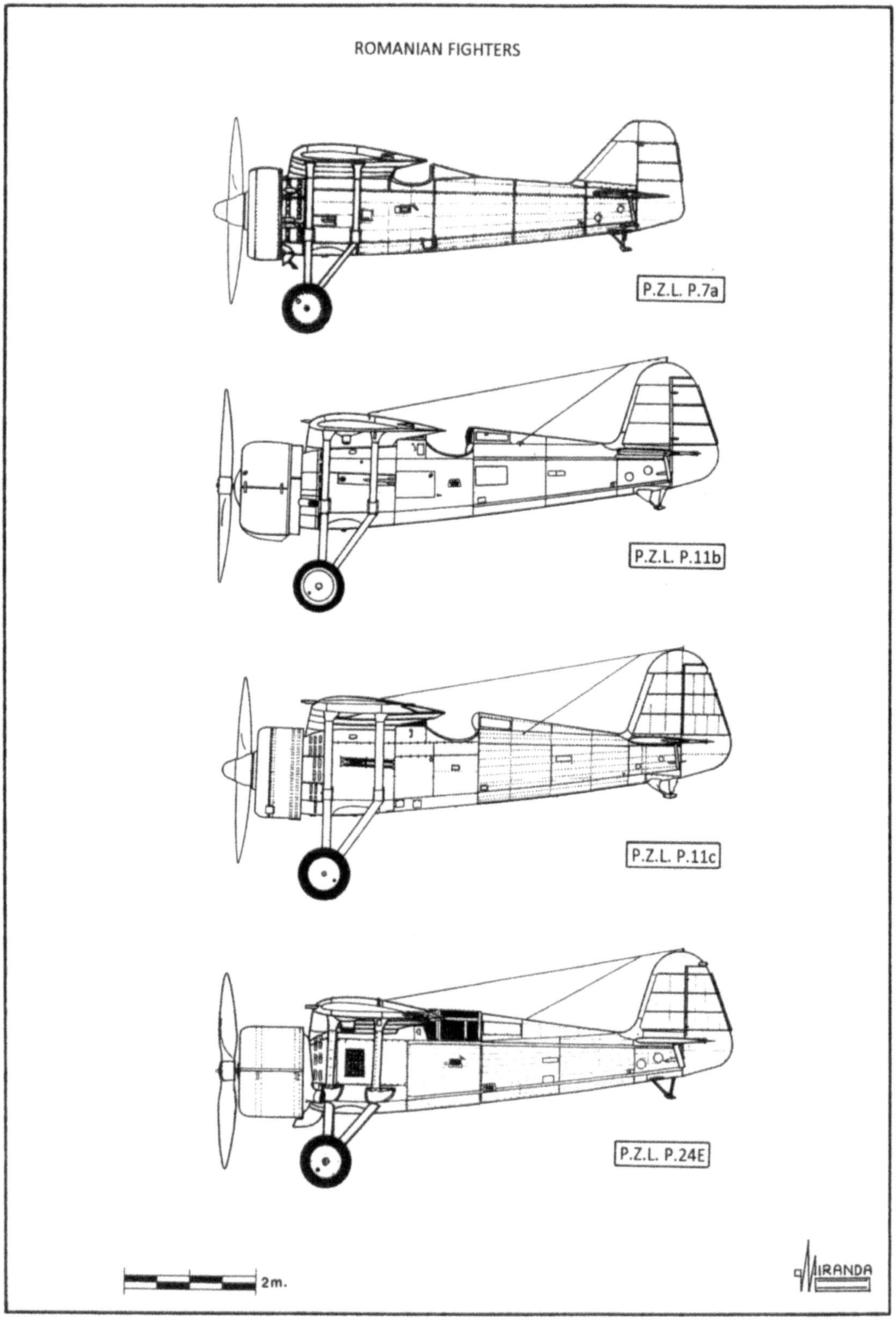

ROMANIAN FIGHTERS

P.Z.L. P.7a

P.Z.L. P.11b

P.Z.L. P.11c

P.Z.L. P.24E

2m.

MIRANDA

ROMANIAN FIGHTERS

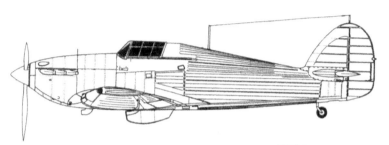

Hawker Hurricane Mk.I

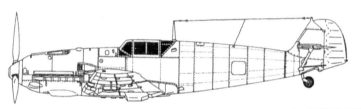

Messerschmitt Bf 109 E-4

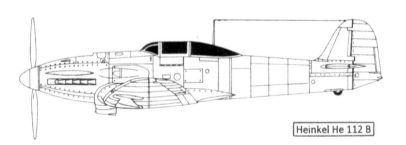

Heinkel He 112 B

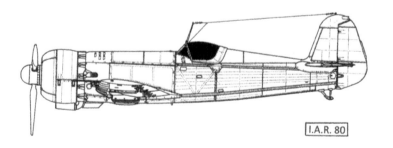

I.A.R. 80

2 m.

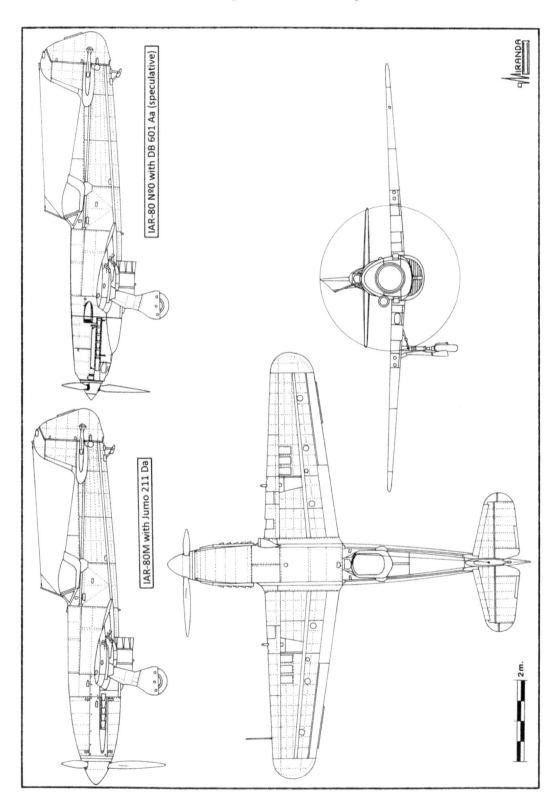

IAR-80 Nº0 with DB 601 Aa (speculative)

IAR-80M with Jumo 211 Da

2 m.

Hungary
(4 April 1941–16 April 1945)

The annexation of Austria to the Third Reich, the loss of credibility of France and Great Britain after the Munich Agreement, and the disintegration of Czechoslovakia contributed to the breaking of the fragile balance between the countries of Eastern Europe since the end of the First World War.

Hungary claimed the Romanian region of Northern Transylvania, and the tension between the two countries led them to enact the total mobilisation on 23 August 1940. At that moment, Germany intervened to prevent the war between its two main suppliers of oil, including them in its area of influence. The pressure on Hungary forced its adhesion to the Axis on 20 November 1940, and five months later, a crisis of government allowed the *Wehrmacht* to cross its territory to invade Yugoslavia.

Following the bombing of Kassa, carried out by Soviet aircraft in 1941, Hungary was forced to participate in the invasion of the USSR during Operation Barbarossa. On March 1944, before the advance of the Red Army, Hungary began peace negotiations with the Allies and the *Wehrmacht* occupied the country to keep its oil supply, resisting until April 1945.

The peace treaty of Trianon, signed in 1920, banned the possession of military aircraft to Hungary. After the Austria *Anschluss*, the Royal Hungary Air Force (MKHL) was started with the acquisition of fifty-two Fiat CR.32 and sixty-eight Fiat CR.42 Italian fighters in 1938. Both models were obsolete in 1941 and were too slow to intercept the Yugoslavian Bristol Blenheim. However, in combat against the Soviet Polikarpov I-16, the CR.42 were superior in manoeuvrability.

The MKHL needed modern fighters, but in 1939, its acquisition was already difficult. Finally, seventy Reggiane Re.2000s were ordered in December that year, as well as the licence to build the fighter. The aircraft were delivered between December 1940 and February 1941, equipped with an unreliable Piaggio P.XI engine and only two machine guns. They also lacked armour. Some aircraft had fuel leaks that made them useless for combat.

All should be modified as *Hejja I* (520 kph), installing them a new 1,000-hp Manfred Weiss WM K-14 B radial engine, driving a Hamilton-Standard three-bladed, constant-speed propeller. Armour plates and one additional fuel tank were installed in the fuselage, and the Italian machine guns were replaced by two 12.7-mm Danubia/Gebauer GKM.

On 11 August 1941, *Hejja I* entered combat for the first time, surpassing the Polikarpov I-16 in speed and manoeuvrability. In 1942, they were overcome by the new Soviet fighters, and in 1943, they were used for home defence duties. Some 203 other units of the Hungarian version *Hejja II* were manufactured under licence by MAVAG between 1942 and 1944.

On September 1938, the Hungarian Ministry of War Affairs ordered thirty-six Heinkel He 112B fighters, but the Germans deliberately delayed the fulfilment of the order for political reasons and refused to hand over the licence for the Jumo 211 engine. Hungary only received two He 112 B-1/U2 demonstrators in 1939 and one He 112 B-1 in 1940.

By the end of 1939, the Hungarian Government took the decision to produce a simplified version of the He 112 adapted to the possibilities of the local aviation industry. The new aircraft, called Weiss Manfréd WM 23 Ezüst *Nyil*, would be propelled by a 1,000-hp Gnôme & Rhône 14 Kfrs radial engine driving a Hamilton-Standard propeller.

The wings, with Fowler flaps, would have been built in wood/plywood and the fuselage in a welded-steel tube with plywood skinning. The armament, installed in the fuselage, would consist of two 8-mm Gebauer machine guns and two 20-mm synchronised Mauser MG 151 cannons. It was built as a prototype (530 kph) that demonstrated good flying characteristics during its first flight on September 1941. It was destroyed in 1942 due to malfunction of the starboard aileron.

The improved version *Ezüst Nyil II*—with all-metal monocoque fuselage and 1,475-hp DB 605 engine (planned for 1943)—was discontinued when the Germans allowed the manufacture under licence of the Messerschmitt Bf 109 G. The availability of the DB 605 engine induced engineer Dezső Marton of the Aviation Technological Institute to design a twin-boom push-pull heavy fighter based on the Fokker D.XXIII. The construction of the prototype, called Marton RMI-8 XV-01, with wooden wings and metal fuselage, started in 1943 but was destroyed by bombing on 13 April 1944. It was expected to have reached a maximum speed of 580 kph and a ceiling of 11,500 m.

The armament would have consisted of a 30-mm Rheinmetall-Borsig MK 108 cannon, firing through the propeller hub, two 20-mm Mauser MG 151 installed in the boom leading edges, and two 8-mm Gebauer machine guns fitted in the front fuselage. The aircraft was to have an ejection seat powered by a spring.

Enemy at the Gates

HUNGARIAN FIGHTERS

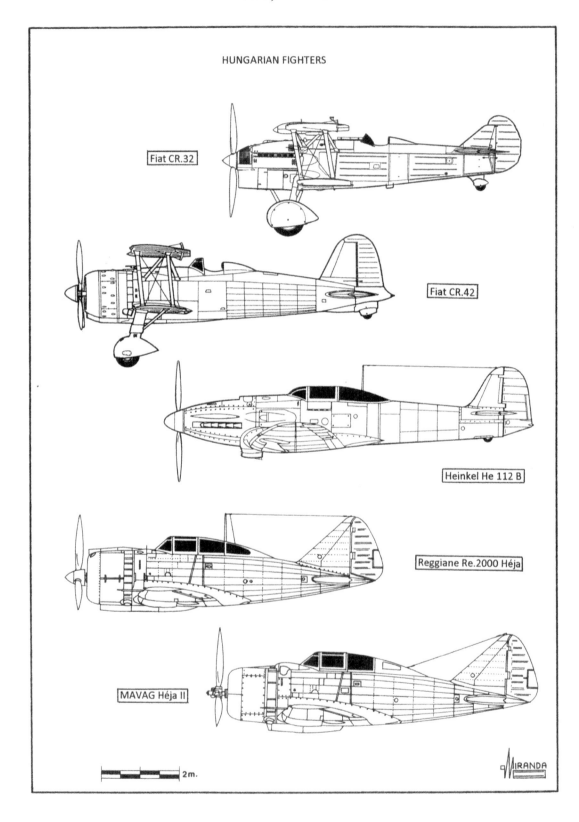

Fiat CR.32

Fiat CR.42

Heinkel He 112 B

Reggiane Re.2000 Héja

MAVAG Héja II

2m.

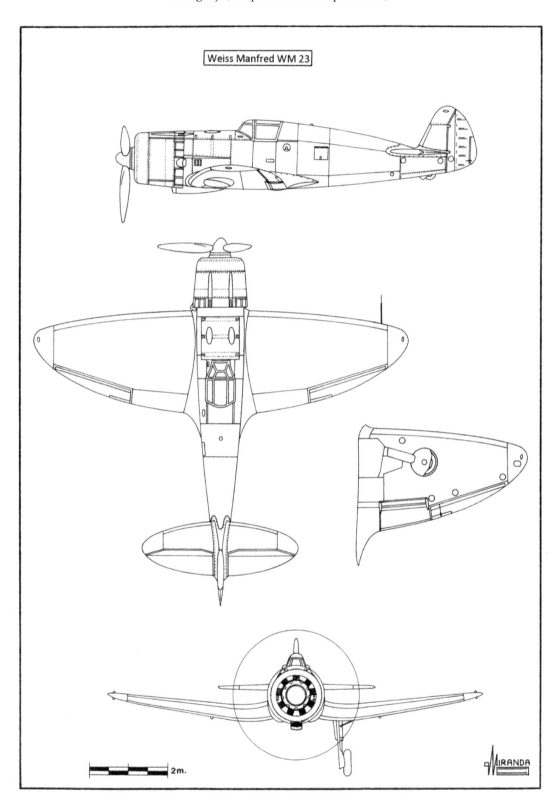

Weiss Manfred WM 23

2m.

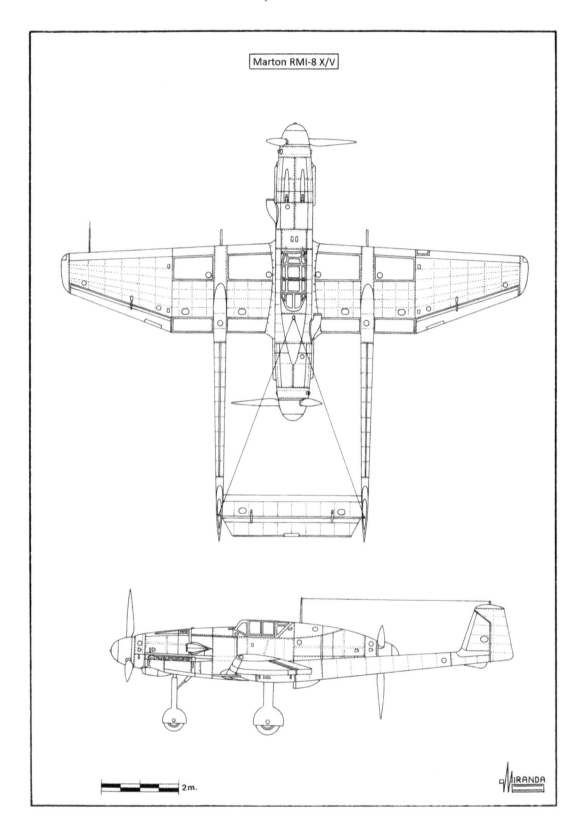

Marton RMI-8 X/V

2m.

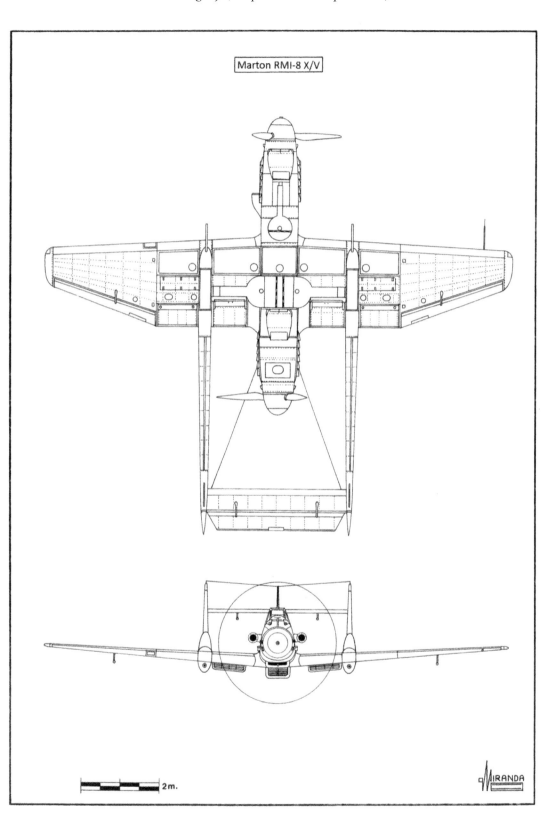

Marton RMI-8 X/V

2m.

13

Yugoslavia
(6–18 April 1941)

On 6 April 1941, eight German, Italian, and Hungarian armies invaded Yugoslavia in a fast campaign of just thirteen days. The attackers used 797 fighters, 965 bombers, and 339 reconnaissance aircraft.

The Royal Yugoslav Air Force (JKRV) had 474 airworthy aircraft: 140 fighters (forty-six Messerschmit Bf 109 E-3as, forty-one Hawker Hurricane Mk Ias, thirty-four Hawker Fury Mk IIs, three Avia BH-33Es, two Potez 63s, eight Ikarus IK-2s, and six Rogožarsky Ik-3s), 172 bombers (fifty-five Bristol Blenheim Mk Is, seventy-two Dornier Do 17 Kas, and forty-five Savoia-Marchetti S.M. 79 Ka), 127 Army cooperation aircraft of the types Breguet Br XIX, Potez 25, and Fieseler Fi 156C, plus thirty-five maritime patrol floatplanes of the types Dornier *Wal*, Dornier Do 22, and Sim XIV.

The JKRV made 1,433 combat sorties. Out of them, 993 were made by fighters who fought hard, shooting down eighty German, fourteen Italians, and six Hungarian aircraft.

The Hawker Fury

In 1931, the Yugoslavian Government acquired three Fury Mk I fighters with a 525-hp Rolls-Royce Kestrel IIS engine; in 1935, they bought ten more units of the Fury Mk II with one 745-hp Kestrel XVI. In 1937, the firm Ikarus built twenty-four Mk II under licence, and Zmaj built sixteen more, armed with two 7.7-mm Darne M.30 machine guns.

On the first day of fighting, fifteen Messerschmitt Bf 109 E-7s of the LG2 and fifteen Bf 110s of the II./ZG 26 attacked Režanovačka Kosa airfield, destroying ten Furies in aerial combat, one strafed on the ground, and one more during a forced landing. One Bf 109 and one Bf 110 were rammed by the Furies, and another Bf 110 was destroyed by the AA. The Furies were too slow (389 kph) to intercept the He 111 and Ju 88, so they were mainly used on strafing and bomber escort missions.

On 9 April 1941, two surviving Furies were burnt by their own crews in Morava valley. The next day, eight more aircraft were damaged, suffering the same fate in Kraljevo. On the 12th, a Fury was destroyed by the Flak. Two days later, another was shot down by a Macchi MC.200. On the 16th, the seven surviving aircraft were captured by the Italians in Kolpino Poje.

The Ikarus IK-2

The Ikarus IK-2 was the first fighter designed in Yugoslavia, inspired on the French prototype Loire 43. Two prototypes and twelve production aircraft were built between 1935 and 1939. They were powered by an 860-hp Avia HS.12 Ycrs, built under licence in Czechoslovakia, driving a three-bladed Ratier airscrew. The armament consisted of a 20-mm HS.9 cannon and two 7.92-mm FN M-38 machine guns. The R/T device was a Telefunken FuG VIIa.

In 1941, the IK-2 was considered obsolete; though it proved to be more manoeuvrable than the modern fighters, it was mainly used in scouting and strafing duties. On 6 April, just eight aircraft were left in flying condition, based at Bosanski Aleksandrovac airfield. They tried to intercept a formation of twenty-seven Bf 109 E-7s, together with eight Hurricanes. During the combat, two Hurricanes, two Bf 109s, and one IK-2 were shot down. On 13 April, four IK-2 were burnt by their own crews, and the three that survived were captured by the Germans two days later.

The Rogožarsky Ik-3

It was a low wing monoplane that was proposed as successor of the IK-2 in 1936. The project was approved in March 1937, after learning that the new Messerschmitt Bf 109 B-1 (462 kph) had entered service with the Luftwaffe. The prototype flew in the spring of 1938, proving to be 40 kph faster than the Morane-Saulnier M.S.405, although equipped with the same engine. Its turning radius was smaller than those of the Hawker Hurricane Mk I and the Bf 109 E.

Twelve production aircraft were built between March 1939 and July 1940, powered by a 980-hp Avia HS.12 Y-29, driving one Hamilton-Standard constant-speed airscrew. The armament consisted of one 20-mm Oerlikon FF/SMK M.39 EM engine-mounted cannon and two 7.9-mm Browning FN M.38 machine guns fitted in the front fuselage. The R/T device was a Telefunken FuG VII.

On 6 April 1941, the JKRV only had six Ik-3 in flying condition, based at Zemun-Belgrade. They were forced to fight on four occasions against the bombers of the Luftflotte IV that attacked the capital that same day during Operation Retribution. The first attack was carried out by seventy-four Ju 87B dive bombers of the StG 77, 160 He 111 of the II./KG 4, and forty-four Do 17Z of the KG.2 and KG.3, escorted by fifty-three Bf 110 of the ZG 26 and 100 Bf 109E-7 of the JG 77. The Ik-3 fighters shot down two Dorniers and five Bf 110s, losing an aircraft in combat and two in forced landings.

The second attack, carried out by fifty-seven Ju 87Bs of the StG 77, escorted by thirty Bf 109s, were intercepted by three Ik-3s and some Yugoslavian Bf 109 E-3a of the 51st Fighter Group, which managed to shoot down two Ju 87s and one German Bf 109. The same fighters entered combat for the third time against ninety-four Ju 88 bombers of the KG.5, escorted by sixty Bf 109s and, for the fourth time, against a formation of ninety Ju 87Bs and sixty Bf 109s, shooting down two Ju 87s of StG 77, one Bf 109 E-4B of the JG54, and a Bf 109 E-7 of the JG 77.

At the beginning of the invasion, twenty-five Ik-3s of the second production series (540 kph) were in the final assembly phase, but only one was completed in time to fight, managing to shoot down a Bf 110 over Fruska Gora. On 11 April, two Ik-3s managed to shoot down two Ju 87Bs, losing one of them over Belgrade. The next day, all the surviving aircraft were burnt by their own crews, but the Germans captured three aircraft damaged in Zemun.

The Hawker Hurricane

At the end of 1937, the Yugoslavian Government acquired twelve fighters Hurricane Mk I, equipped with fabric wings and a Rolls-Royce Merlin II engine, driving a two-blade Watts wooden propeller. Between February and March 1940, a second batch delivery included twelve Mk Ias with metal wings, a 1,030-hp Merlin III engine, and three-blade, variable-pitch de Havilland propellers. Twenty additional Mk Ias were built under licence by Zmaj Zemun. At the time of the German onslaught, a total of forty-one Hurricanes were in service with the JKRV.

During the second attack over Belgrade, the Hurricanes of the 52nd Fighter Group shot down a Ju 87B of the StG.77. On 8 April, a Hurricane was shot down by the Flak during a strafing mission. In a combat over Rovine, on 9 April, Hurricanes of the 33rd and 34th Fighter Group shot down a Bf 109 E in exchange of two aircraft of their own.

The next day, another Bf 109E was shot down by the 34th F.G., three aircraft of the 52nd F.G. were destroyed in accidents, and others by their own crews to prevent their capture in Veliki Radinci. On 11 April, aircraft of the 34th F.G. shot down a Bf 110 over Nova Gradiška and a Ju 88 over Bosanka Gradiška. A Hurricane was strafed by Bf 109 in Zemun.

The next day, the Hurricanes of the 33rd F.G. were strafed by Bf 110 in Bijeljina airfield, surviving just one aircraft. Two more Hurricanes were downed by the Ju 88 of the KG.5 and the Bf 110 of escort over Banja Luka. A Ju 88 and a Bf 110 were shot down by Hurricanes of the 34th F.G. near Banja Luka. Two Hurricanes from the Air Training School were shot down over Mostar by the Ju 88 and the Bf 109 of escort.

On 13 April, a Bf 110 was shot down by the 34th F.G. over Banja Luka. On 16 April, the three surviving Hurricanes were captured by the Germans.

The Messerschmitt Bf 109

On April 1939, the Yugoslav Government signed a contract for the acquisition of fifty Messerschmitt Bf 109 E-3as, followed by a new contract for another fifty aircraft on 23 June of the same year.

A total of seventy-three fighters were delivered, without spares, before the cooperation with Germans would be interrupted for political reasons. On 6 April 1941, the JKRV had forty-six serviceable Bf 109. Thirteen of them were downed during fighting over Belgrade while the Germans lost one Ju 87B and one Hs 126.

The Bf 109 of the Luftwaffe differed only externally from the Yugoslavs in their yellow nose, which caused numerous confusions. On 7 April, the JKRV lost twelve Bf 109s in combat over Belgrade. On the 10th and 11th, all serviceable Bf 109 were burned at Veliki Radinci.

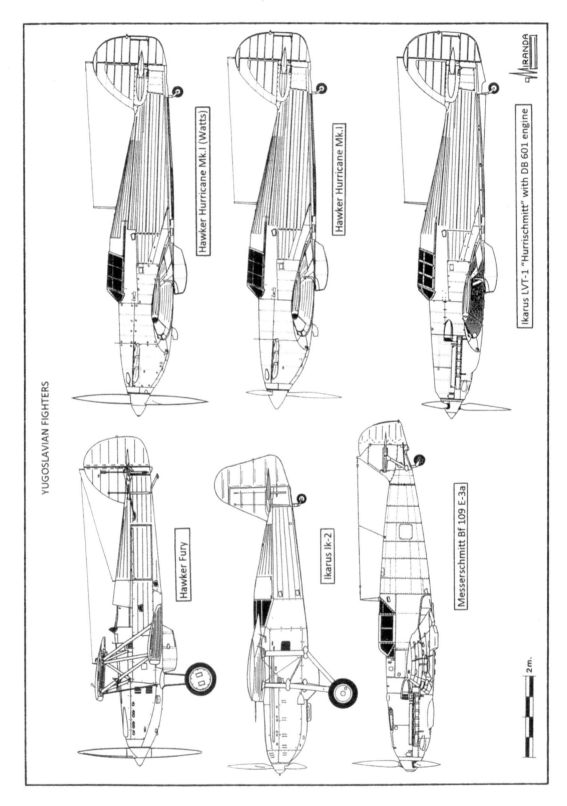

YUGOSLAVIAN FIGHTERS

Hawker Hurricane Mk.I (Watts)

Hawker Hurricane Mk.I

Ikarus LVT-1 "Hurrischmitt" with DB 601 engine

Hawker Fury

Ikarus Ik-2

Messerschmitt Bf 109 E-3a

2 m.

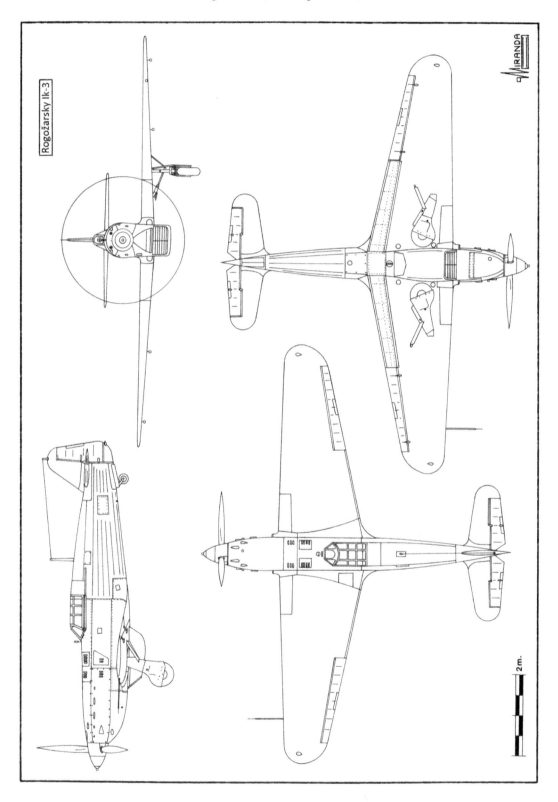

Rogožarsky Ik-3

2 m.

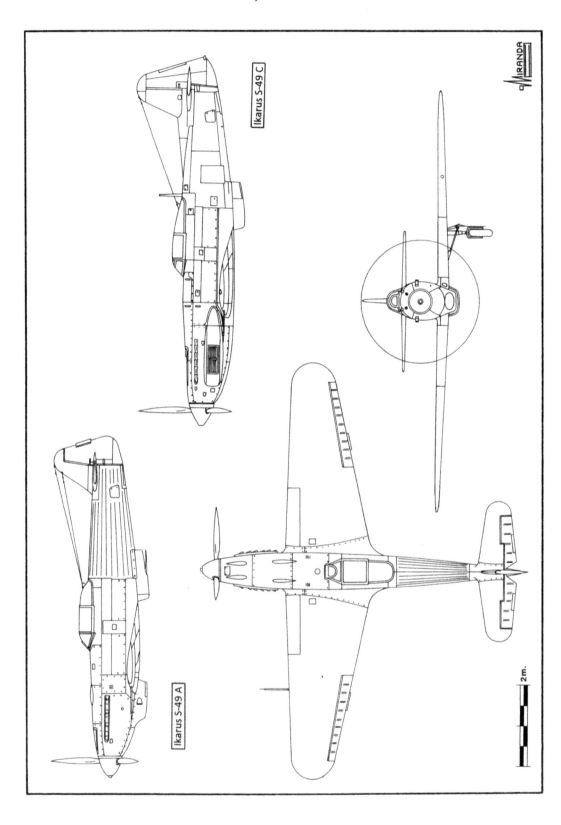

Ikarus S-49 C

Ikarus S-49 A

2 m.

14

Greece
(6–27 April 1941)

On 2 October 1940, during Operation *Esigenza G*, an Italian army of 40,000 men supported by 300 aircraft attempted to invade Greece, being rejected in a week with the help of three RAF squadrons.

After their expulsion from Dunkirk, the British tried to return to continental Europe by increasing their influence in the Eastern Mediterranean. They took part in Greek politics, forcing the rejection of Yugoslavia to the Tripartite Pact, prompting the French forces in Syria to resume the fight against the Axis, eroding the Turkish neutrality and humiliating to the Italian Regia Marina in Taranto, Genoa, and Matapan.

Establishing air bases in Crete would have allowed the bombers of the RAF to attack the oilfields of Ploesti, and the new Yugoslavian policy would have permitted the Royal Navy to carry out a landing at the Dalmatian coast without opposition. This situation forced the Germans to postpone the invasion of the USSR, attacking Yugoslavia and Greece on 6 April 1941 (Operation Marita) and Crete on 20 May 1941 (Operation Mercury) with twenty-eight divisions and 1,200 aircraft.

The Royal Hellenic Air Force (EVA) order of battle in October 1940 consisted of fifty-three Avia BH-33, Avia B-534 III, Gloster Gladiator Mk I, PZL P.24 F/G, and Marcel Bloch MB. 151 C.1 fighters; twenty-nine Potez 633 B2, Bristol Blenheim Mk IV, and Fairey Battle Mk II bombers; forty-one Breguet Br XIX A2/B2, Potez 25 A2, and Henschel Hs 126 K-6 reconnaissance aircraft; and thirty Fairey IIIF, Dornier Do 22, and Avro Anson Mk I naval aircraft.

On 18 August 1936, the Greeks acquired four Yugoslavian Avia BH-33 fighters and two Czech Avia B-534 Serie III on 3 November 1940. Both B-534 (363 kph) fought against the Italians and were still part of the 24th Squadron in 1941.

On 16 November 1936, the Greek Government placed an order for thirty PZL P.24F and six P.24G. The fighters were delivered in the spring of 1937, fitted with a 970-hp Gnome-Rhône 14 N 07 radial engine, an armoured windshield, a dorsal armour plate, a Telefunken R/T device, and Gaertner oxygen equipment. The P.24G was armed with two

20-mm Oerlikon FF cannons and two 7.92-mm Colt Browning MG 40 machine guns, the P.24F with four MG 40.

In October 1940, the EVA had thirty P.24 serviceable aircraft with the 21st, 22nd, and 23rd Squadrons. In April 1941, only nineteen were in flying condition, nine were destroyed in combat (two of them by ramming), and the rest strafed. During the combats in Greece, they managed to shoot down five CANT Z.1007biss, five Fiat CR.42s, one Caproni Ca.314, one IMAM Ro.37bis, five Fiat B.R.20s, four Fiat G.50s, one Savoia-Marchetti S.M.79, one Dornier Do 17Z, and three Henschel Hs 126s.

In 1938, the Greeks acquired two Gloster Gladiator Mk I (413 kph) equipped with four 7.92-mm machine guns, a Telefunken stat 276 AF R/T device, and a Gaertner oxygen supply system. One of them was still in service in November 1940 in the Fighter Training Centre. On December 1940, nineteen ex-RAF Gladiators Mk I/II entered service with the 21st Squadron, managing to shoot down one Fiat CR.42, two Fiat B.R.20s, three Fiat G.50s, two CANT Z.1007biss, and one Junkers Ju 87, losing four planes of their own in combat.

Out of twenty-five Bloch MB.151 C.1s (415 kph) ordered before the German invasion of France, only nine were delivered (without spares) in April 1940, equipped with a 900-hp Gnome-Rhône 14 N. These engines were often well-used, suffering problems of warming, and they only generated a real power of 700 hp, they were optimised to operate at a 3,000-m ceiling and could not compete with the DB 601 of the German fighters.

The aircraft lacked oxygen equipment, were only armed with four 7.5-mm MAC 34 M39 machine guns, and their R/T device was not compatible with that of other Greek fighters. Despite these shortcomings, the Bloch managed to destroy a Fiat B.R.20, three CANT Z.1007 bis bombers, and a Dornier Do 17Z reconnaissance aircraft. On 14 April 1941, they still had three aircraft in flying condition operating with the 24th Squadron. One was shot down that same day by a Bf 109E-4 of II/JG 27, and the two remaining aircraft were strafed by Bf 109s four days later, along with eleven P.24s and eight Gladiators.

At the time of the German attack, the continuous clashes with the Italians had reduced the EVA strength to only forty-one combat aircraft in flying condition. A few days before the invasion, the Greek Government ordered ninety 'panic fighters'—Grumman G-36A Wildcat, Curtiss P-40, and ex-French Curtiss H.75A types—but none came to Greek territory, being retained in Suez at the service of the RAF.

Despite the British aid, the German forces quickly established air superiority. The Allied troops retreated to Crete until it was also occupied by the Axis. When the Greek forces were defeated on 27 April, only five Ansons, one Do 22, and three Avro 626s survived, flying to Egypt along with some Yugoslavian aircraft.

GREEK FIGHTERS

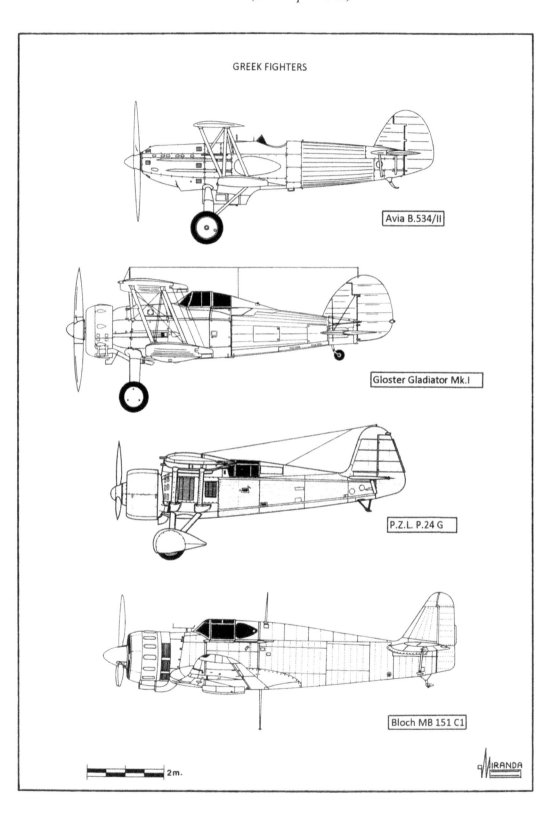

Avia B.534/II

Gloster Gladiator Mk.I

P.Z.L. P.24 G

Bloch MB 151 C1

2m.

15

The Russian Aggressor
(28 May 1939–25 August 1941)

After the defeat suffered against the Polish Army in 1920 and lacking enough aircraft, the Soviets decided to build a powerful Red Air Force (VVS RKKA) formed by 2,500 aircraft to 'liberate' the neighbouring countries. On 28 May 1939, they attacked Manchuria, Poland on 17 September, Finland on 30 November, Lithuania on 15 June 1940, Estonia and Latvia on 16 June, Bessarabia and Northern Bukovina on 28 June, and Iran on 25 August 1941.

In 1923, they built the first indigenous fighter—the Polikarpov I-1. It was a low-wing monoplane built in wood/plywood/fabric with a 300-hp Liberty L-12 engine. The prototype was designed according to the trial and error principle and proved to be unstable and structurally fragile. After suffering several accidents, its serial production was declined in 1927. Its successor, the I-3, was a biplane powered by a BMW VI German engine that generated 750 hp but weighted 540 kg, raising the weight of the aircraft to 1,850 kg. When the I-3 came into service with the VVS in 1929, it could not compete with the agile Fiat CR.20 and Bleriot SPAD 61 fighters used by Lithuanians and Poles. The Soviets acquired some of these aircraft to study their manufacturing secrets, but their industry was unable to duplicate the sophisticated duraluminium structure of their wing. The indigenous engines M-15 and M-17 also proved a failure due to vibration and excessive weight.

The US Navy allowed a public demonstration of the Boeing XF4B-1 prototype fighter at the National Air Races of Los Angeles in 1928. Designed to operate from aircraft carriers, the aircraft was of reduced dimensions, with wings built of wood/plywood/fabric and a fuselage made of welded steel tubing. Its simple construction technique proved more accessible to the Soviets, who used the XF4B-1 as a source of inspiration to design the Polikarpov I-5. The prototype flew in 1930, powered by a Shvetsov M-22, the Russian version of the Bristol Jupiter VI, with 30 hp less. The I-5 was armed with two 7.62-mm Maxim-Nagchkevitch PV-1 machine guns, which were installed on the sides of the fuselage, in order to use the same synchronisation device as the Bristol Bulldog British fighter. The Polish racer PZL P.6 also used the Jupiter VI, but the advanced aerodynamics of its Pulawski wing allowed it to exceed the maximum speed of the I-5, fourteen months before entering service with the VVS.

During the winter of 1932–1933, the PZL P.7 came into service with the Polish Air Force. It was the military version of the P.6 with a maximum speed of 320 kph. The Pulawski gull-wing allowed the Polish fighters to make very steep turns without losing height thanks to the additional lift generated by the 'Vee' central section. The Soviets wanted to improve the manoeuvrability of the I-5 with a similar design but retaining the advantages of the biplanes. For this, they copied the structural solutions devised by the Americans for the Curtiss XP-10 fighter, a prototype built to be fast and manoeuvrable enough to win in a dogfight.

In 1928, the XP-10 proved its superiority over the Curtiss Hawk, but the project was discontinued by deficiencies in the Conqueror V-12 engine.

When the Polikarpov I-15 flew for the first time in October 1933, it had important aerodynamic solutions (from Curtiss XP-10 and F9C 'Sparrowhawk' fighters) incorporated in its design, making it exceptional in handling and manoeuvrability.

The plan had been that the production version would be powered with the M-25 engine, a Soviet version of the Wright Cyclone SGR-1820-F-3 with 80 hp less, but its entry into service was so urgent that the 384 aircraft manufactured in the USSR were equipped with an M-22.

In service with the VVS, the poor view from the cockpit during landing and take-off, produced by the gull wing configuration, were the cause of numerous accidents. The VVS higher officials wanted the production to stop prematurely at the end of 1935.

Some 130 aircraft were sent to Spain between October 1936 and February 1937, achieving some initial successes against the Junkers Ju 52/3m and the Heinkel He 51 of the Condor Legion. However, they failed in their attempts to intercept the new German Dornier Do 17 (315 kph) and Heinkel He 111 (395 kph) bombers flying at 4,000 m. The I-15 had a maximum speed of only 360 kph and lacked oxygen equipment to combat above 3,500 m.

Thanks to its manoeuvrability, it could evade the attacks of the Messerschmitt Bf 109 B, C, and D; however, after the arrival of the Bf 109 E to Spain, the I-15 were earmarked for strafing and night fighting duties to avoid being exterminated. The next Polikarpov fighter—the I-152—was built with a reinforced structure and a 775-hp M-25V engine to improve the performances of the I-15 in speed and dive, but it did not work and only could survive to the Japanese fighters in Khalkhin Gol and China thanks to the protection of the I-16 monoplanes.

Faced with this new failure, the designer continued his unfortunate strategy of trial and error, returning to the gull wing configuration with the I-153. It was basically an I-15 with retractable landing gear that was outdated from its very beginning, in October 1938.

A feature common to all the Polikarpov fighters was their longitudinal instability, caused by the short length of their fuselage that had been designed to save weight and building materials. For their part, the Polikarpov fighters suffered snaking problems that affected weapon accuracy during combat manoeuvres.

The Soviets believed to have found the solution by increasing the rate of fire of the machine guns. In 1933, they began to build the ShKAS, a 7.62-mm gas-operated machine gun that used the Polish Szakats revolver-feed system and the French Berthier gas regulator.

The ShKAS had a rate of fire of 1,300–1,800 rounds per minute, but it presented numerous problems of maintenance and jamming, due to the low manufacturing quality of the 7.62×54mmR ammunition.

The reality of the aerial combat in Spain showed that the ShKAS was effective against slow aircraft built in wood and fabric, but to destroy the new German fast bombers, it was necessary to use more powerful weapons.

The British chose to equip their fighters with eight or even twelve 0.303-inch Browning machine guns. That proved to be a wrong solution, which allowed too many German bombers to escape during the Battle of Britain. The Americans and Italians preferred to use a lower number of 12.7-mm heavy machine guns, and the French trusted the destructive power of its 20-mm Hispano-Suiza HS.404 cannons.

The Soviets failed with the 12.7-mm ShVAK of 1932 and could only build the version of 20 mm after studying the gas-operated locking bolt of the French cannons. The HS.9 technology was acquired on February 1936, together with the Dewoitine D.510R c/n 45, while the HS.404 was considered a secret weapon by *l'Armée de l'Air* and not authorised for export. However, in May 1936, the communists of the *Front Populaire* stole an entire set of drawings from the HS.404 from the Bois-Colombes Hispano-Suiza headquarters.

By the beginning of 1933, the Soviets had nothing that could overcome the PZL fighters and looked for new ideas in the world of air races. In 1931 and 1932, the Gee Bee aircraft had achieved great publicity with reported speed records in the Shell Speed Dash. In 1932, also, five low-wing monoplanes managed to overcome the Hall's Bulldog, a racer equipped with Pulawski wing, in the Thompson Trophy.

In January 1934, the Soviet prototype TsKB-12 flew for the first time. It incorporated in its design many of the innovations used by Gee Bee Model Z and R-1, as well as some of its dangerous defects. It had a small low-wing without flaps, based on structural solutions of the Lorraine Hanriot 41 and 130, designed for the Coupe Michelin air races of 1930–1932.

The retractable undercarriage, which was operated by use of a hand crank, had been copied from the Lockheed Altair model 1930 but never worked properly. The wheels did not completely retract frequently due to an abnormal extension of the cables, generating considerable drag and turbulence. At other times, the mechanism was flattened, and the pilots had to free it by cutting the cables with pliers.

The production version—Polikarpov I-16 Type 4—had been intended to use the M-25 engine, but its availability was delayed by the difficulty in copying the American engine, and the new fighter entered service propelled by an old M-22.

The new fighter was presented to the public by the Soviet propaganda services as the most advanced in the world in May 1935. In fact, the insane tendency to flat spin—caused by its longitudinal instability, the high landing speed due to the absence of flaps, and the unreliable undercarriage—killed almost as many pilots as the Axis fighters.

The I-16 failed in Spain, Finland, Khalkhin Gol, China, and in its own country, having been unable to stop the Luftwaffe in 1941, even resorting to carry out numerous *Taran* suicide attacks. It also failed the more modern MiG-3; burdened by the 830 kg of its

Italian engine, it could only carry three machine guns and was finally used in *Taran* attacks against German reconnaissance planes. These acts of desperation, caused by the low level of Soviet technology, were presented by the official propaganda in heroic terms.

During the Second World War, the Soviets made massive use of French Hispano-Suiza HS.12 Y engines, version Klimov M-105, to propel their Yak and LaGG fighters. The M-22 did not have the Bristol licence and it was manufactured in accordance with the Gnome-Rhône French version. The M-85 used by the Ilyushin DB-3 bombers was also a version of the Gnome-Rhône 14 Kdrs.

The German attack forced the Soviets to interrupt the production of armament while they moved their industry to new locations, to the east of the Urals. The former offender was forced to survive thanks to the massive aid sent by Americans and British—18,000 aircraft, 500,000 vehicles, 20,000 tanks, 16,000 km of telephone cable, 35,000 R/T devices, 380,000 phones, chemicals product to improve the poor quality of Soviet fuel, 100 octane fuel for the fighters, information about the movements of the *Wehrmacht* provided by the British Intelligence Centre of Bletchley Park, millions of boots, and all types of military equipment for the Red Army.

Actually, the VVS could only fight the Luftwaffe on equal terms after receiving 143 Lend-Lease Spitfire Mk VBs through Iran in February 1943 and 1,183 Mk IXs almost a year later. It was not selfless aid—the democracies could not afford the millions of casualties that the defeat of the Reich required.

Enemy at the Gates

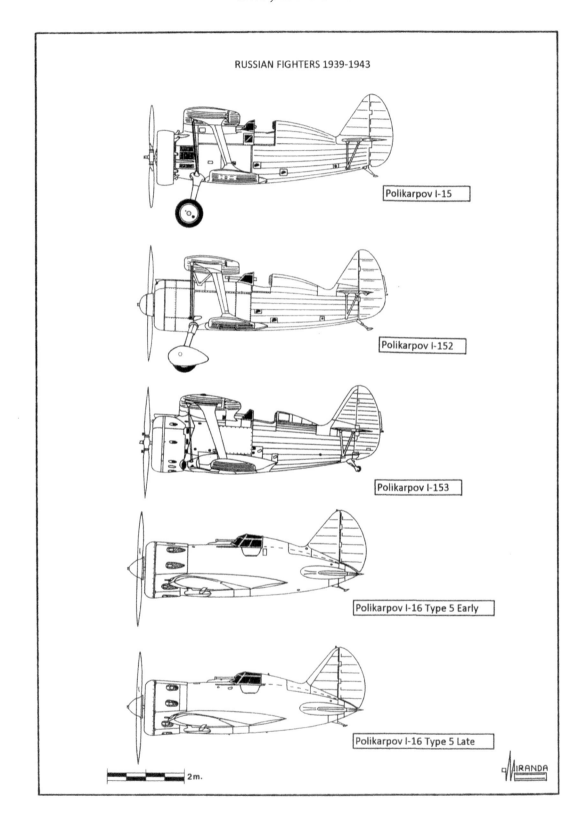

RUSSIAN FIGHTERS 1939-1943

Polikarpov I-15

Polikarpov I-152

Polikarpov I-153

Polikarpov I-16 Type 5 Early

Polikarpov I-16 Type 5 Late

2 m.

MIRANDA

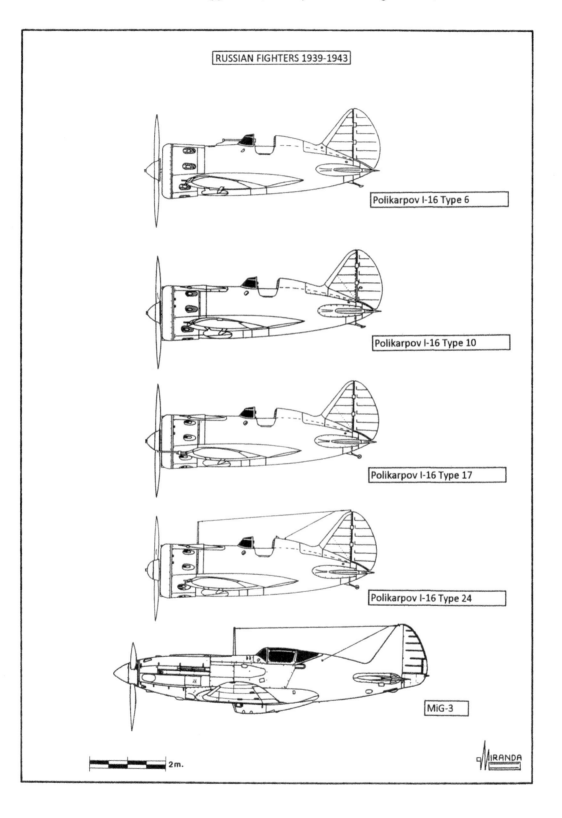

RUSSIAN FIGHTERS 1939-1943

Polikarpov I-16 Type 6

Polikarpov I-16 Type 10

Polikarpov I-16 Type 17

Polikarpov I-16 Type 24

MiG-3

2 m.

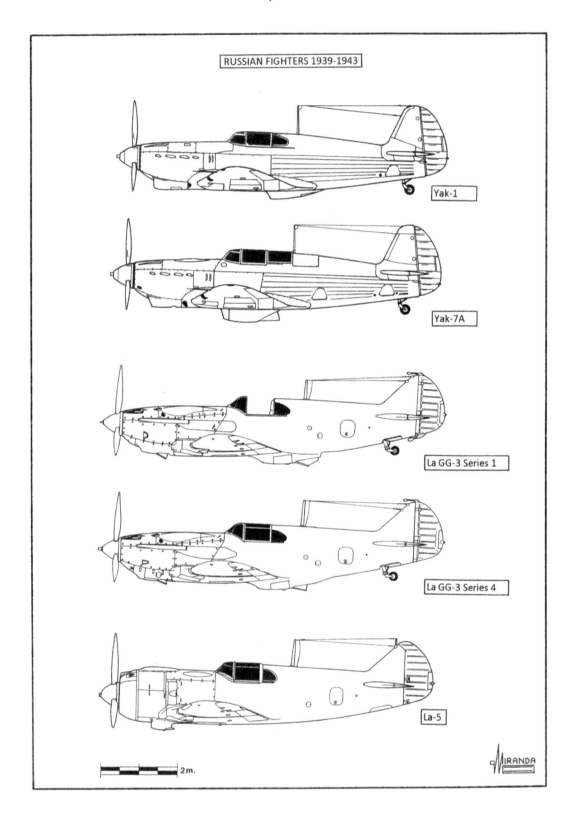

RUSSIAN FIGHTERS 1939-1943

Yak-1

Yak-7A

La GG-3 Series 1

La GG-3 Series 4

La-5

2 m.

MIRANDA

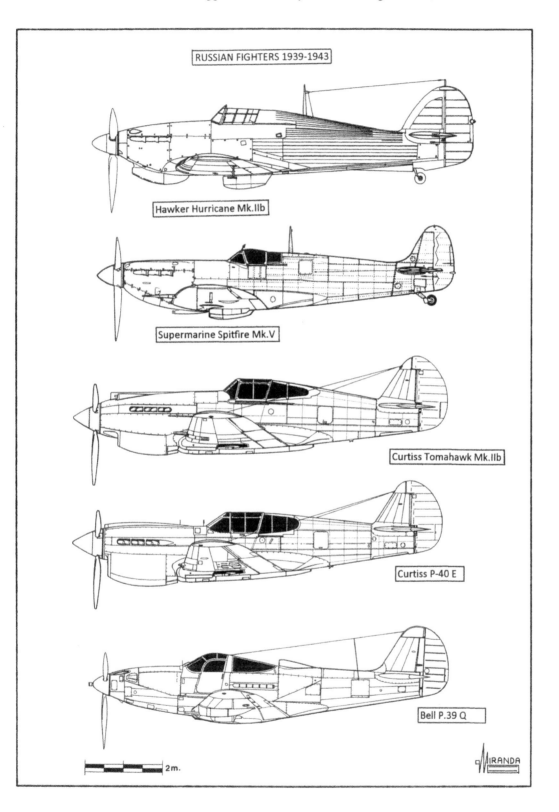

RUSSIAN FIGHTERS 1939-1943

Hawker Hurricane Mk.IIb

Supermarine Spitfire Mk.V

Curtiss Tomahawk Mk.IIb

Curtiss P-40 E

Bell P.39 Q

2m.

MIRANDA

Finland
(30 November 1939–
4 September 1944)

After obtaining its independence in 1917, the new state created the *Ilmailuvoimat* (Aviation Force) with Russian and French war surplus aircraft. In 1920, Finland signed the Dorpat peace treaty with Russia, and in January 1930, the Aviation Force was renamed *Ilmavoimat* (Air Force).

Between 1929 and 1934, the Finnish Air Force was strengthened with the acquisition of twenty Gourdou-Lesseurre GL-22C fighters, twelve Koolhoven FK.31 two-seat fighters, sixteen Aero A.32 light bombers, twenty-five Blackburn Ripon IIF bombers, seventeen Bristol Bulldog Mk IVA fighters, six Junkers K-43 bombers, and eighteen de Havilland DH.60 Moth elementary trainers

In 1935, thirteen Fokker C.VE reconnaissance aircraft were acquired. A year later, the Finns launched an urgent aircraft modernisation programme by acquiring three Avro Anson Mk I transports, four Fokker C.X light bombers (along with the licence to manufacture another thirty units), seven Fokker D.XXI fighters (along with the licence to manufacture thirty-five units more), and eighteen Bristol Blenheim Mk I bombers (along with the licence to manufacture forty-five additional units).

In 1937, a five-year development plan for the *Ilmavoimat* started. It consisted of the creation of four army-cooperation squadrons, three bomber squadrons, three fighter squadrons, and one maritime squadron.

On 30 November 1939, the Soviets attacked Finland's eastern border with 450,000 men (twenty divisions), 2,000 tanks, 2,050 cannons, and 3,250 aircraft from types Polikarpov I-152, I-153, I-16, R-5, R-Z and U-2, Tupolev SB-2M103 and TB-3, Ilyushin DB-3 M, and Beriev MBR-2.

The Finnish Armed Forces had 327,000 men (five divisions), twenty tanks, 425 cannons, two armoured ships, and five submarines. The Ilmavoimat strength was 135 aircraft: thirty-six Fokker D.XXIs, ten Bristol Bulldog Mk IVAs, seventeen Bristol Blenheim Mk Is, thirty-two Fokker C.Xs, seven Fokker C.VEs, fourteen Blackburn Ripon IIFs, four Junkers F.13s, three de Havilland Moths, three VL *Saaskis*, and one VL *Kotka*.

The Finns fought fiercely, causing so many losses to the Soviets that they were forced to sign an armistice on 13 March 1940. The international community condemned the aggression by expelling the Soviet Union from the League of Nations on 14 December 1939 and offering military aid to Finland.

The *Ilmavoimat* received 210 new planes: thirty Gloster Gladiator Mk IIs, twenty-two Bristol Blenheim Mk IVs, thirty Morane-Saulnier M.S.406s, thirty-two Fiat G.50s, forty-four Brewster B-239s, twenty-five Gloster Gauntlet Mk IIs, ten Hawker Hurricane Mk Is, one Douglas DC-2, twelve Westland Lysander Mk Is, three Fokker C.Vs, and one Fokker F.VIIa. Many of these models were technologically superior to the Soviets, as were the tactics used by the Finnish pilots, as proved in combat.

In December 1939, the Finnish fighters shot down sixty Soviet aircraft and the *Ilmavoimat* lost fourteen. In January 1940, the Soviets lost fifty-three aircraft in air combat against ten Finnish loses. In February, the Soviets changed their aerial tactics, using formations of up to 350 bombers and fighter escorts to air support the land forces and bomb the population centres.

The Finnish fighters carried out 2,000 sorties and 300 aerial combats, shooting down seventy-one Soviet aircraft. Nine others were shot down by *Flygflottilj* 19, a Swedish volunteer air unit that operated in Northern Finland with twelve Gloster Gladiator Mk Is and five Hawker Harts. In March, the *Ilmavoimat* destroyed twenty more Soviet aircraft, losing eight aircraft of their own.

The period between 30 November 1939 and 13 March 1940, known as the Winter War, cost the Soviets 579 aircraft and the Finns seventy-four. The loss of prestige inflicted on the USSR during the unequal fight convinced the Germans that its advanced technology could easily neutralise the numerical superiority of the Red Army in a future *Blitzkrieg*.

The German-Soviet war, launched on 22 June 1941, also signalled the end of peace for Finland. The bombing carried out by the Red Air Force against several Finnish cities on 25 June was considered an act of war and the combats continued. The new period of clashes lasted until September 1944 and was named the Continuation War by historians.

At this stage, the Finns also got local air superiority using fighters Brewster, Hawk, and Messerschmitt against the Soviet MiG-3, LaGG-3, Yak-7, La-5, Il-2, and Pe-2, which were joined by 10,377 Lend-Lease Hurricane, Airacobra, and Tomahawk fighters. The expected defeat of the *Wehrmacht* led the Finns to initiated efforts to reach a peace settlement with the Soviets.

On 4 September 1944, a peace treaty was signed by which Finland retained its independence in exchange for losing some territories. During the Continuation War, 3,313 Soviet planes were shot down by Finnish fighters and 1,345 by the anti-aircraft artillery. The *Ilmavoimat* lost 257 aircraft in combat, 100 in training, and 215 due to other causes.

Finnish Fighters

Bristol Bulldog Mk IIA (286 kph)
Two aircraft were supplied by Sweden on 15 December 1939. They crashed in accidents in 1940 and 1942.

Engine: one 440-hp Bristol *Jupiter* VIIF.
Armament: two 0.303-inch Browning machine guns.

Bristol Bulldog Mk IVA (362 kph)

On April 1934, Finland ordered seventeen units. During the Winter War, they shot down two I-16 and two SB-2M103.
Engine: one 654-hp Bristol *Mercury* VI S.2.
Armament: two 0.303-inch Browning machine guns.

Gloster Gauntlet Mk II (370 kph)

On February 1940, twenty-five aircraft were supplied by the South African Government as support to Finland. They were used as advanced trainers.
Engine: one 645-hp Bristol *Mercury* VI S.2.
Armament: two 0.303-inch Vickers machine guns.

Gloster Gladiator Mk I (407 kph)

On 10 January 1940, the Swedish *Fligflottilj* 19 arrived in Finland with twelve aircraft who managed to shoot down four SB-2M103s, one TB-3, one DB-3M, and three I-152s. One Gladiator was lost in combat and two in accidents.
Engine: one 830-hp Bristol *Mercury* IX.
Armament: four 0.303-inch Browning machine guns.

Gloster Gladiator Mk II (414 kph)

Thirty aircraft were delivered to Finland between January and February 1940.
During the Winter War, three I-152s, two I-153s, seven I-16s, nine SB-2M103s, one DB-3, one R-5, and four R-Zs were shot down. During the Continuation War, they shot down one MiG-3, two U-2s, and one R-5, losing eleven Gladiators in combat and two in crashes.
Engine: one 830-hp Bristol *Mercury* VIIA.
Armament: four 0.303-inch Browning machine guns.

Fokker D.XXI Mercury (418 kph)

Seven aircraft with 840-hp Bristol *Mercury* VII engines were acquired on 18 November 1937. Another fourteen were built under licence by *Valtion Lentokonetehdas* (VL) in Tampere-Härmälä, powered by Bristol *Mercury* engines manufactured by P. Z. L. in Poland and delivered between November 1938 and March 1939. A second batch of twenty-one aircraft with *Mercury* engines, built in Tampere-Tampella, was delivered between March and July 1939.
Armament: a pair of 7.7-mm Vickers machine guns fitted in the front fuselage and two wing-mounted 7.7-mm Vickers.

Fokker D.XXI Wasp (434 kph)

On May 1939, fifty planes with 825-hp Pratt & Whitney R-1535-SB4-C Twin Wasp Junior American engines, were ordered to VL-Kuorevesi. They did not arrive in time to participate in the Winter War as they were delivered between January and June 1941. Less manoeuvrable than the Polikarpov fighters, the Fokker flew in 'finger four' formations and used 'zoom-and-climb' combat tactics. During the Winter War, they shot down seventy-three SB-2M103s, twenty-two DB-3Ms, two R-5s, twelve I-16s, and three I-152s, losing twenty-three aircraft that were shot down in combat, one that was rammed by I-153, one by friendly anti-aircraft artillery, and forty-two due to crashes, sabotage, and strafing.

Armament: four wing-mounted 7.7-mm Vickers machine guns.

Hawker Hurricane Mk I (518 kph)

In the second week of March 1940, twelve aircraft were donated by Great Britain.

Two planes were destroyed in transit. Ten were delivered too late to see action in the Winter War. Due to scarcity of replacement parts, only five and a half kills were achieved with these planes. Five Hurricanes were destroyed in battle during the Continuation War and two from anti-aircraft fire.

Engine: one 1,030-hp Rolls-Royce Merlin II.

Armament: eight wing-mounted 0.303-inch Browning machine guns.

Morane-Saulnier M.S.406 C1 (486 kph)

Thirty units were donated by French Government on February 1940. Twenty-five ex-*Armée de l'Air* fighters were supplied by Germans on October 1940 and two more on October 1942. Between July and September 1942, another thirty aircraft were purchased from the Vichy Government. The aircraft were delivered without the engine-mounted cannon HS.404 and the Finns instead installed a 12.7-mm Berezin UB or a Colt M-2 heavy machine guns. They also replaced the two wing-mounted 7.5-mm MAC 34 A (drum feed) machine guns by two 7.7-mm (belt feed) Brownings and the Chauvière airscrew by a Hamilton Standard.

Between 17 February 1940 and 12 July 1944, the Moranes shot down twenty SB-2M 103s, fourteen I-153s, twelve I-16s, fourteen MiG-3s, ten I-152s, six Hurricanes, five DB-3Ms, six Tomahawks, four Airacobras, five IL-2s, four MBR-2s, two LaGG-3s, one La-5, three Pe-2s, two R-5s, one R-Z, one Boston, one Yak-9, and one U-2, fourteen of them during the Winter War.

Engine: one 860-hp Hispano-Suiza HS.12 Y-31.

Morane-Saulnier M.S.410 C1 (509 kph)

Fifteen ex-*Armée de l'Air* units were supplied by Germany between July and November 1941.

Engine: one 860-hp Hispano-Suiza HS.12 Y-31 driving one Ratier airscrew.

Armament: five 7.5-mm (belt feed) MAC 34 M39 machine guns.

Mörkö Moraani (525 kph)

Starting from June 1944, forty-one Moranes were re-engined with one 1,100-hp Klimov (Hispano-Suiza) M-105 P driving one VISh-61P constant speed airscrew.

Only three modified aircraft entered combat during the Continuation War, shooting down one La-5 and two Airacobra.

Armament: one engine-mounted 20-mm MG 151 cannon and two wing-mounted 7.7-mm (belt feed) Browning machine guns.

Fiat G.50 (472 kph)

Thirty-two aircraft were donated by Italy between 18 December 1939 and 19 June 1940. Two were lost in transit, one in combat, another by the anti-aircraft artillery, and six in crashes.

Engine: one 840-hp Fiat A74 R1 C38 engine, driving one Fiat 3D 41-1 airscrew. Forty-two ex-CR.42 Swedish-made spinners were installed to protect the variable-pitch mechanism from frost damage.

During the Winter War, the Fiat fighters shot down one I-16, four DB-3Ms, one SB-2M103, and two I-153s. During the Continuation War, twenty-two SB-2M103s, two MiG-3s, fifteen I-153s, two MBR-2s, two I-16s, three I-152s, and one DB-3M.

Armament: two 12.7-mm Breda-SAFAT MC machine guns.

Brewster Model 239 (484 kph)

Out of the forty-four aircraft purchased on 16 December 1939, six arrived in Finland before the Winter War ended and the rest continued arriving until 1 May 1940.

During the Continuation War, the Brewsters shot down sixty-two I-153s, thirty-five MiG-3s, thirty-nine Hurricanes, twenty-three SB-2M103s, fifteen I-16s, nine LaGG-3s, eight R-5s, five Pe-2s, four MBR-2s, three I-152s, three DB-3Ms, and one Airacobra. They lost nineteen aircraft of their own.

Engine: one 950-hp Wright R-1820 G-5. Armament: one 0.30-calibre MG 40 and three 0.50-calibre MG 53-2 machine guns. The Finns installed new Revi 3/c reflector gunsights, an armoured headrest, and seat back plates. Six aircraft were equipped with captured Russian M-63 engines.

Curtiss Hawk 75 (500 kph)

Nine H.75 A-2 and seven H.75 A-4 ex-*Armée de l'Air* fighters were supplied by Germany in June 1941 and another fifteen H.75 A-4 between June 1943 and January 1944. Eleven ex-Norwegian H.75 A-6s were additionally supplied between July and August 1941.

During the Continuation War, the Hawks managed to shoot down twenty-one I-153s, eleven I-16s, three DB-3Fs, fifteen MiG-3s, sixteen LaGG-3s, two Yak-1s, nine Pe-2s, three MBR-2s, two U-2s, one Boston, and two La-5s. They lost eight aircraft of their own.

The A-2 and A-6 models were powered by a 1,200-hp Pratt & Whitney R-1830-SC3-G engine and A-4 models by a 1,200-hp Wright Cyclone R-1820-95.

Armament: six 7.5-mm FN/Browning Mle 38 machine guns.

Caudron C-714 (465 kph)

Six aircraft were donated by France on 12 March 1940, being delivered in May. Assigned to the LeLv 60 reconnaissance squadron, after a few crashes due to the fragility of the landing gear, flying them was prohibited in September 1941.

Engine: one 500-hp Renault 12 R-03.

Armament: four 7.5-mm MAC M39 (drum feed) machine guns.

Messerschmitt Bf 109 G-2 (522 kph)

On 1 February 1943, forty-eight ex-Luftwaffe fighters were ordered and delivered between March and May.

Engine: one 1,475-hp Daimler-Benz DB 605 A-1.

Armament: one 20-mm MG 151 cannon and two 7.9-mm MG 15 machine guns.

Messerschmitt Bf 109 G-6 (621 kph)

Between May and August 1944, 109 aircraft were delivered, along with two G-8 reconnaissance fighters. Between 24 March 1943 and 4 September 1944, the Bf 109 Finns shot down 663 Soviets aircraft, losing thirteen in combat of their own, five shot down by anti-aircraft fire, seven in crashes, and five due to technical failures.

Engine: one 1,475-hp DB 605 AM.

Armament: one 30-mm MK 108 cannon and two 13-mm MG 131 machine guns.

Indigenous Designs

Ilmailuvoimain Lentokonethdas—IVL (Aviation Force Aircraft Factory)—made under licence, between 1922 and 1925, 120 Hansa-Brandenburg W.33 floatplanes, thirty-four Caudron C.60s, and six Morane-Saulnier M.S.50cs.

The first indigenous fighter, the prototype IVL C.24, with a parasol wing inspired by Morane designs, was flown on 16 April 1924; the C.25, an improved version with narrower-chord wing, was flown in June 1925. Both models suffered longitudinal stability problems caused by the excessive weight of the Siemens Sh 3A engine. Its serial production was dismissed after an accident suffered by the C-25.

The next attempt to provide the *Ilmailuvoimat* with an indigenous fighter was the IVL D-26 *Haukka*. The biplane prototype was flown on 17 March 1927, manifesting structural faults and flat spin tendencies. Both problems were not fully resolved in its successor D-27 *Haukka* II and its production was again dismissed in favour of licence-built Gloster Gamecock Mk II.

In 1928, the IVL became *Valtion Lentokonetehdas*-VL (State Aircraft Factory). Before the war, VL had built some self-designed trainers and second line aircraft: it produced thirty-three units of the *Saaski* reconnaissance aircraft in 1928, seven *Kotka* light bombers in 1930, thirty-one *Tuisku* advanced trainers in 1933, twenty-four *Viima* elementary trainers in 1935 and forty-one *Pyry* advanced monoplane trainers in 1939, but no fighters.

VL *Myrsky* (470 kph)

On 8 June 1939, the Ministry of Defence instructed VL to design a new single-seat fighter powered by a Bristol *Taurus* III engine.

VL did not have experience with high speed aircraft, there was not any duraluminium production in Finland, and no one would sell aluminium in 1939. The *Taurus* engine was not available due to war, so a 1,065-hp (with 87 octane fuel) Swedish-built civilian version of the Pratt & Whitney R-1830 was chosen. VL then decided to use the same construction system of the Fokker D.XXI. The wings and tail surfaces were made of wood/plywood and the fuselage structure was welded chromium-molybdenum steel tube with fabric and plywood coating.

The prototype was flown on 23 December 1941, manifesting serious yaw to port, excessive wing loading, and engine problems. On 30 May 1942, the Department of War Supplies had placed an order for three pre-production aircraft called *Myrsky* I.

Built between April and June 1943, the three planes suffered accidents and two of them were destroyed during diving tests because of fractures of the wing attachment bolts and plywood skinning under stress, due to defective bonding.

The investigation board confirmed that flutter had caused the wings to break up and recommended that they be strengthened in the forty-seven *Myrsky* IIs (525 kph) that began to be manufactured in July 1944. The fuselage fabric covering was replaced in these aircraft with plywood sheeting, the elevators and the landing gear were strengthened, and a VLS 8002 constant-speed propeller (with wooden blades and cooling fan) was installed. The construction of the *Myrsky* II complicated when the availability of the German *Tego-film* glue ended, after the destruction of its manufacturing plant in 1943. It was replaced by bad Finnish glues based on casein.

Maximum permissible diving speed was raised to 650 kph and maximum engine revolutions were restricted to 3,060 rounds per minute. The armament consisted of four 12.7-mm VKT LKk/42 machine guns. The *Myrsky* II entered service with *Ilmavoimat* in July 1944, being used mainly in reconnaissance missions.

In August and September, the *Myrsky* II fought against two Yak-7s, three Yak-9s, and two La-5s of the 195 IAP, damaging several of them but without achieving any victory before ceasefire. Until being retired from service, on February 1948, the *Myrsky* fighters had suffered a total of fifty-one accidents, with the loss of twenty-one aircraft and four pilots.

VL *Pyörremyrsky* (522 kph).

At the end of 1942, VL tried to negotiate a full reparation licence for the Messerschmitt Bf 109 G-2, but complete sets of drawings and tools were never delivered.

The *Ilmavoimat* had been particularly concerned with the debut in some numbers of the Lavockin La-5 Soviet fighter and the possibility of the Germans to suspend the supply of fighters. The *Pyörremyrsky* programme began when the *Ilmavoimat* ordered two new Finnish fighters into design phase: *Pyörremyrsky* and *Puuska*.

The design was given the following basic parameters: At least 50 km/h faster than the fastest enemy bomber; if faster than enemy fighters, it may be less agile and a worse climber; if slower than enemy fighters, it must be better climber and more agile.

By early 1943, VL was instructed to design a single-seat fighter powered by one 1,475-hp Daimler-Benz DB 605 AC engine driving a VDM three-bladed airscrew. Since it was impossible to import aluminium due to the war, the *Pyörremyrsky* was to be built using only domestic materials, incorporating the lessons learned from the construction of the *Myrsky*.

The single-spar wing was built in wood/plywood, with metal-framed, fabric-covered ailerons and electrically operated metallic flaps. The tail assembly was also built in a similar way with metal-framed movable surfaces. The forward fuselage structure was welded chromium-molybdenum steel tube, and the aft fuselage was a Soviet-style wooden monocoque structure. The armament consisted of one engine-mounted 20-mm MG 151 cannon and two 12.7-mm LKk 42 machine guns in the nose.

Prototype construction was low, affected by the unavailability of the German *Tego-film* glue and the aircraft was still not completed in September 1944, when the peace treaty was signed. On 21 November 1945, during their flight tests, the new fighter proved to be more manoeuvrable than the Bf 109 G-6, with an outstanding climb rate and few teething troubles.

Unfortunately, the series production was dismissed because of the difficulty in obtaining a supply of Daimler-Benz engines.

VL *Puuska* (650 kph)

In the fall of 1943, VL was instructed to design a single-seat lightweight fighter, with narrow-track undercarriage, powered by one 1,475-hp Daimler-Benz DB 605 AC engine driving three-bladed VDM airscrew.

The design should adapt to the new fighter tactics of the *Ilmavoimat*, which was considered outdated the dogfight, preferring the 'zoom and climb' to either repeat the attack or break off the contact with an advantage in speed and climb. To meet the specification, it was necessary to design a light airframe to take full advantage of the 1,475 hp of the available engine.

The result was the *Puuska*, an 80 per cent smaller and light version of *Pyörremyrsky* that VL offered to the *Ilmavoimat* at the end of 1943. Out of the five proposed designs, the Finnish Air Force Material and Procurement staff selected two on 24 January 1944— PM-3 and PM-5—to be built as prototypes that were to be ready on 1 July 1945.

The PM-3

The PM-3 should use the under-nose oil cooler and two radiators from Bf 109 G-2 under the wings, local manufacture Sperry artificial horizon, Hollsman compass, and Vaisala reflector gunsight.

The double-joint undercarriage retraction system would use Siemens and Stromberg electrical motors and two 660 × 160-mm wheels from Bf 109 G-2. The proposed armament was one engine-mounted 20-mm MG 151 cannon, with 300 rounds, and two 12.7 VKT LKk/42-mm nose-mounted machine guns.

Wingspan: 9.2 m.
Length: 7.5 m.
Wing area: 13.5 sq. m.
Maximum weight: 3,200 kg.
Maximum speed: 620 kph.
Climb rate: 6.2 min to 6,000 m.
Service ceiling: 12,000 m.

The PM-5

The PM-5 was designed as a point-defence interceptor, very fast and with amazing climb rate. To save weight, they decided not to install armour and the armament was reduced to a MG 151 with 210 rounds. The internal fuel was also reduced to only 400 litres, with the possibility of carrying two drop tanks of 140 litres each under the wings. Oil and glycol radiators were grouped in a ventral nacelle to save drag.

It was expected that series aircraft were equipped with a Telefunken FuG-7a R/T device and used the main wheels from Soviet LaGG-3 and the retractable tail wheel from DB-2 bomber. The building system should be the same used in the *Pyörremyrsky*, but the project was cancelled on March 1944 due the low availability of DB engines.

Maximum weight: 2,650 kg.

Maximum speed: 682 kph.

Climb rate: 4.7 min to 6,000 m.

Service ceiling: 14,000 m.

VL *Humu* (430 kph)

In October 1942, the *Ilmavoimat* placed an order with the VL for four prototypes of the *Humu*, a copy of the Brewster 239 fighter that should be built in wood/plywood/steel with the same technique used in the Fokker D.XXI. It was expected to build a series of fifty-five aircraft, using instrument and M-63 engines from captured Soviet aircraft.

On 8 August 1944, the prototype was flown, powered by a 930-hp Shvetsov M-63, reaching 420 kph. A surplus Brewster fuselage and new wings built in wood/plywood by VL had been used for its construction. It turned out to be too heavy (2,895 kg), manifesting problems of longitudinal stability, and the initiation of series production was delayed pending the results of flying tests. The proposed armament were three 12.7-mm LKk / 72 machine guns. The project was cancelled in the summer of 1944.

Fokker D.XXI Modified

Earlier, in 1939, the Finns had experimentally fitted two underwing 20-mm Oerlikon cannons in the Fokker FR-76. On 29 January 1940, the FR-76 shoot down a Soviet DB-3M bomber with just eighteen rounds, but the excessive weight limited its performances and the experiment was discontinued.

Another attempt to improve the outdated fighter consisted in installing a modified wing (the so-called E-wing) in the FR-121. It had more dihedral and was more tapered that the standard wing. During flight tests, it was found that the gun access panel blew off as a result of the air pressure in the gun bay.

Finally, two Fokkers were modified with a retractable landing gear: the FR-117 (*Mercury*) on 27 April 1941, and the FR-167 (Twin Wasp) on 2 March 1942. Both aircraft were later equipped with a fixed gear, and the whole idea was dropped because the speed improvement was only 15–37 kph depending on altitude.

VL *Vihuri*

In 1943, the Finns were waiting to receive two crashed British de Havilland Mosquito, requested from Germany to serve as models for planned production. One would be repaired and another one would be teared into parts to make blueprints. The Finns are great wood workers and probably would have been able to circumvent the unavailability of balsa and *Tego-film*, with the technique used by the Soviets in the construction of the Polikarpov I-16, which already had been tested in the *Pyörremyrsky*. The Polikarpov fuselage was built in two halves, like the Mosquito, and each half was comprised of pine frames and longerons. The monocoque skin was produced from layers of birch strips glued cross-grained and moulded on a former.

The new aircraft—the *Vihuri*—would have possibly been used as fighter-bomber with nose-mounted machine guns. It would have been powered by two 1,475-hp German Daimler-Benz DB 605 AC engines and used the landing gear of the Bristol Blenheim. It was estimated that its performances would have been inferior to those of the Mosquito because of its greater structural weight. Production plans would have delivered between the middle of 1946 and December 1947 due to the overload of work that represented for VL the repair of fighters in service, the production of the *Myrsky* and the *Mörkö-Moraani* conversion.

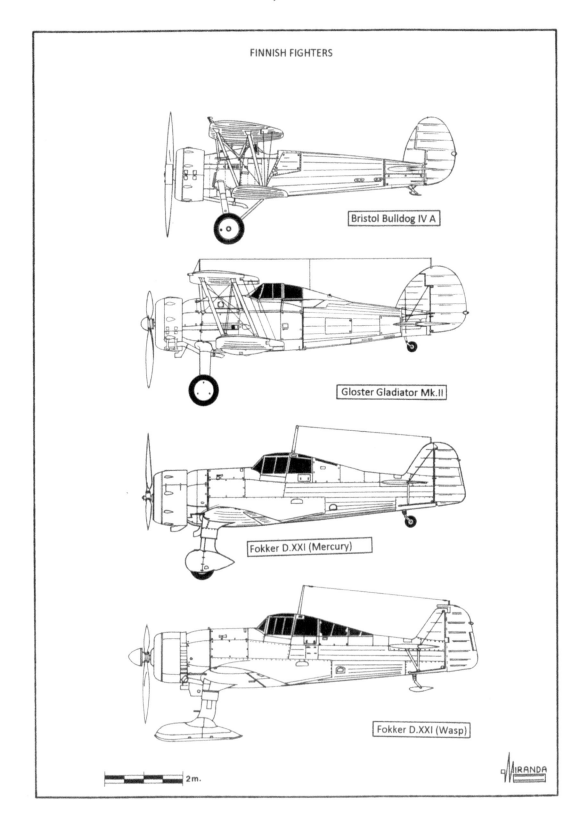

FINNISH FIGHTERS

Bristol Bulldog IV A

Gloster Gladiator Mk.II

Fokker D.XXI (Mercury)

Fokker D.XXI (Wasp)

2 m.

MIRANDA

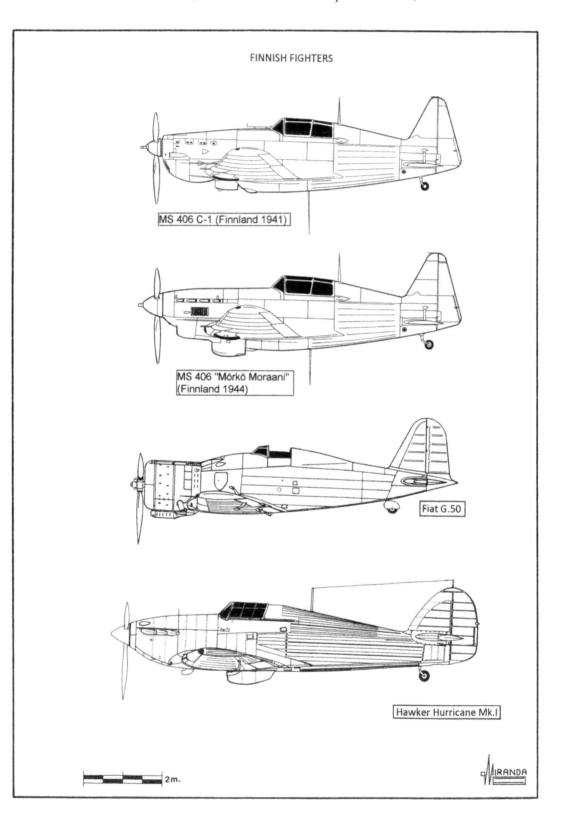

FINNISH FIGHTERS

MS 406 C-1 (Finnland 1941)

MS 406 "Mörkö Moraani" (Finnland 1944)

Fiat G.50

Hawker Hurricane Mk.I

2m.

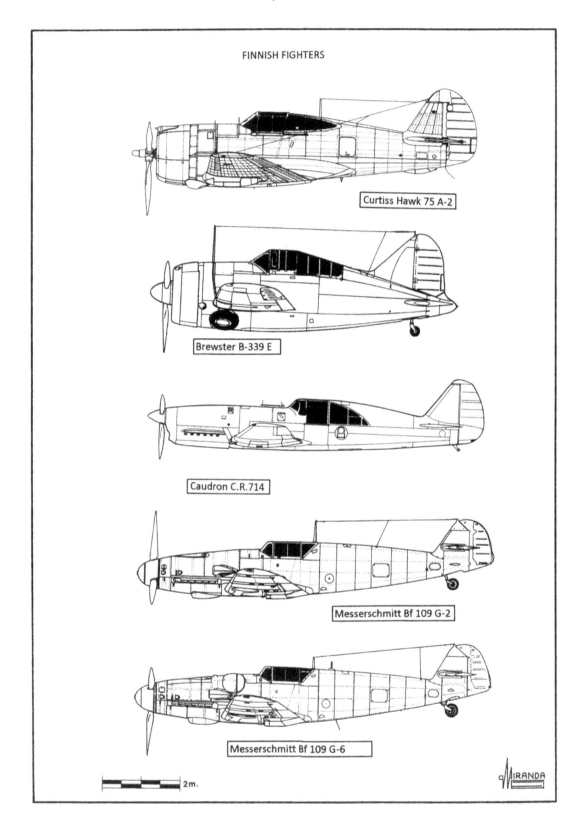

FINNISH FIGHTERS

Curtiss Hawk 75 A-2

Brewster B-339 E

Caudron C.R.714

Messerschmitt Bf 109 G-2

Messerschmitt Bf 109 G-6

2m.

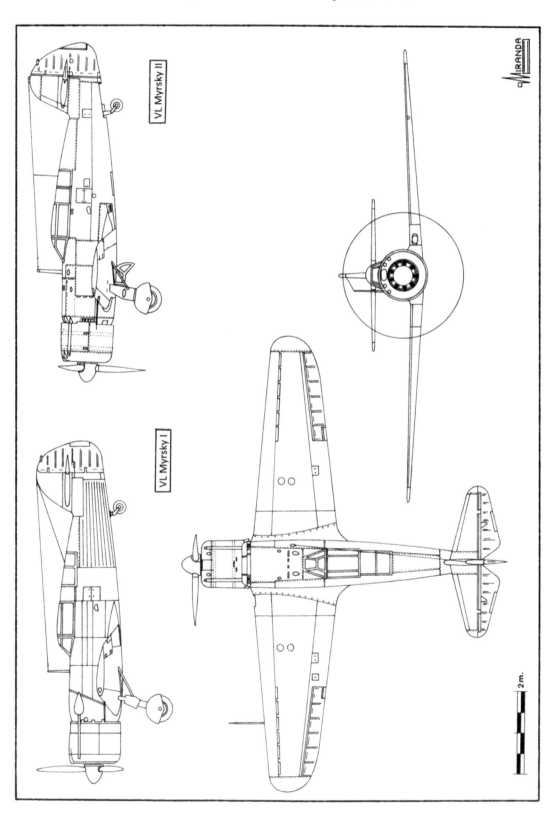

VL Myrsky II

VL Myrsky I

2 m.

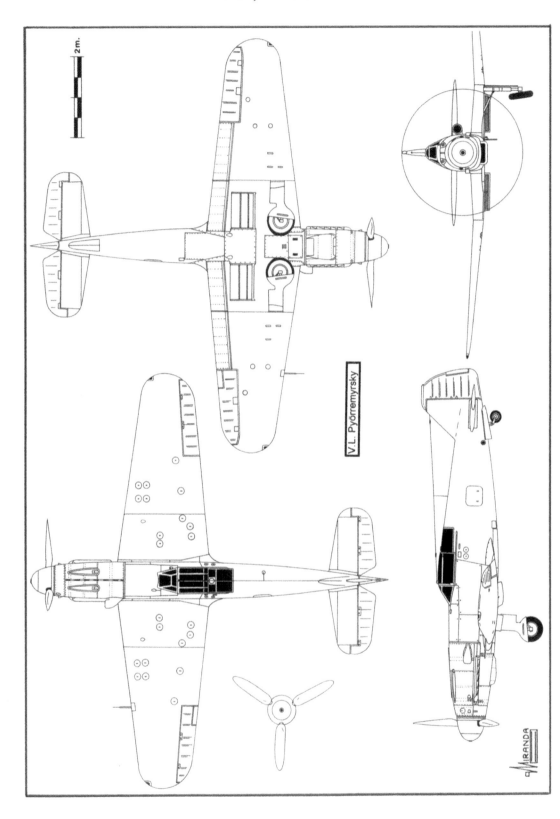

V.L. Pyörremyrsky

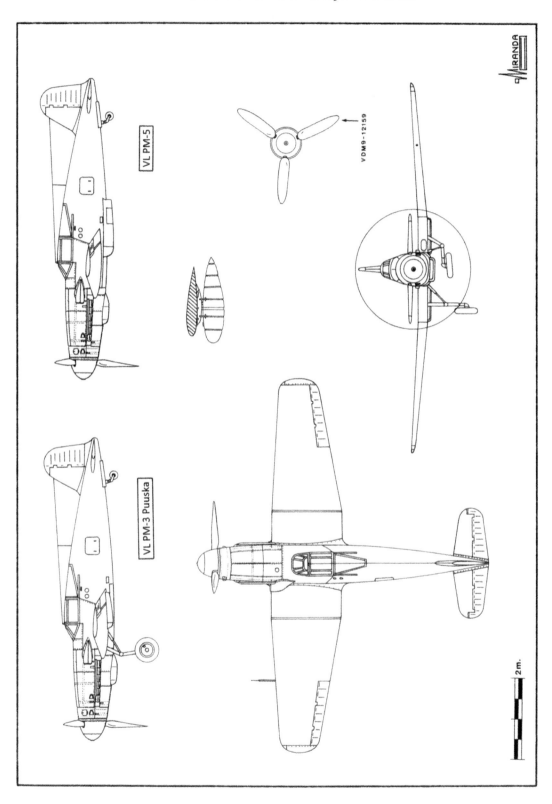

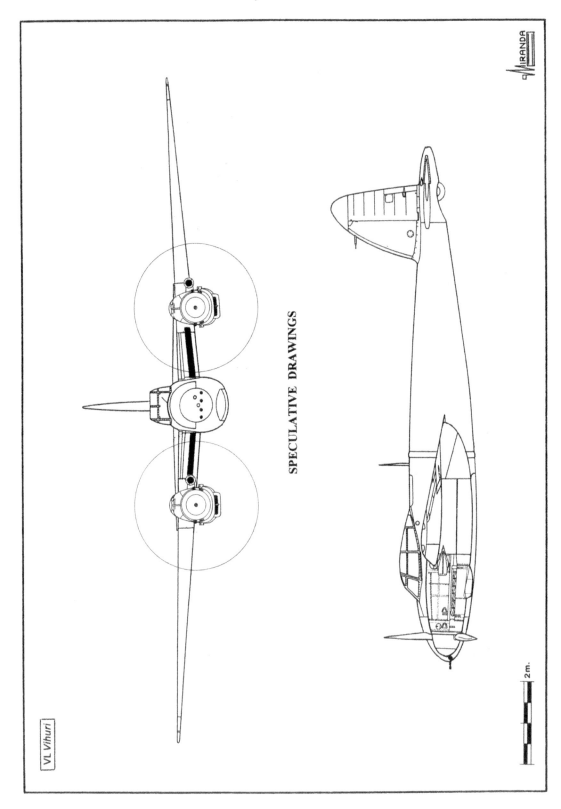

SPECULATIVE DRAWINGS

VL Vihuri

2 m.

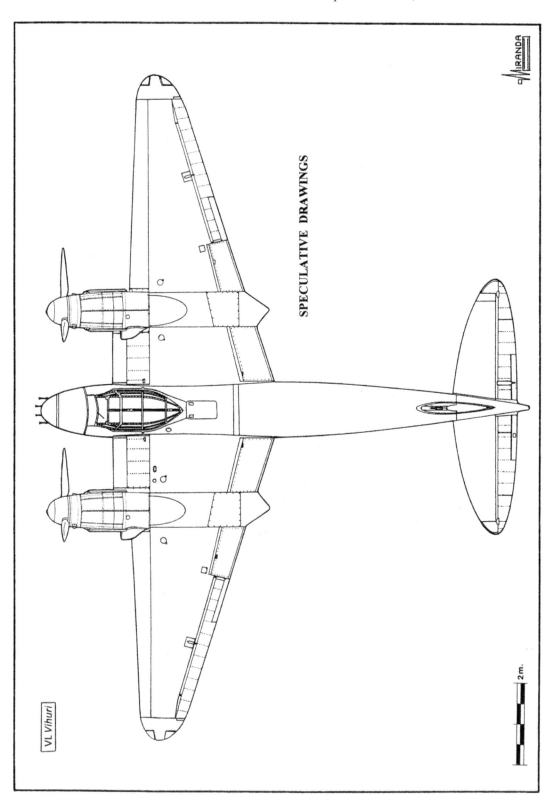

SPECULATIVE DRAWINGS

VL Vihuri

2 m.

17

Lithuania
(15 June 1940)

To protect their independence, obtained on 16 February 1918, this small Baltic country was forced to create an Air Force (*Karo Aviacija*) formed by twelve Ansaldo SVA 10 reconnaissance aircraft and twelve fighters of the Martinsyde F.4 and Letov S.20L types.

In the mid-1920s, these aircraft were enough to deter the Soviets, whose VVS strength was of 340 aircraft only. However, in 1928, the potential aggressor started a series of five-year plans for the massive production of weapons. In 1929, the VVS had already 1,280 aircraft; in 1933, 3,150; and in 1937, 8,140. Although they lacked the quality of Western designs, their large number was worrisome for countries bordering the USSR; this was the cause of the beginning of an arms race.

Following the entry into service of the Polikarpov I-3 (279 kph) in 1929, Lithuania ordered fifteen Fiat CR.20s (270 kph) that were superior to the Russian aircraft in dogfight and climb. From mid-1934, the VVS based its strategy in the use of large mixed formations of Polikarpov I-15 (286 kph) biplanes and Polikarpov I-16 Type 4 (362 kph) monoplanes armed with four 7.62-mm machine guns.

To counter the new threat, Lithuania ordered twenty Dewoitine D.371L (359 kph) monoplane fighters armed with four 7.7-mm machine guns. By the end of 1936, the Polikarpov I-16 Type 5 (445 kph) entered service with enhanced armament and Lithuania decided to change their D.371 by thirteen Dewoitine D.501Ls armed with a 20-mm HS. 9 cannon and two 7.7-mm machine guns.

In 1937, the Polikarpov I-152 (397 kph) fighter biplane appeared, designed to replace the I-15. Lithuania ordered fourteen Gloster Gladiator Mk I (407 kph) biplanes, which were superior in manoeuvrability and climb. In 1939, the Polikarpov I-16 Type 17 (425 kph) armed with 20-mm cannons came into service and Lithuania ordered thirteen Morane-Saulnier M.S.406L monoplane fighters armed with a 20-mm HS.404 cannon and two 7.7-mm machine guns. Unfortunately, the French needed these aircraft to defend themselves against the Luftwaffe and decided not to honour the agreement.

Between 1925 and 1939, the Lithuanians created a small aeronautical industry capable of supplying ANBO-III trainers and ANBO-41 reconnaissance aircraft to the *Karo Aviacija*.

They also built the prototype of the ANBO-VIII, a dive bomber that flew for the first time on 5 September 1939, but they lacked the technology required for the construction of advanced fighters. When the Red Army occupied Lithuania on 15 June 1940, the *Karo Aviacija* only had fourteen Ansaldo A.120s, seven Fiat CR.20s, fourteen ANBO-41s, one ANBO-VIIIs, thirteen Dewoitine D.501Ls, fourteen Gladiator Mk Is, and three interned aircraft: one Messerschmitt Bf 109, one Henschel Hs 126, and one PZL P.37.

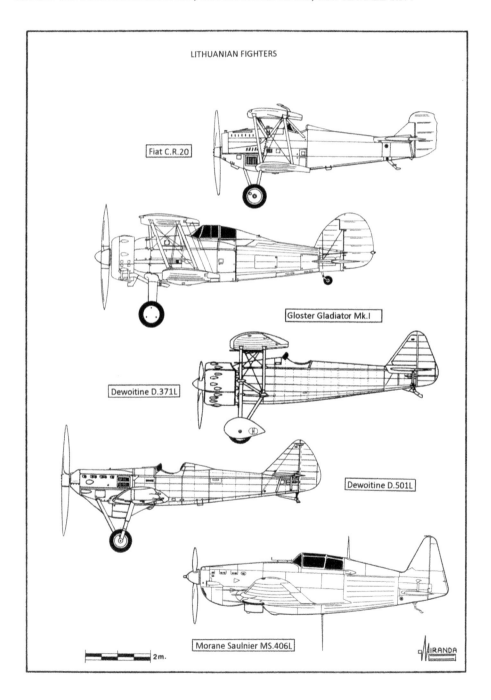

LITHUANIAN FIGHTERS

Fiat C.R.20

Gloster Gladiator Mk.I

Dewoitine D.371L

Dewoitine D.501L

Morane Saulnier MS.406L

2 m.

18

Estonia
(17 June 1940)

After achieving independence on February 1918 and signing a peace treaty with the USSR in 1920, Estonia created an aviation regiment equipped with some German and British aircraft surviving from the First World War.

In 1924, the government managed to neutralise a communist coup that had been seconded by the aviation regiment. It was necessary to reform the Estonian Army and to create a new air force. In 1925, fifteen Gourdou-Lesseurre GL-32 monoplane fighters were acquired, followed by nine Potez 25 A.2 light bombers in 1926, twelve Bristol Bulldog Mk II biplane fighters in 1930, and eight Hawker Hart fighter-bombers in 1932.

The growing Soviet threat required the assignment of 20 per cent of their annual state budgets to defence, a burden that the economy of the small Baltic state could not support indefinitely. By the middle of the 1930s, Estonia had four infantry divisions, two submarines, one torpedo boat, six gunboats, four minelayers, and fifty combat aircraft.

In early 1937, the government of Estonia sold seven Bristol Bulldog Mk IIs and eight Potez 25 A.2s to Spain through a Czech import company to circumvent the arms embargo imposed by the non-intervention committee. The operation turned out to be very lucrative and Estonia decided to act as an intermediary in the sale of twenty-six Fokker G.I heavy fighters, two Fokker C.X light bombers, two Fokker D.XXI monoplane fighters, and seven Letov S.231 biplane fighters to the Spanish communists.

On 8 July 1937, after Hendon Air Show, the Estonian Military Purchasing Committee placed an order for twelve Supermarine Spitfire Mk Is with the money obtained from the illegal arms trade. The price of a Spitfire of the time was equivalent to 40 per cent of the annual budget of Estonia. The Spitfires were to be delivered between July 1939 and June 1940, but the British cancelled the operation twelve days after the German attack on Poland.

The attempt to acquire some PZL P.24 fighters also failed because of the excessive demand from other countries. The Molotov–Ribbentrop Pact signed in August 1940, the Mutual Assistance Pact imposed by the Soviets in September to the Baltic States, and the beginning of the Second World War took the Estonian Air Force by surprise with a strength of four Gladiators and seven Harts.

The local aeronautical industry reached the capacity to manufacture the PON-1 biplane trainer in 1935 and the PTO-4 monoplane trainer in 1938. The first flight of the prototype Aviotehas PN-3, designed as a conversion trainer for the Spitfire, took place in January 1939. It could fly at 395 kph, powered by a Rolls-Royce Kestrel XI and was armed with two 7.62-mm machine guns. It would have served as the basis for the construction of an advanced fighter, but its development was interrupted by the Soviet occupation on 17 June 1940.

Enemy at the Gates

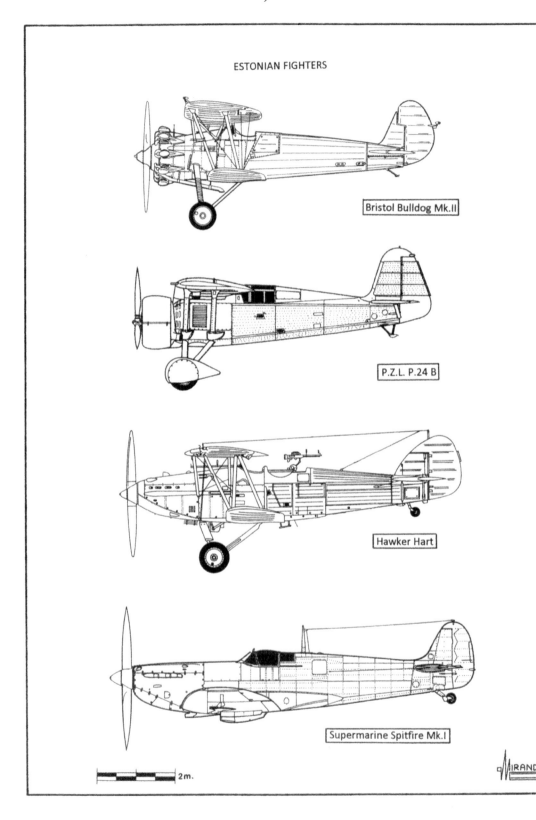

ESTONIAN FIGHTERS

Bristol Bulldog Mk.II

P.Z.L. P.24 B

Hawker Hart

Supermarine Spitfire Mk.I

2 m.

MIRANDA

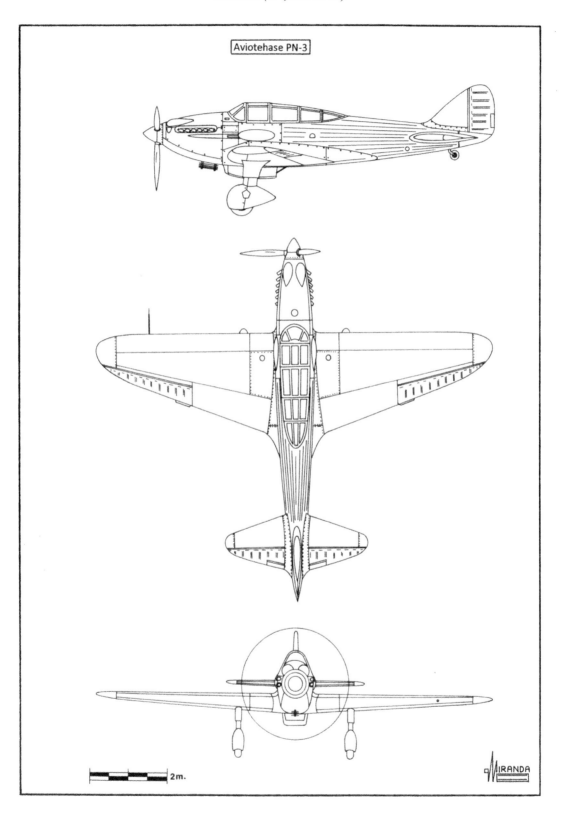

Aviotehase PN-3

2m.

19

Latvia
(17 June 1940)

Just eight months after having gained independence, the Latvian Air Force (LAR) was founded on 7 June 1919, using Nieuport 24 bis and Sopwith Strutters. In 1920, the Baltic State reached some political stability by signing the Soviet-Latvian peace treaty.

From 1921, the LAR was reorganised with the acquisition of seven Ansaldo A.1 fighters and four Ansaldo SVA 10 light bombers. They acquired eight Martinsyde ADC-1 fighters in 1926 and four Fiat CR.1 fighters a year later. Once mass production of Soviet armament started, with the first five-year plan of 1928–1932, Latvia purchased eighteen Letov Š-16L bombers in 1928, five Bristol Bulldog Mk II fighters in 1929, and seven more in 1930 to counter the threat posed by the new Polikarpov I-3.

Upon learning the performance of the Polikarpov I-16 Type 6 (440 kph) in Spain, Latvia acquired thirteen Gloster Gladiator Mk I (407 kph) fighters in 1937 and thirteen more in 1938, after the Polikarpov I-16 Type 10 (448 kph) entered service. That same year, they also acquired three Hawker Hind bombers. The Polikarpov I-16 Type 24 (470 kph) appeared in 1939 and Latvia tried to acquire thirty Hawker Hurricane Mk Is and twelve Westland Lysanders, but the British cancelled after the German invasion of Poland.

Between 1937 and 1940, the local industry *Valsts Elektro-Fabrika* (VEF) produced several all-wood monoplane trainers, with fixed landing gear, that proved to have exceptional flight performances and a great potential, susceptible of being used as 'emergency fighters'. The VEF I-12 light trainer, with twelve units built, reached 230 kph powered by a Cirrus engine of 90 hp only. In 1938, four aircraft were converted to single-seat fighters, armed with a light machine gun, to be used by the Latvian National Guard.

The VEF I-15, built in 1939, was a single-seat training aircraft with two machine guns that could fly at 330 kph with a 210-hp Gipsy Six engine. The VEF I-16—which performed its first flight in 1940, with a maximum speed of 460 kph, a 520-hp Walter Sagitta ISR engine, and four machine guns—was roughly the equal of Polikarpov I-16 Type 24. Construction began on a series of twelve aircraft, which was interrupted by the Soviet occupation on 17 June.

After the purchase of Hurricane fighters was cancelled, the Latvian Government ordered the design and construction of the air superiority fighter VEF-19 capable of competing with the MiG-3 and the Bf 109E. The complexity of the hydraulic equipment for the retractable landing gear was above the VEF capabilities and it did not seem possible to obtain engines with more than 500 hp.

These difficulties did not stop the resourceful designer Karlis Irbitis who proposed building a composite engine connecting three de Havilland Gipsy Six to each other to make an inverted 'Y', six-bank, thirty-six-cylinder, 36-l, air-cooled powerplant, driving a three-bladed variable pitch airscrew. The monster, denominated MI-02, could possibly develop up to 1,800 hp at take-off and 1,470 hp at 3,670 m.

The VEF-19 would be built of wood/plywood and armed with four machine guns. It would have had an 11-m wingspan, a 9.2-m length, and a 650-kph maximum speed. The plan was to use the American engine Allison V-1710 for the preliminary calculations and for the flight of the first prototype. It was also considered to obtain some Rolls-Royce Merlin and Hispano-Suiza HS.12 engines.

In the autumn of 1939, the Cukurs C-6 record aircraft was converted into the C-6bis dive bomber with the installation of a 280-hp Hispano-Suiza 6 Mb engine, two machine guns and underwing racks for 150 kg of bombs. After being tested by the LAR, reaching a speed of 440 kph (clean), the manufacture of twelve units was ordered only ten days before the Soviet occupation.

The LAR strength on 17 June 1940 was ten Letov Š-16Ls, six Bristol Bulldog Mk IIs, twenty-five Gloster Gladiator Mk Is, three Hawker Hinds, four VEF I-12s, two VEF I-15s, one VEF I-16, one Cukurs C-6bis, twenty R.W.D. 8s, and six VEF I-16s in construction.

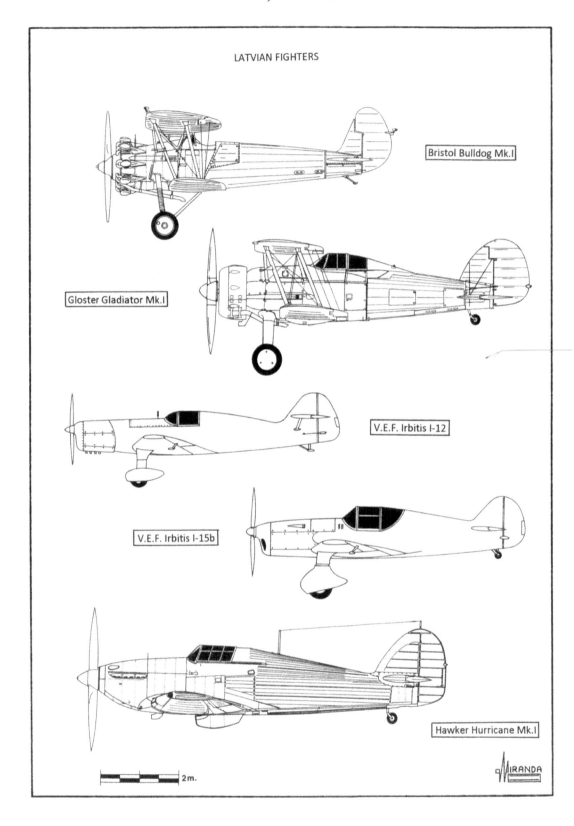

LATVIAN FIGHTERS

Bristol Bulldog Mk.I

Gloster Gladiator Mk.I

V.E.F. Irbitis I-12

V.E.F. Irbitis I-15b

Hawker Hurricane Mk.I

2 m.

MIRANDA

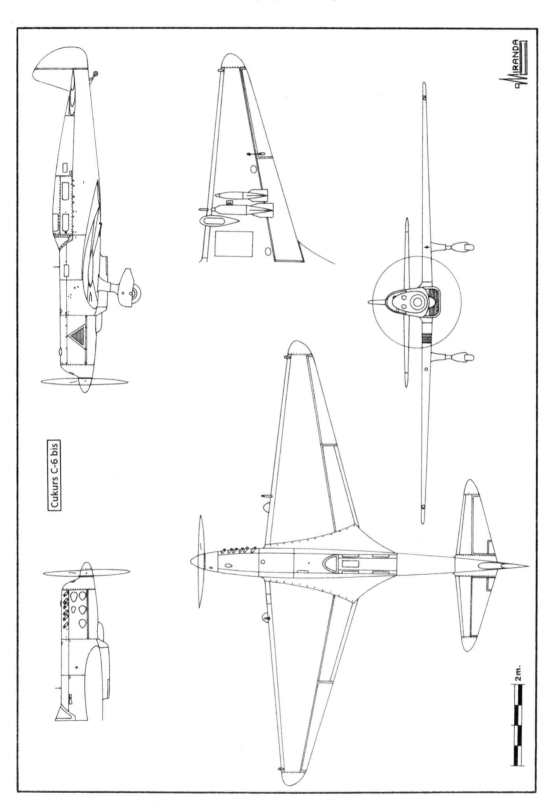

Cukurs C-6 bis

2 m.

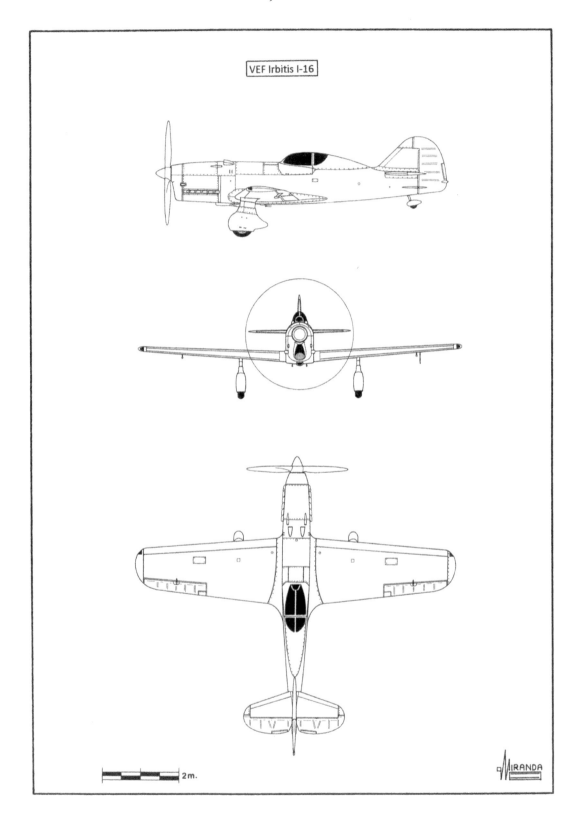

VEF Irbitis I-16

2 m.

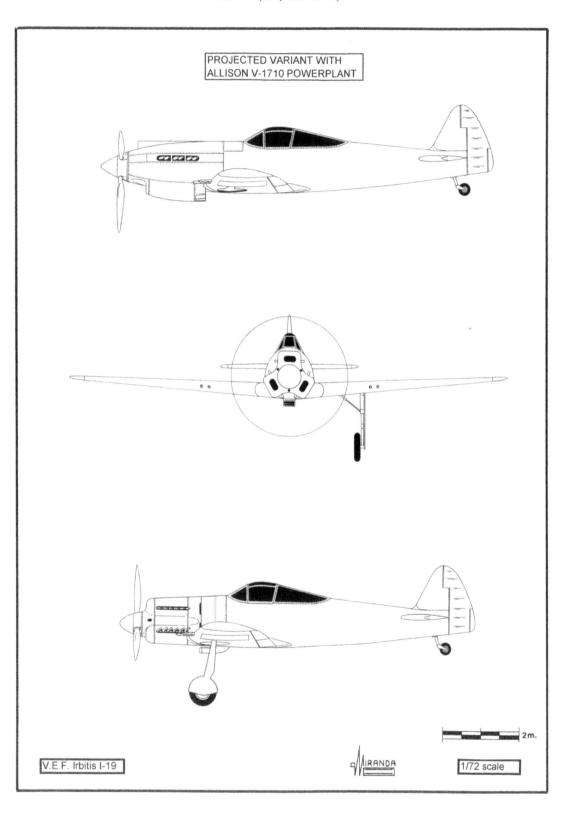

PROJECTED VARIANT WITH
ALLISON V-1710 POWERPLANT

V.E.F. Irbitis I-19

MIRANDA

1/72 scale

2m.

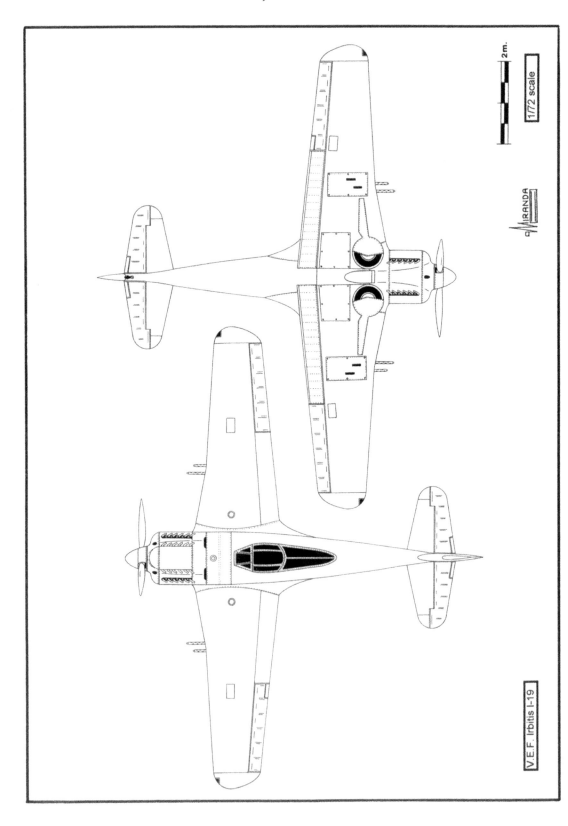

2 m.

1/72 scale

MIRANDA

V.E.F. Irbitis I-19

20

Sweden
(30 November 1939–
4 February 1945)

In 1919, the Swedish Army had an aircraft division formed by twelve war surplus Phönix D.III fighters joined by twenty-four FVM Öl *Tummelisa* advanced trainers in 1921.

Four years later, they acquired ten units of the Nieuport-Delage NiD 29 ex-French fighters. The Swedish Air Force (*Flygvapnet*) was created in 1926, unifying any army and navy aviation. The new service required the use of two-seat long-range fighters. They acquired fifteen Fokker C.Vds in 1927 and the following year six Heinkel HD 19 seaplane fighters.

The arms race started by the Soviet five-year plan in 1928 prompted the countries close to the USSR to modernise their combat aircraft. After the entry into service of the Polikarpov I-3, in August 1929, Lithuania ordered fifteen Fiat CR.20 fighters and Latvia ordered seven Bristol Bulldog Mk IIs. In March 1930, the prototype of the first Polish monoplane fighter—PWS-10—flew for the first time, and four months later, the prototype of the Polikarpov I-5 also flew. At that time, the VVS already had 250 I-3 in service.

In August, Sweden ordered three Bristol Bulldog Mk II and eight Bulldog Mk IIA (286 kph) fighters in May 1931. That same year, the Swedish Government ordered the construction of eighteen units of the indigenous fighter Svenka Aero *Jaktfalk*. The VVS fighter strength was of 389 I-3s and sixty-six I-5s. In 1932, the expansion of the *Flygvapnet* was planned, with the construction under licence of thirty-six Tiger Moth and twenty-five *Tigerschwalbe* elementary trainers, joined by ten *Sparmann* S-1A advanced trainers in 1934.

Between 1936 and 1938, the USSR made a demonstration of force by sending 108 Polikarpov I-15s, ninety-three Polikarpov I-152s, ninety-three Polikarpov I-16 Type 5s, sixty-eight Polikarpov I-16 Type 6s, 124 Polikarpov I-16 Type 10s, thirty-one Polikarpov R-5 Army cooperation aircraft, thirty-one Polikarpov R-5 Cht strafers, sixty-two Polikarpov RZ light bombers, and ninety-three Tupolev SB-2 medium bombers to Spain. They also sent 347 tanks, sixty armoured vehicles, 1,186 cannons, 340 mortars, 20,486 machine guns, 497,813 rifles, 862 million cartridges, 3.5 million artillery shells, 10,000 aviation bombs, and four torpedo boats.

Lithuania ordered thirteen Dewoitine D.501 L monoplane fighters.

With the publication of the Defence Act in December 1936, the second plan of expansion of the *Flygvapnet* to five combat wings started. To equip these units with enough aircraft, it was necessary to organise the indigenous production of forty-two Hawker Hart light bombers, eighty Junkers Ju 86 K-1 medium bombers, 102 Douglas 8 A-1 attack bombers, 190 SAAB 17 dive bombers, eighty-five Focke-Wulf Fw 44 elementary trainers, and 136 North American NA-16-4M advanced trainers, which were to be delivered between 1937 and 1941.

In 1937, the VVS strength was of 8,139 front-line aircraft, including 443 medium and heavy bombers. The Polikarpov I-152 started fighting in China. In June, Sweden ordered thirty-seven Gloster Gladiator Mk I fighters. In 1938, the production of Polikarpov I-153 started, and Sweden ordered eighteen Gloster Gladiator Mk IIs (414 kph). At the end of that year, Soviet aviation was defeated in Spain thanks to the technological superiority of the Condor Legion.

On 11 May 1939, the VVS entered into combat against fighters of the Imperial Japanese Army (IJA) in Khalkhin Gol. In September, the Soviets were forced to sign an armistice as they were overcome by the technical quality of Japanese planes and pilots. On 29 June, Sweden ordered fifteen Seversky EP-1-106 fighters.

After its defeat in Spain, the USSR was also forced to sign the Molotov–Ribbentrop Pact and be satisfied with 'freeing' weaker objectives by occupying eastern Poland when the Polish Army had already been defeated by the *Wehrmacht*. That same month, the ANBO VIII indigenous dive bomber took its first flight in Lithuania and its government ordered thirteen Morane-Saulnier M.S.406 fighters that the French never delivered because of the war. Nor did the British deliver the Spitfires acquired by Estonia or the Hurricanes acquired by Latvia. On 11 October, Sweden ordered a second batch of forty-five Seversky fighters.

Despite the losses suffered in Spain, Manchuria, and China, the VVS strength was of 7,320 aircraft. On 30 November, the Soviets began the invasion of Finland. At that time, the *Flygvapnet* possessed a front-line strength of only 140 aircraft (of which about half consisted of Harts and Gladiators biplanes) but went to their aid forming the *Flygflottilj* 19, a volunteer unit with four Hawker Harts and twelve Gladiators equipped with ski undercarriages.

On 1 January 1940, the Swedish Government ordered a third batch of sixty Seversky EP-1-106 and two Republic 2PA attack bombers. On 6 February, they also ordered 144 Vultee Model 48C fighters; however, fearing that the aircraft might fall into Soviet hands, the US State Department placed an embargo on the export of military aircraft to Sweden on 18 October.

The embargo also included the export of engines, so the Douglas 8 A-1 attack bombers had to use the Bristol Pegasus XII, the SAAB 17 used the Bristol Pegasus XXIV and the Piaggio P.XII bis RC 40D, and the North American trainers used the Piaggio P. VII RC 16, which were less powerful and reliable than the original Pratt & Whitney and Wright Whirlwind. The situation resulted in panic, and the Swedish Government ordered seventy-two Fiat CR.42 bis and sixty Reggiane Re.2000 fighters from Italy as a stop-gap solution until the indigenous industry could build their own fighters.

Unfortunately, the SAAB 19—a fighter based on the Bristol Type 153, whose manufacture started in 1941—had been cancelled when the British refused to continue the production of the 1,400-hp Bristol *Taurus* II engine. The SAAB 19 would have been a low wing monoplane with a 10.5-m wingspan, an all-metal construction, a retractable undercarriage, and armed with four wing-mounted 13.2-mm m/39A machine guns. Its estimated maximum speed would have been 605 kph and the maximum take-off weight of 2,690 kg.

On 1 January 1941, the design work of the J 22 'panic fighter' was started under the leadership of Bo Lundberg. General Nils Söderberg established the FFVS workshop, a temporary organisation intended solely for the production of the new aircraft. As the Swedes expected to get the fighters in the USA, all available aluminium 2024 T3 was already being used in the production of the S 17 and S 18 bombers.

The construction system of the J 22, based on that of the Finnish *Myrsky*, consisted of a welded chromium-molybdenum steel tube structure covered with plywood panels. To circumvent the engine embargo, Sweden managed to purchase a batch of 100 Pratt & Whitney R-1830-45 Twin Wasp engines in 1942, from the Vichy-French Curtiss H-75 fighters, and *Svenska Flygmotor-Trollhättan* started a programme to copy the Twin Wasp as the Swedish-made 1,050-hp STWC-3G.

The J 22 prototype made its first flight on 20 September 1942, reaching 575 kph.

Between 1943 and 1946, 198 units were built. Of these, the first 143 units were J 22 A (with two 13.2-mm m/39A and two 7.9-mm Bofors m/22F machine guns) and fifty-five units of the J 22 B version (with four m/39 A). The J 22 was a light and very manoeuvrable fighter equivalent to the Spitfire and Messerschmitt Bf 109 of 1940, but it could not compete with the latest German and British designs when it entered service.

This did not represent a serious problem as Sweden already maintained good relations with both, and the J 22 exceeded or equalled the Soviet fighters Polikarpov, LaGG, Hurricane Mk II, and Airacobra, which posed the real threat. In March 1941, the *Flygvapnet* Air Board managed to reach an agreement for *SFA-Flygmotor* licence manufacture of the German Daimler-Benz DB 601 engine. Subsequently, the licence upgraded to the latest version (DB 605B with 1,475 hp). The new engine was acquired to improve the performances of the SAAB 18 bomber and propel the fighter that would replace the J 22. On 5 April 1941, the design team of SAAB, under the leadership of Frid Wänström, proposed the construction of the J 21, an unconventional fighter with twin tail booms, nose wheel, and pusher propeller.

The radical nature of the new fighter presented unknown development problems: the technological risk of the design of a high speed laminar flow wing, the serious cooling difficulties of the radiator installation buried inside of the wing (that never really overcome), the adoption of a nose wheel that required to train the pilots again using a specially modified North American NA-16 and the development of the SAAB-Bofors Mk I ejector seat to prevent the pilot from being hit by the airscrew during the bail out.

In October 1941, fearing that the J 21 presented insurmountable development difficulties, the *Flygvapnet* suggested the design of a more conventional fighter, as a fall-back option, and the SAAB J 23 parallel project was proposed on November. It was a low-wing monoplane with 11.28 wingspan, all-metal construction, conventional landing gear and armed with a 20mm Bofors M/45 engine-mounted cannon and four 13.2-mm Bofors m/39A wing-mounted machine guns.

The J 23 would be propelled by one DB 605B driving a VDM propeller and cooled by one Mustang-style ventral radiator. Wind tunnel tests in the Technical High School-Stockholm showed that the J 23 would have superior maximum speed and climb, but the J 21 was more manoeuvrable thanks to the central position of the engine. When the J 21 development problems were surmounted, the J 23 design work was discontinued on 5 December 1941.

At the end of 1944, the latest models of German and British fighters already reached speeds that the J 21 could not match because of the excessive drag generated by their tail surfaces. In April 1945, SAAB started the design work on the J 27, a conventional fighter with elliptical wings, Youngman flaps, tear drop canopy, and ejector seat, capable of flying at 700 kph powered by a 2,200-hp Rolls-Royce Griffon engine driving contra-rotating airscrews. The foreseen armament was four 13.2-mm Bofors-Colt m/39A wing-mounted machine guns.

It was expected to build a more advanced version, with butterfly tail, four 20-mm Hispano cannons, and a 740-kph maximum speed, when the 2,500-hp *Svenka Flygmotor AB Mx* would be available—a 54-l engine with twenty-four cylinders in 'X' configuration to be ready in 1947.

At the end of 1945, the *Flygvapnet* chose one brute force solution, acquiring the manufacture licence of the Havilland Goblin Mk II British turbojet (1,360 kg thrust), to power an advanced version of the J 21 that flew at 800 kph in 1947.

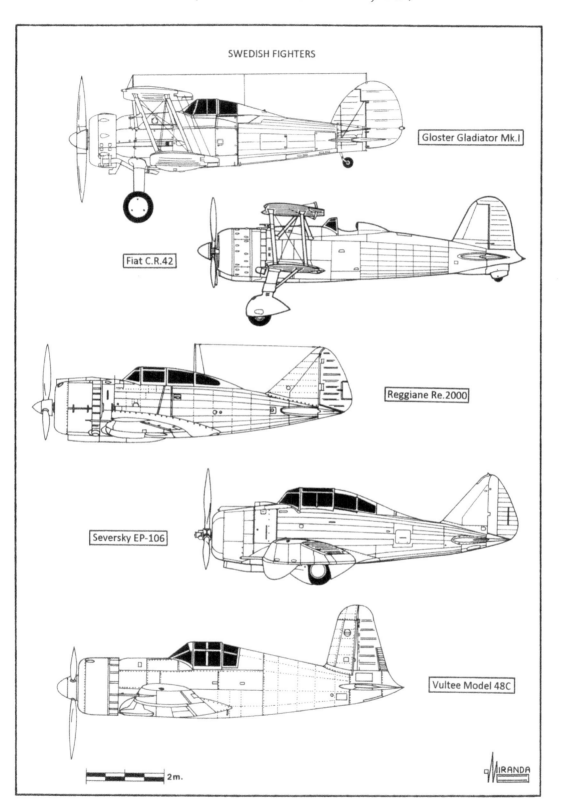

SWEDISH FIGHTERS

Gloster Gladiator Mk.I

Fiat C.R.42

Reggiane Re.2000

Seversky EP-106

Vultee Model 48C

2 m.

MIRANDA

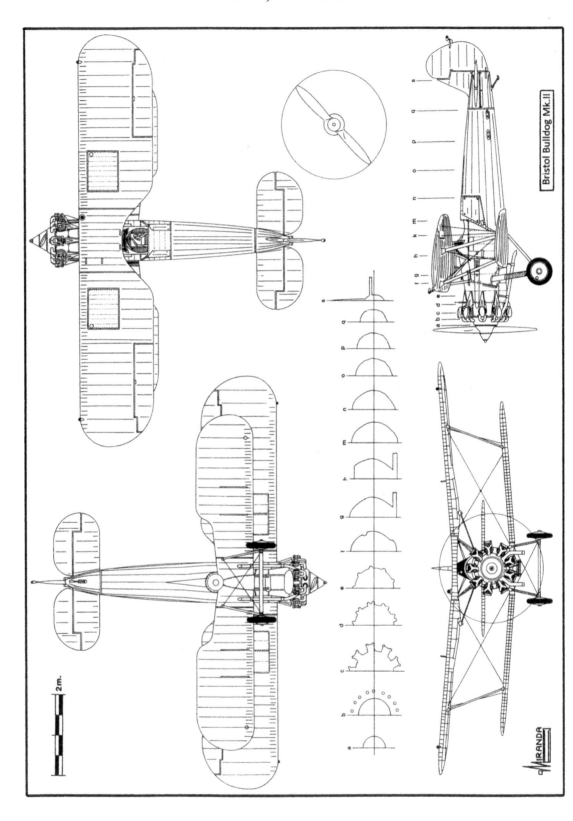

Bristol Bulldog Mk.II

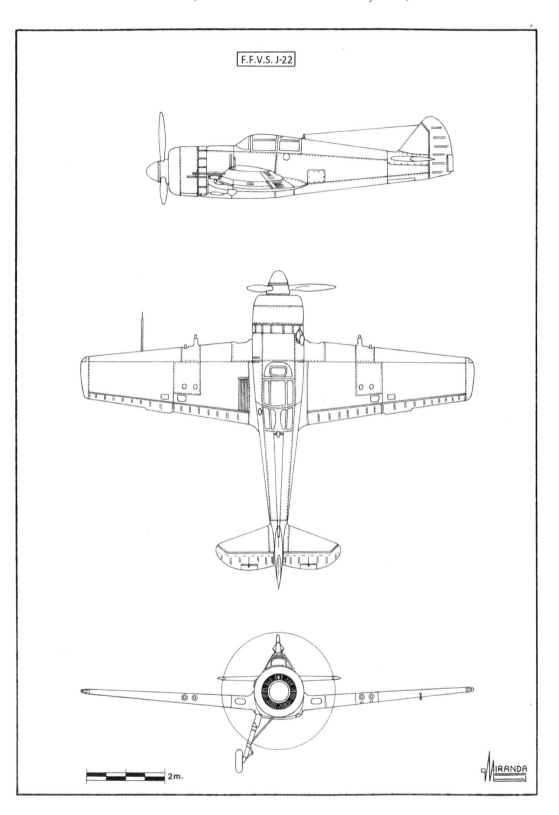

F.F.V.S. J-22

2m.

MIRANDA

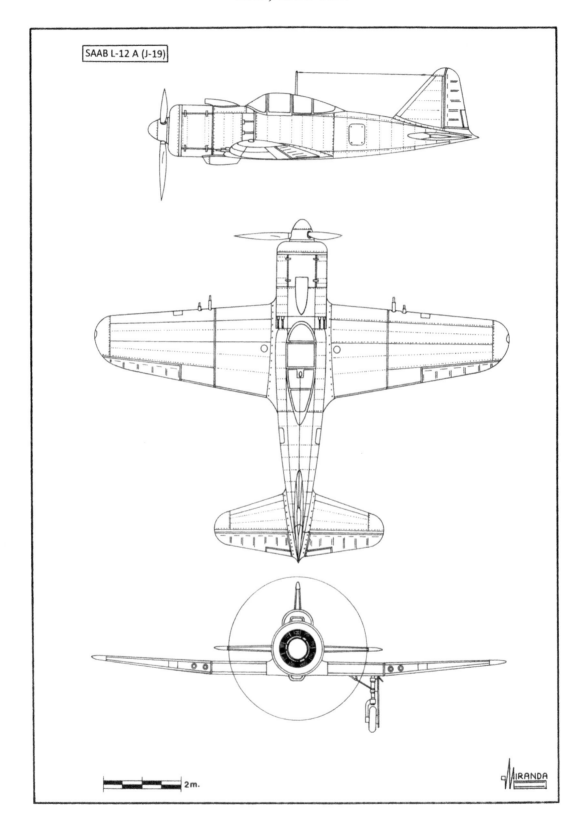

SAAB L-12 A (J-19)

2m.

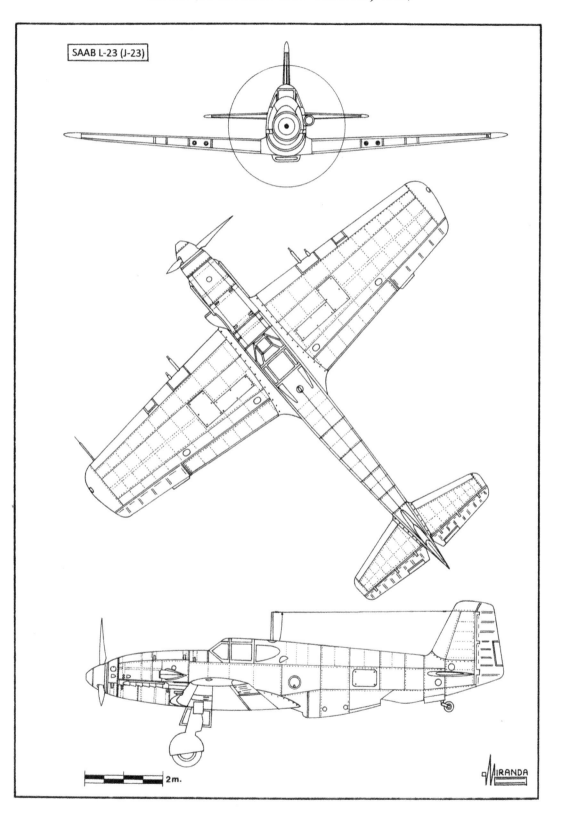

SAAB L-23 (J-23)

2m.

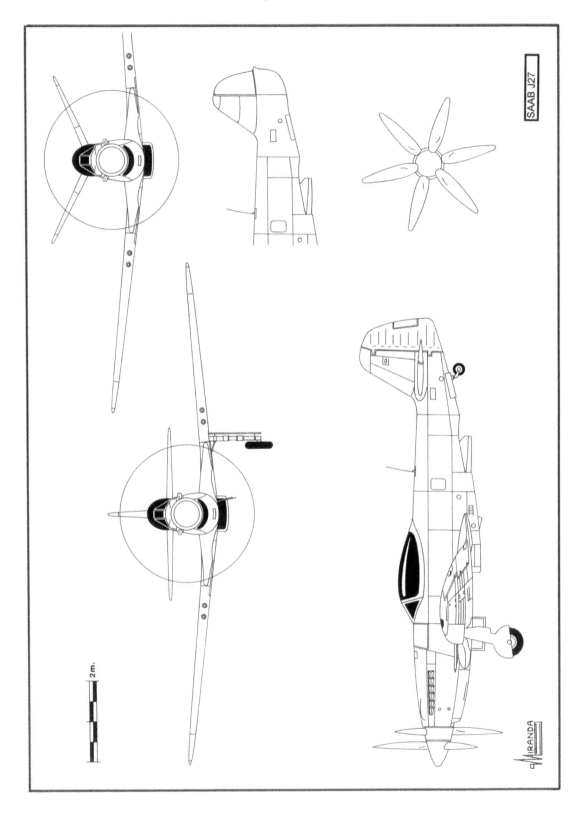

SAAB J27

2 m.

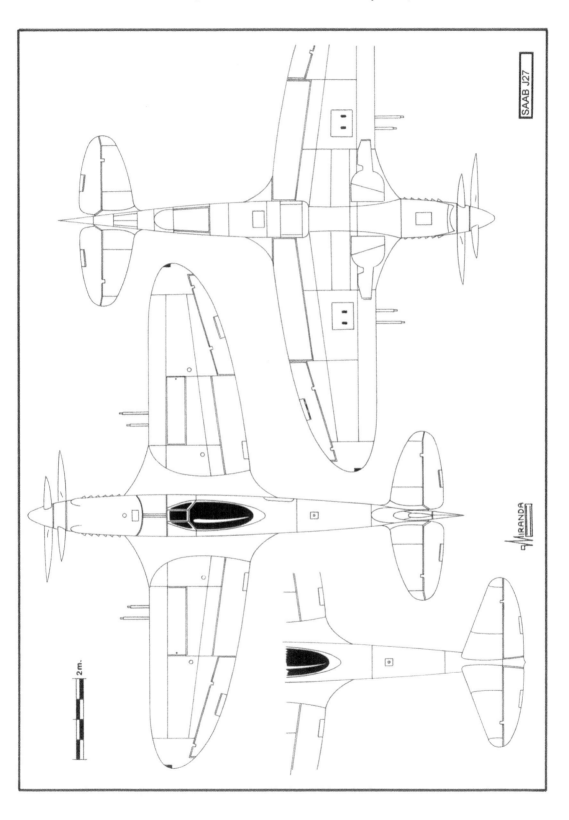

SAAB J27

2 m.

21

The Japanese Aggressor
(28 January 1932–15 August 1945)

After the abolition of feudalism in 1871, Japan hastened to create an industrial monster that quickly exceeded the very few natural resources of the country. The inertia generated by the machines led the Japanese to a militaristic spiral that only a major defeat could stem.

They annexed Taiwan in 1895, defeated Russia in 1905, and invaded Korea in 1910 to seize large amounts of coal. To save Japan from the effects of the Great Depression, the Imperial Japanese Army occupied Manchuria in 1931, giving the Japanese industry access to its numerous natural resources of iron, aluminium, coking coal, soybeans, and salt. In 1933, Japan occupied the Chinese province of Jehol, and in 1937, they initiated large-scale warfare that alarmed the international community. After the short war with the Soviets in Nomonhan, Japan lost its access to oil concessions in Northern Sakhalin.

When France capitulated in June 1940, Japan moved into French Indochina and the US Administration reacted by banning the export of essential defence materials: aviation motors, high-octane aviation fuel, lubricants, melting iron, and steel scrap. The embargo was expanded in July 1941 to such grades of oil. The British and the Dutch followed suit and embargoed export to Japan of copper, tin, bauxite, rubber, and petroleum from their colonies in Southern Asia. The Allies were putting Japan in an untenable position that would force oil-starved Japan to seize the oil fields of the Dutch East Indies.

For this purpose, the Imperial Japanese Army wanted to neutralise the powerful Singapore British defences, and the Imperial Japanese Navy wanted to make landings in the Philippines, defended by the Americans. The war would be inevitable and the Allies knew it, but they did not expect the attack to be successful and were surprised when only seventeen Mitsubishi G4M bombers, from the IJN Genzan Kokutai, managed to sink two of the most modern British battlecruisers in a few minutes.

Shortly afterwards, eighty-seven Nakajima Ki.27bs and fifty-nine Nakajima Ki.43-Ias, from the IJA, destroyed the 114 Brewster Buffalos and fifty-one Hawker Hurricanes that defended Malaya, pushing back the British to Sumatra and Burma initially, then up to

Ceylon and Australia. The Mitsubishi A6M2 *Zero-Sen* wrought havoc in Pearl Harbor, the Philippines, Java, and Ceylon by annihilating most of the P-35, P-36, P-40, Hurricane Mk II, Curtiss CW.21B, and Fairey Fulmar fighters that opposed them.

The exceptional dogfighting capabilities of the Japanese fighters and the ferocity and experience of their pilots had been virtually ignored by the Allied intelligence officers—how could this happen?

The Nakajima Ki.27 had been operating in China since March 1938, and several units were captured and tested by Chinese and Soviets. Its performances were known in the West, but the archaic aspect of its airframe, with fixed undercarriage (inspired by that of the Northtrop XFT of 1934), made the Allies think that it was a design technologically surpassed.

Actually, under the protection of 600 Ki.27 fighters, the IJA conquered 90 per cent of the territories occupied during the Second World War. The Ki.27 was not examined by experts of the Allies until the capture of one from the 77th Sentai in Burma in April 1942.

The *Zero* was also unknown to the Allies. In spring 1941, the Chinese succeeded in shooting down an A6M2 over Chengdu. They managed to assemble a very accurate data sheet and three-view drawings were given to the US Navy and War Departments, but the experts did not consider the data credible and the report was ignored.

The *Zero* was designed to meet specification IJN 19 May 1937, which required a fighter capable of flying at more than 500 kph and with an exceptional range to escort the bombers on the specific conditions of the war in China. Its construction was only made possible by adopting a retractable landing gear (based on that of the prototype Chance Vought V.143 acquired by the Japanese in 1937) and removing the armour and all the auxiliary equipment typical of a naval fighter, until the aircraft weighted 25 per cent less than the Grumman F4F, even keeping its powerful armament. No one in the Western countries believed that a fighter with these characteristics could exist until the attacks on Pearl Harbor, the Philippines, and Java.

In July 1942, American experts examined a *Zero* captured in Akutan Island and identified the weak points of its construction, information that saved the lives of US airmen and that was used to design the Grumman Hellcat. On the other hand, the Nakajima Ki.43 was completely unknown outside of Japan. The success of the Ki.27 had delayed the start of production until April 1941 with only forty units having entered service in December. That was a complete surprise to the Allies, who at first mistook it for the *Zero*. The Japanese Army decided to reveal its existence in April 1942.

Equipped with butterfly combat flaps and weighting 33 per cent less than the P-40B, the Ki.43 was able to outmanoeuvre Buffaloes, Hurricanes, and Tomahawks. The first unit was captured at Chittagong in spring 1942. Tested by the Australians, the Chinese, and the Americans, it revealed some shortcomings in combat: a lack of pilot armour and self-sealing fuel tanks. The Allies soon developed 'hit and run' tactics that could be used successfully against it.

The Japanese R/T devices never worked air-to-air. The pilots used to uninstall them to save weight and communicated with each other by wing movements. The telescopic gunsight restricted the vision of the environment, and many pilots of Ki.27 and Ki.43 were surprised by 'hit and run' attacks during the strafing of an airfield.

After initial successes, obtained by attacks with local numerical superiority against the second line Allied fighters, the Japanese Sword was blunted in Midway, Guadalcanal, and New Guinea. The Allies reacted by designing and building thousands of Hellcats, Seafires, Corsairs, Mustangs, Thunderbolts, and Lightings in record time, while the Japanese kept on manufacturing the same models as in 1941.

The effective blockade made by the US Navy submarine force prevented the Japanese industry from acceding to the Chinese coal; the sugarcane of the Philippines; the petroleum from Sumatra, Celebes, and Burma; the tin and bauxite from Malaya; and the rice from Thailand and Cochinchina, which had cost so much blood to obtain.

The Japanese defeat was a matter of industrial production and resources. Without them, Japanese aviation was forced to retreat to the mother islands, finally losing air superiority even over them and sacrificing themselves in useless suicide attacks.

Japanese 'Panic Fighters'

Readers interested in this subject can find detailed descriptions of the Japanese rammers Nakajima Ki.27-*Otsu*, Nakajima Ki.43-III-*Ko*, Nakajima Ki.44-II-*Hei*, Kawasaki Ki.61-I-KAI-*Hei*, Nakajima Ki.84-I-*Ko*, Kawasaki Ki.45-KAI-*Hei*, Mitsubishi Ki.46-III-*Ko*, Kawasaki Ki.100, Mitsubishi A6M Series, Nakajima J1N1-*Hei*, and the projects Mizuno *Shinryu* II and Kakukyoku *Rammer* in my book *Axis Suicide Squads: German and Japanese Secret Projects of the Second World War*, published by Fonthill Media Ltd in 2017.

You may also find descriptions of the projects Manshu Ki.98, Mitsubishi J4M *Senden*, Mitsubishi A7M *Reppu*, Yokosuka *Ginga* night fighter variant, Rikugun Ki.202, Kyushu *Shinden* turbojet variant, Tachikawa Ki.94, Nakajima Ki.87, Nakajima C6N2 with turbocompressor, Yokosuka D4Y2 with turbocharger, Nakajima Ki.201 *Karyu*, Kayaba Katsudory ramjet fighter, Nakajima *Kikka*, and Yokosuka R2Y turbojet variants in my forthcoming book *Fighters of the Dying Sun: The Most Advanced Japanese Fighters of the Second World War*.

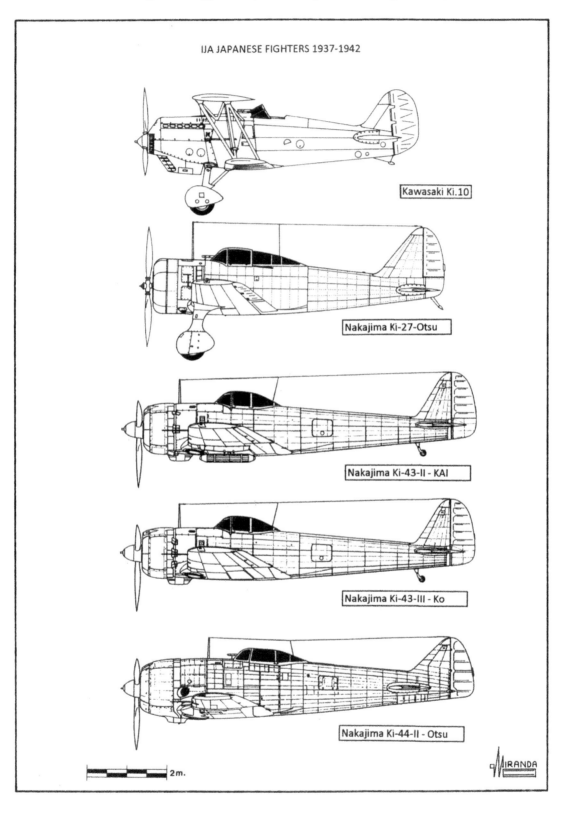

IJA JAPANESE FIGHTERS 1937-1942

Kawasaki Ki.10

Nakajima Ki-27-Otsu

Nakajima Ki-43-II - KAI

Nakajima Ki-43-III - Ko

Nakajima Ki-44-II - Otsu

2 m.

MIRANDA

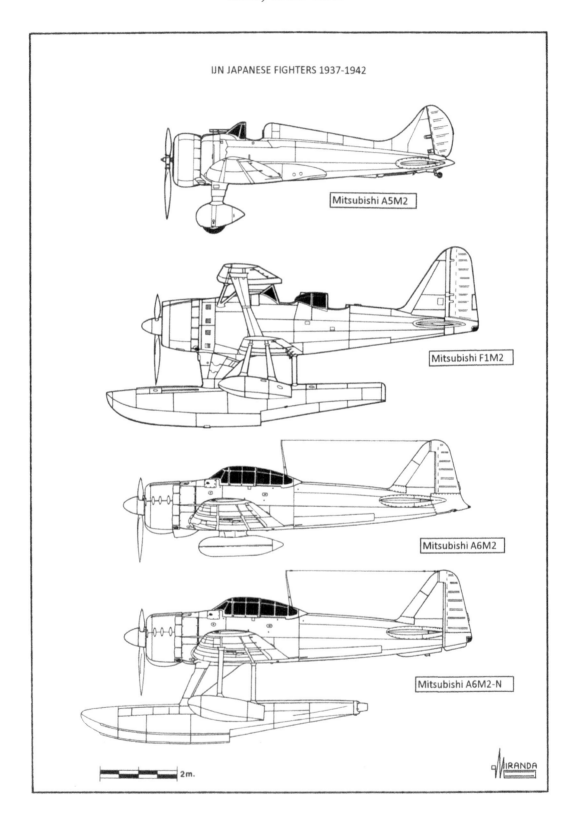

IJN JAPANESE FIGHTERS 1937-1942

Mitsubishi A5M2

Mitsubishi F1M2

Mitsubishi A6M2

Mitsubishi A6M2-N

2 m.

MIRANDA

22

China
(28 January 1932–15 August 1945)

In September 1931, taking advantage of a period of political weakness in China, Japan declared the independence on Manchuria and proclaimed it the new protectorate of Manchukuo.

At the beginning of 1932, Mitsubishi B1M-3 bombers from IJN carrier *Kaga*, escorted by Nakajima A1N-2 (239 kph) fighters from IJN carrier *Hosho*, launched attacks against Shanghai. China's air defence consisted of two Blackburn Lincock III (264 kph) fighters, the prototype Boeing 218 (304 kph), and five Vought V-65C (269 kph) fighter-bombers.

The Chinese fighters were superior to the Nakajima in speed and rate of climb, but they were surprised by the exceptional manoeuvrability of the Japanese planes. During combat over Shanghai on 5, 22, and 26 February, the Japanese downed the Boeing, one Blackburn, and two Vought.

As opposed to the heterogeneous collection of aircraft that the Chinese strove to acquire overseas, the Japanese had the advantage of the standardisation of models and excellent maintenance onboard the *Kaga* and *Hosho*, as well as the local numerical superiority they could achieve by displacing the aircraft carriers.

When the Japanese occupied the Jehol province in 1933, the Chinese Central Government started contacts with American and Italian aircraft manufacturers to import the modern Curtiss Hawk II (335 kph), Curtiss Hawk III (386 kph), Fiat CR.30 (370 kph), Fiat CR.32 (375 kph), and Breda 27 (380 kph) fighters.

In 1934, they also acquired ten Boeing 281 (376 kph) monoplane fighters and components to assemble ninety Hawk IIIs in the new CAMCO-Shaoguan plant.

On 7 July 7 1937, an international incident was used by the Japanese to declare war on China and begin the occupation of a large part of its territory. At that time, the Chinese Air Force (CAF) consisted of twenty-nine Curtiss Hawk IIs, seventy-six Curtiss Hawk IIIs, ten Boeing 281s, ten Breda 27s, three Fiat CR.32 fighters, and 170 bombers of the types Northrop 2E, Douglas O2MC, Curtiss A-12, Fiat B.R.3, Heinkel He 111A, Martin 139, Savoia S.M. 72, and Vought V-92C.

The Imperial Japanese Navy started its attacks with seventy-six fighters (Nakajima A1N-2 Type 3 (239 kph), A2N-3 Type 90 (300 kph), and AN4-1 Type 95 (352 kph)), 148 bombers (Aichi D1A-2, Mitsubishi B1M-3, B2M-2, G2M-1, and G3M-1), and twenty-seven Nakajima E8N-1 Type 95 floatplanes. The Imperial Japanese Army initially used seventy-two Ki.10 Kawasaki type 95 (400 kph) fighters, 105 Nakajima Ki.1, Ki.2, and Ki.3 bombers, and twelve Nakajima Ki.4 Type 94 reconnaissance aircraft.

Again, the use of easily replaceable self-manufactured aircraft and expert pilots favoured the Japanese. On the contrary, the level of training of the Chinese pilots was so low and the maintenance of their aircraft so poor that only a third of them were in flying condition. During August, the Hawk II of the 28th Pursuit Squadron obtained some successes against the G3M bombers operating without an escort of fighters, but they suffered large losses against the Ki.10 of the 16th Hiko Rentai. Henceforth, the Hawk II were used in training and night fighter duties only.

The Hawk III were biplane fighters with retractable undercarriage and a very robust airframe, originally designed to operate from the US Navy aircraft carriers. Superior in manoeuvrability to the A4N-1 and Ki.10, they were too slow to intercept the G3M2 Type 21, which arrived in China in September. The Hawk fought hard for two months but lost the initiative with the appearance of the new Mitsubishi A5M1 Type 96 (370 kph) monoplane fighters from IJN *Kaga*, based in Kunda airfield, which surpassed them in manoeuvrability, shooting down three Hawk without suffering any losses. The CAF tried to counter the new threat by using mixed formations of Hawk III and Boeing 281, a monoplane fast enough to intercept the G3M2 but it was inappropriate for the dogfight because of its high wing load.

It was expected that the Hawk, fitted with oxygen equipment, would fly at 6,000 m in order to surprise the Type 96 with 'hit and run' attacks, but they rarely managed to achieve at height for lack of time. The available reserves of oxygen were not enough to make high-altitude patrols in a systematic way. The Chinese technical units used oxygen from the repair depots without checking its quality, and at altitude, the tubes and masks sometimes froze, causing accidents.

The Chinese Air Raid Warning Net (VNOS) was not a sufficiently effective organisation as its alarm signal often sounded only five to ten minutes before the Japanese fast bombers flew over the target. As a result, the Hawk IIIs were often surprised by the Type 96 climbing at medium level, suffering heavy combat losses. The Boeing also did not achieve much success because of its scarce armament. A single fighter equipped with two 0.30-inch machine guns, attacking three G3M2s in an auto defensive formation, could face nine rear gunners firing from several angles.

The same thing occurred with the Fiat CR.32 fighters, which had armament that proved insufficient when confronting the Kisarazu Kokutai G3M1 bombers during the Battle of Nanking. Its manoeuvrability turned out to be inferior to the new Mitsubishi A5M2 (370 kph). The Italian engines ran with a mixture of gasoline, alcohol, and benzene; its maintenance was very problematic at that time. On October 1937, just one Fiat was in flying condition.

In China, poor maintenance of aircraft and airfields, insufficiently trained pilots, and a lack of spares managed to disable three times the number of aircraft than all the Japanese attacks. By the beginning of November, there was no more than forty serviceable aircraft and the best Chinese pilots had died, so the CAF retired to the western region of Hankow, far from the reach of the Aichi dive bombers.

Until 1945, the Japanese aircraft practically every year annihilated the CAF, systematically destroying aircraft, airfields, and aircraft-assembling factories and firing on its pilots as they descended in parachutes.

Each year, the CAF would be reconstructed with aircraft acquired abroad and new promotions of inexperienced pilots with little chance of survival. Yet each year was more difficult to compensate losses, and each year, the Japanese aircraft were more numerous and more technologically advanced.

In 1937, China needed a 'Panic Fighter' able to stop the Japanese aggressor and believed found in the Polikarpov I-16, a small monoplane that had achieved good results in Spain last year, fighting against the Heinkel He 51 of the Condor Legion.

The Chinese Central Government decided to request military assistance from the USSR, acquiring Soviet aircraft worth $100 million of gold.

Between September 1937 and April 1941, the CAF received 656 Polikarpov fighters, of which 272 were classic biplanes of the type I-152 (379 kph), ninety-three were biplanes with retractable landing gear of the type I-153 (444 kph), and various other versions of the I-16: twenty Type 5s (457 kph), thirty Type 6s (440 kph), ninety-two Type 10s (448 kph), seventy-five Type 17s (425 kph), and seventy-four UTI-4 two-seat trainers. They also acquired 292 modern Tupolev SB-2 bombers and a large amount of auxiliary equipment for the maintenance of the aircraft.

The contract with the Soviets also included support technique, searchlights, acoustic detectors, squads of 'voluntary' Russian pilots with combat experience in Spain, and training of Chinese pilots and mechanics in the USSR, but the Japanese remained invincible in China until the end of the Second World War.

The Soviets tried to use their numerical superiority in combat tactics based on the use of large mixed formations of biplanes and monoplanes, which supported each other flying at different heights. Yet, as occurred during the Battle of Britain, the use of large formations only managed to aggravate the problem of rapid interception.

The Polikarpov fighters lacked the automatic starting system of the Boeing and Hawks. Their engines were to be put into operation using a Hucks starter truck that made the axis propeller turn through a system of pulleys. The procedure was slow and it was customary for the biplanes to take off first to protect the I-16s, which had small wings without flaps that were inefficient to operate from the poorly equipped Chinese airfields.

This delayed the formation of a fighting force even more because according to Soviet air doctrine, the monoplanes were to occupy the higher level. The slowness and clumsiness of the system benefited the Japanese, and their fast bombers often managed to surprise the Chinese fighters in the ground, causing heavy losses.

The I-152 (379 kph) was superior in armament and manoeuvrability to the Japanese fighters. It could turn 360 degrees in eleven seconds against the fifteen seconds of the A5M2 and seventeen seconds of the Ki.10, but it had already given bad results in Spain because of the poor design of the central section of the upper wing, which made it lose excessive height during the horizontal turns. Besides, its armament and armour made it too heavy, making it inferior to the Japanese fighters in climb rate and maximum speed.

At the beginning of 1938, it became evident that the I-152/I-16 combination did not work against the A5M2. On February, during the defence of Hankow, the pilots of the 4th FG were forced to use the ramming against the fighters of the 13rd Kokutai. On April, the I-152 clashed for the first time with the new Nakajima Ki.27 (460 kph) monoplanes of the IJA 2nd Daitai suffering serious losses on Kuei Teh.

By the mid-1930s, the design teams of the firms Fokker, Nakajima, and Mitsubishi independently arrived at the same aerodynamic solution; a detailed study showed that with the engines of fewer than 1,000 hp available at the time, it would not be effective to provide a fighter monoplane with a retractable undercarriage.

The designers estimated that disadvantages in increased weight and mechanical problems would not justify the 3 per cent increase in overall speed and so decided to build the D.XXI, Ki.27, and A5M2 fighters with fixed undercarriage streamlined to the greatest extent possible.

During the flight tests with the prototype of the Fokker D.XXI, it was found that the drag generated by the undercarriage was only 10 per cent of that generated by the entire airframe. Subsequent experiments carried out in Finland with a D.XXI equipped with retractable landing gear, confirmed the calculations of the contractor. On the contrary, the Type 5 fastest version of the Polikarpov I-16 did not exceed the overall speed of the Ki.27 and was only 20 kph faster than the A5M2. The cause was the poor aerodynamic design of the engine cowling, equipped with a shuttered front plate.

The Type 5 also proved to be inferior in manoeuvrability regarding the Japanese monoplanes. The too-short fuselage created longitudinal instability, affecting the accuracy of the weapons, and its small wings did not generate sufficient lift, penalising their rate of climb, which was just of 73 per cent compared to the climbing rate of the Japanese fighters. The absence of flaps made manoeuvrability difficult at low speeds and caused so many landing accidents in the poorly equipped Chinese airfields that it was necessary to import several two-seat trainers of the UTI-4 type to retrain the pilots.

The firepower was increased in Type 6 with two additional 1,800 rpm rapid-fire ShKAS machine guns, to improve its effectiveness against the G3M bombers. However, excess weight caused by the extra weaponry, the ammunition, and the dorsal plate armour was not fully compensated by the installation of a more powerful engine, and Type 6 turned out to be even slower than its predecessor. During his first combat on Nanking, on 21 November, the Type 6 proved inferior to the A5M2.

In spring 1938, the Soviets introduced the Type 10 in China, armed with four ShKAS—effective against the G3M but too heavy for a dogfight against the agile Japanese fighters. The designers tried to solve the problem of excessive landing speed, installing flaps powered by compressed air, but its use required some practice and even veteran pilots continued to suffer accidents. Numerical superiority was not enough to defeat the Japanese planes, which continued occupying territories. The Polikarpov fighters were abundant and cheap, but they lost all the wars in which intervened.

At the beginning of 1938, faced with the failure of the Soviet material, the Chinese decided to try their luck with British technology, acquiring thirty-six Gloster Gladiator

Mk Is, considered the most effective biplane fighter of its time. In March, the A5M2 began to use oxygen equipment that allowed them to fly at more than 6,000 m. The only Chinese fighters who could fight at that point were the Gladiator of the 5th PG, which finally obtained some successes against the Mitsubishi fighters, to which they exceeded in manoeuvrability and armament.

Unfortunately for the CAF, the British could only give away thirty-six planes that were soon affected by the usual problems in the maintenance of oxygen equipment. The Gladiators also suffered frequent stoppages in the four Browning M1919 machine guns due to the poor quality of the Belgian ammunition they used. Weapons failing, some Chinese pilots carried out ramming against the A5M2. At the end of 1939, only three Gladiators were serviceable.

During the summer of 1938, the scale of resistance of the CAF dramatically decreased as a third part of its 200 pilots had died and the survivors avoided the confrontation with the Japanese fighters, limiting themselves to carrying out missions of strafing or night fighting with their I-152. At the end of August, the CAF began its annual retreat to Western bases, leaving the burden of combat to Soviet 'volunteers'.

To keep in touch, the Ki.27 and A5M2 were equipped with belly fuel tanks that increased their operational range. They used to escort the bombers at a distance to surprise the Chinese fighters who dared to take off believing that the bombers attacked without protection. On November, the Soviets received an order to temporarily discontinue their participation in battle.

At the end of 1938, the CAF had lost 202 aircraft and had only 170 in flying condition, but the country was too large to be completely defeated. In any case, the IJA started a long-range annihilation campaign against Chinese aircraft based on Lanchow and Chungking using its new Mitsubishi Ki.21 Type 97 and Fiat B.R.20 bombers. For their distant targets, bombers were to carry out missions of 1,600 km without an escort of fighters, being occasionally intercepted by the I-16 Type 10 that the Chinese still kept. On February 1939, the losses of the IJA reached 10 per cent and the offensive was limited only to night attacks.

In May, the IJA received orders to relocate their planes to Manchuria to fight against the Soviets in Nomonhan, and the IJN preferred to concentrate their attacks only on Chungking, the new Chinese capital. The city was defended by the new American fighters Curtiss H-75M (450 kph). They were monoplanes with a fixed undercarriage, as fast as the Ki.27 but less manoeuvrable and with lower rate of climb due to the large weight of auxiliary equipment: armour plates, R/T device, oxygen equipment, and 12.7-mm machine guns.

Its structural resistance prevented the H-75 from suffering too many losses. However, they suffered numerous accidents due to a defect in the design of the undercarriage that used to lock the wheels. The Curtiss stayed in the front line until the arrival of the Mitsubishi A6M2 Type 11 *Zero-Sen* (533 kph) in September 1940.

The G3M bombers also evolved, becoming faster and harder to shoot down. At the end of 1939, the CAF began to fight them with some French Dewoitine D.510C (367 kph) fighters, armed with a 20-mm HS.404 cannon that allowed them to shoot the G3M without exposing themselves to the defensive fire of the rear gunners.

The Dewoitine was only 55 kph faster than the G3M and had to attack it from a higher altitude using the half-roll diving technique. However, it was discovered during the first combats that this manoeuvre impeded the proper functioning of the cannon that had a tendency to jam when firing in a dive This design flaw forced the French fighter to attack flying at the same level as the G3M, losing the speed advantage and increasing its exposure to defensive fire.

The situation worsened with the entry into service of the new G3M2 Model 21, as fast as the Dewoitine and armed with a 20-mm cannon Type 99 on a dorsal turret. The D.510 were used in the defence of Chengdu until 4 December 1940, when they were decimated by the *Zeros* in a single combat. The two surviving aircraft continued to operate as night fighters with the 17th PS.

After the IJA failure in its ambitious offensive of strategic bombing, the IJN decided to accelerate the entry into service of the Mitsubishi A6M2 Type 11 *Zero-Sen*, a predator able to fly to any part of China, overcoming any opposition thanks to its manoeuvrability and powerful armament.

On July 1940, fifteen pre-production *Zeros* were sent to China to perform operational tests with the 12th Kokutai. They entered combat for the first time over Chungking on 13 September against twenty-seven Polikarpov I-152 and I-16, shooting down all them without losses of their own.

The CAF tried to counter the threat using mixed formations of Curtiss H-75 Q (490 kph) and Curtiss-Wright CW-21 (476 kph). The first model was an improved version of the H-75M equipped with retractable landing gear. It was not as fast as the *Zero* but armed with two 23-mm Madsen cannons, which were more powerful than the 20-mm Oerlikon Type 99-1 of the Japanese fighter. The Madsen would be lethal for the G3M2 and could also be used in ground attack duties. The CW-21 'Interceptor' was a high-altitude light fighter with a phenomenal climb rate of 24.4 m/second.

On March 1939, the demonstration prototype was flown in mock combats against Chinese I-152, I-16, and D.510 fighters proving its superiority in climb rate and speed. Surprisingly, the CW-21 also proved to be superior in manoeuvrability through usage of step climbs and wing overs by an experienced driver.

The Central Government acquired the prototype, three pre-production aircraft, and thirty sets of components for local assemblage at CAMCO-Loiwing facilities. It was to carry an armament of two 7.62-mm Madsen machine guns, with 1,000 rounds per gun and two 11.35-mm Madsen heavy machine guns with 400 rounds per gun, mounted in the cowl.

In the production version, the original Pyrolin plastic windscreen was to be replaced by a three-piece armour-glass assembly. Provision for belly tanks was to be added. The modifications would increase the take-off weight to 1,975 kg with a 4 per cent reduction of the maximum speed.

On 26 October 1940, the CAMCO factory was bombarded by fifty-nine G3M2 Model 21 from 15th Kokutai, escorted by forty *Zeros*; many of the partially assembled CW-21 were destroyed. In autumn 1941, the three pre-production machines were transferred to the AVG's 3rd Squadron, operating from the Rangoon-Mingaladon airfield.

The slow-climbing P-40B could not catch the high-flying Mitsubishi Ki.46-II *Dinah* reconnaissance aircraft of the IJA 8th Sentai and three CW-21 were sent to the AVG

'Flying Tigers' base at Kyedaw with the mission to intercept them. Unfortunately, all the 'Interceptors' were destroyed during the ferry flight as a consequence of the poor quality of the 70-74 octane fuel supplied by the CAF.

There is no reliable data on the career of the CW-21 in China. The prototype shot down a Fiat B.R.20 over Chungking on 2 April 1939, but this was not confirmed by Japanese sources. In 1942, the Chinese rebuilt at least two aircraft with parts recovered in CAMCO, but it is ignored if they were even involved in fight.

The 'Interceptor' surpassed the Ki.27-II, Mitsubishi A5M4 Type 96, and A6M2 Model 11 in climb and roll. It was the only Allied fighter in the Far East able to match the performance of the Japanese fighters, but it did not have the opportunity to prove it, neither in China nor in the Dutch East Indies, for reasons beyond their original design.

The contract with the firm Curtiss included the import of an H-75Q and components for the manufacture of forty-nine H-75Qs in CAMCO. Unfortunately for the Chinese, the *Zero* could fly for 3,100 km, remaining more than eight hours in the air. This capacity allowed them to escort the G3M2 to the most remote sanctuary bases of the CAF, preventing its annual reorganisation.

In May 1940, the G3M2 Model 22 started to be used in China. They used oxygen equipment and 87 octane fuel to fly at 7,000 m, attacking the Chinese airfields with the new Type 2, Mk 21 bombs of 52.5 kg. Each of them consisted of a canister containing thirty-six high-explosive submunitions. The G3M2 was used to operate in collaboration with the Mitsubishi C5M2 Type 88 fast reconnaissance aircraft that informed them by radio when the Chinese fighters landed for refuelling.

During August, the IJA continued the attacks against Kunming and Chengtu using the new Mitsubishi Ki.21 bombers. Between 19 August 1940 and 15 September 1941, the *Zeros* downed 103 planes of the CAF and destroyed 162 others in strafing missions. The Soviets tried to fight the *Zeros* using mixed formations of I-153, I-16 Type 10, and Type 17 fighters flying in three levels at 7,500 m, 7,000 m, and 6,500 m.

After numerous tests with an A5M2 captured in China, the Soviets came to the conclusion that the Polikarpov I-153 (444 kph) were more capable of tracking the Japanese monoplane on equal terms. The I-153 was as fast as the I-16 Type 6, its climb rate the highest of all Soviet fighters, and its gull wing configuration allowed it to turn 360 degrees in 13.3 seconds without losing height at every turn. It was very well armed with four rapid-fire ShKas machine guns and equipped with a PAK-1 reflex gunsight, oxygen, armour plates, and RSI-3 R/T device. The I-16 Type 17 was slower, with a rate of climb of just 9.4 m/second (the *Zero* had 15.75 m/second) consequence of the additional weight of the two 20-mm ShVAK cannons and their ammunition.

The Soviets considered this armament was necessary to combat the new G4M1 weapons bombers. However, it turned out that both the *Zero* and the G4M1 were equally armed with cannons and the Japanese fighter not only was 100 kph faster than the I-153, but it could also turn on only 11.2 seconds.

Confronted with the *Zero*, the Polikarpov I-153 could not flee, and if they decided to fight, they were systematically shot down. On 14 March 1941, in their first combat over Shuang-Liu airfield, the I-153 lost thirteen to zero. After this last failure, the USSR decided to abandon the China adventure to concentrate on defending its European borders.

Foreign observers doubted the combat potential of the CAF's remaining force. In April 1941, the situation alarmed the US Administration, who authorised the creation of the AVG, an expeditionary force consisting of three squadrons of Curtiss P-40B (566 kph) Flying Tigers. In August, the US Administration imposed an oil embargo on Japan and the 87-octane gasoline would no longer available.

In September, the IJN started to concentrate its forces in Japan and Taiwan to prepare the attack against the Philippines and Pearl Harbor. Until then, the Japanese losses were of 287 aircraft shot down in combat and 100 in accidents. Those of the CAF were 355 aircraft downed and 1,230 in strafing and accidents. By early November, the CAF had been reduced to twenty-nine fighters, sixty bombers, and forty-two various other aircraft.

After the destruction of the only Curtiss 'Interceptor' available in China, the AVG had no means to intercept the high-flying Mitsubishi Ki.46-II *Dinah* reconnaissance aircraft from the IJA 8th Sentai. To provide high-altitude cover to the slow P-40B, the US Administration authorised the export to China of seventy-two Republic P-43 'Lancer' and 108 P-43 A-1 'Chinese Lancer' fighters through Lend-Lease Act.

The long sea voyage damaged the Fairplane cement used to seal the wing fuel tanks, a circumstance that went unnoticed during its assembly in India and that caused the loss of 139 aircraft during the Karachi-Chengtu ferry flight. Most of the accidents were fires caused by the fuel dripping under the fuselage belly until reaching the hot turbo-exhaust.

On July 1942, ten P-43As were delivered to the AVG. The turbo-supercharger provided the Lancer good power through 9,000 m and American pilots who tested it in flight were satisfied with its good handling and rapid rate of roll, but the AVG staff did not trust them as interceptors and chose to use them as reconnaissance aircraft. However, one of them managed to shoot down a *Dinah* over Bhamo.

The P-43 A-1 were used by the CAF against the Ki.46 with little success since both models had the same speed at 6,000 m. On 24 October 1942, the 24th Sqn 'Chinese Lancers' downed a *Dinah,* from 18th Dokuritsu Chutai, over Si Bao and one Kawasaki Ki.48 from 16th Sentai over Han-Sou on 12 January 1943.

The turbo-supercharger was a complex piece of equipment and the CAF simply did not have the resources to train people to properly maintain the units. The P-43 A-1 had a limited use in combat and the *Dinah* completely lost its immunity only when the Lockheed P-38 began operating in the Far East.

In 1939, the firm Vultee Aircraft developed the Model 48C, a monoplane light fighter based on the airframe of the Valiant trainer. On 6 February 1940, the Swedish Government ordered 144 fighters Vultee Model 48C, but fearing that the aircraft might fall into Soviet hands, the US State Department placed an embargo on the export of military aircraft to Sweden in 18 October. In February 1942, the Roosevelt Administration allowed the export to China via Karachi of 119 fighters Model 48C, under the designation P-66 'Vanguard'.

They fought against the Ki.48 Type 99 bombers of the 90th Sentai and their escort fighters Nakajima Ki.43-I east of Enshih airfield on 6 June. In August, twenty-one Type 97 bombers from 58th Sentai performing a raid over Chungking, escorted by thirty-one Ki.43-Is from 25th and 33rd Sentais, were intercepted by ten P-40Bs, eight P-43 A-1s, and eleven P-66s. Two 'Vanguards' were shot down by the Nakajima fighters.

In October 1942, the CAF tried to use them against the *Dinah*, again without any success. In China, the 'Vanguard' did exhibit some handling problems during high speed dives, poor lateral stability, and undesirable stalling characteristics during landing. Corrosion problems resulting from an inadequate maintenance of the weak landing gear caused frequent ground loops and broken tailwheels. In December 1943, the fifty-three serviceable Vanguards were removed from to combat status and used only for training duties.

At the time of their acquisition the Polikarpov I-16 Type 5, the Dewoitine D.510C, the Curtiss H-75M, the Curtiss CW-21, the Republic P-43, and the Vultee P-66 were considered 'Panic Fighters' although none of them managed to overcome its Japanese equivalents in this long war. However, the real Chinese 'Panic Fighters' were some indigenous aircraft designed and built in desperate circumstances.

At the beginning of 1937, the designer Chee Wing Jeang built the Kwangsi Type 3, a biplane fighter developed at the Liuchow Mechanical Aircraft Factory for the Kwangsi Independent Air Force. The only prototype was built with wood/plywood wings and steel-tube/fabric fuselage. It flew for the first time on July, powered by a 260-hp Armstrong Siddeley Cheetah IIA air-cooled radial engine. Its performances proved insufficient to justify further development.

In the summer of 1937, Japanese bombers bombarded the Shaoguan Aircraft Factory, where the Hawk III fighters were assembled, and the factory was moved to Hangzhou. However, it was also bombed there before entering service. Production continued in the First Aircraft Factory of Kun-Ming in Yunnan Province in 1938. After a new attack, they moved to Loiwing by mid-1939, but the new location was destroyed in the bombing of 26 October 1940 and occupied by Japanese troops on May 1942.

In 1943, the Aircraft Factory was dispersed in several locations, around Kun-Ming, where seven Hawk 75 A-5 and two CW-21 were built using parts recovered from the destroyed factories. The Aviation Research Institute was installed in one Yangling cave, where General Major Chu Chia-Jen designed the new Chinese XP-0 fighter in 1941.

A unique prototype was manufactured in 1943 by AFAMF-Yangling, using the tail surfaces of a Hawk 75, the centre section of the wing and the landing gear of a North American NA-6, the tailwheel from P-43 and the engine and cockpit of a P-66. The wings were built in wood/plywood. It made its first flight in Yangling, without weapons, and being destroyed during the landing.

The next attempt, called XP-1, was designed in 1942 by Constantin Zakharchenko and built in Guiyang in 1944. It also destroyed during its first flight, with fixed undercarriage, on January 1945. The XP-1 was powered by one 1,200-hp Wright Cyclone R-1820-71 from one C-49D. It had wood/plywood inverted-swept wings, with automatic flaps, and the fuselage was built in steel tube/fabric.

In the meantime, the availability of advanced US fighters had removed the need for Chinese indigenous fighters and further development was discontinued.

CW-21 Technical Data

Wingspan: 10.66 m.
Length: 8.03 m.
Height: 2.60 m.
Wing area: 16.19 sq. m.
Max. weight: 1,896 kg.
Maximum speed: 476 kph.
Range: 853 km.
Power plant: one 1,000-hp Wright Cyclone R-1820-G5 air-cooled radial engine.

P-43 A-1 Technical Data

Wingspan: 10.97 m.
Length: 8.68 m.
Height: 4.26 m.
Wing area: 20.72 sq. m.
Max. weight: 3,846 kg.
Max. speed: 573 kph.
Range: 2,333 km.
Power plant: one 1,200-hp Pratt & Whitney R-1830-57 air-cooled radial engine.
Armament: two 12.7-mm heavy machine guns mounted in the cowl and two 12.7-mm guns in the wings.

P-66 Technical Data

Wingspan: 10.97 m.
Length: 8.66 m.
Height: 2.87 m.
Wing area: 18.30 sq. m.
Max. Weight: 3,221 kg.
Max. speed: 574 kph.
Range: 1,386 km.
Power plant: one 1,200-hp Pratt & Whitney R-1830-33 air-cooled radial engine.
Armament: two 12.7-mm heavy machine guns mounted in the cowl and four 7.62-mm guns in the wings.

Kwangsi Type 3 Technical Data

Wingspan: 8.0 m.
Length: 6.25 m.

Height: 2.5 m.
Wing area: 22 sq. m.
Max. weight: 1,043 kg.
Max. speed: 283 kph.
Rate of climb: 5.28 m/second.
Armament: one 7.7mm machine gun synchronised with the propeller.

XP-0 Technical Data

Wingspan: 11.4 m.
Length: 8.8 m.
Height: 3.70 m.
Wing area: 22 sq. m.
Max. weight: 2,990 kg.
Estimated max speed: 504 kph.
Range 1,400 km.
Armament: four 20-mm Hispano cannons mounted in the wings.

XP-1 Technical Data

Wingspan: 12.10 m.
Length: 8.72 m.
Max. weight: 2,930 kg.
Estimated max. speed: 580 kph.
Armament: two 12.7-mm machine guns in the wings.

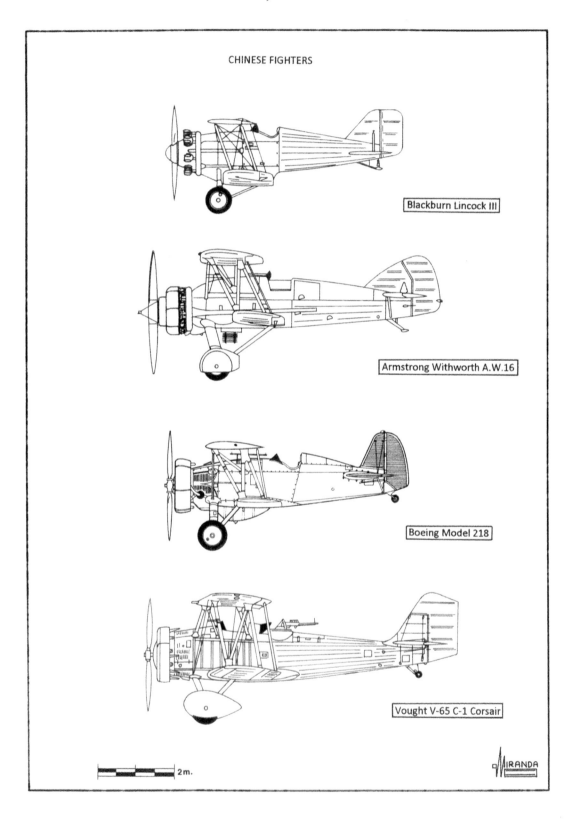

CHINESE FIGHTERS

Blackburn Lincock III

Armstrong Withworth A.W.16

Boeing Model 218

Vought V-65 C-1 Corsair

2 m.

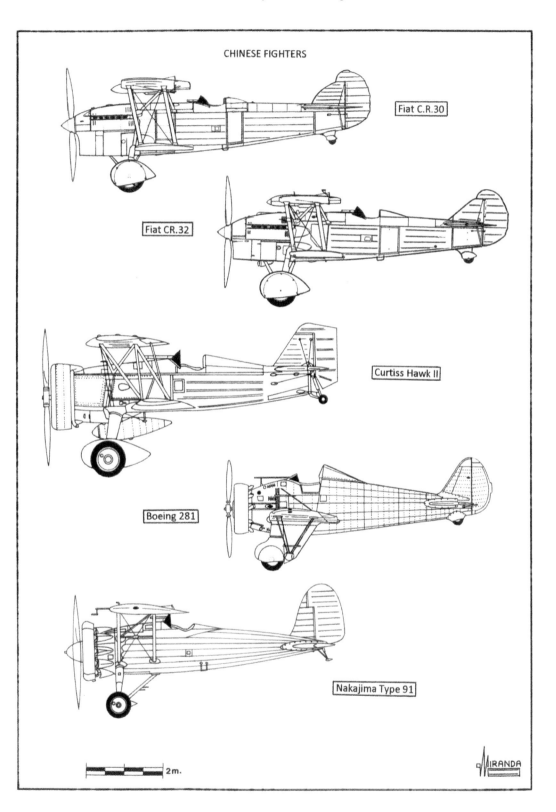

CHINESE FIGHTERS

Fiat C.R.30

Fiat CR.32

Curtiss Hawk II

Boeing 281

Nakajima Type 91

2m.

MIRANDA

CHINESE FIGHTERS

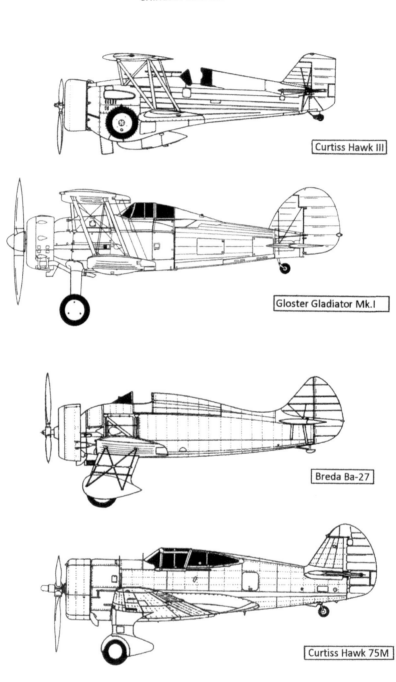

Curtiss Hawk III

Gloster Gladiator Mk.I

Breda Ba-27

Curtiss Hawk 75M

2 m.

CHINESE FIGHTERS

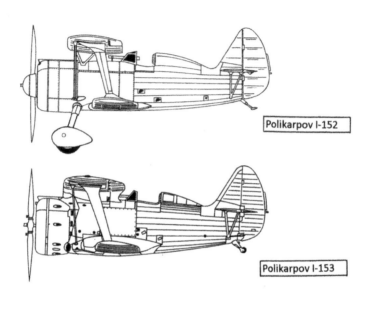

Polikarpov I-152

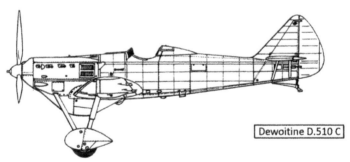

Polikarpov I-153

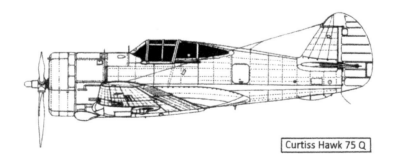

Dewoitine D.510 C

Curtiss Hawk 75 Q

2m.

Enemy at the Gates

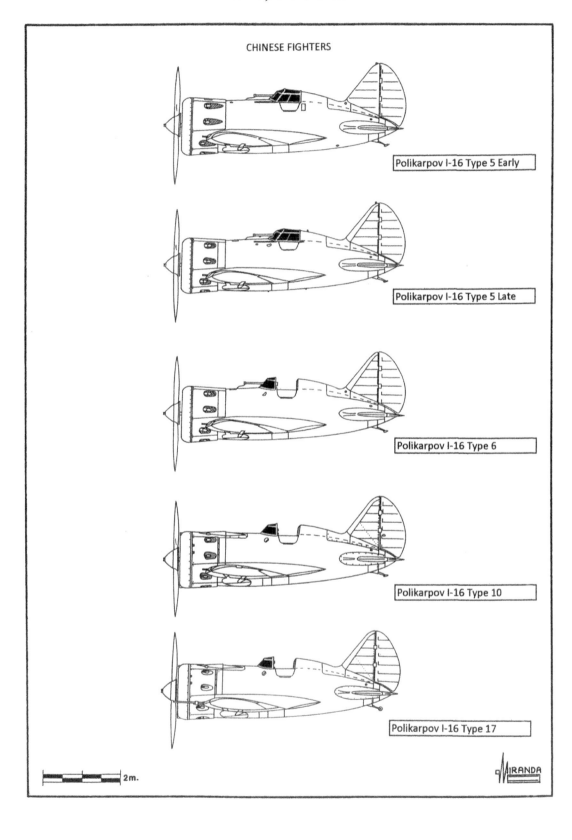

CHINESE FIGHTERS

Polikarpov I-16 Type 5 Early

Polikarpov I-16 Type 5 Late

Polikarpov I-16 Type 6

Polikarpov I-16 Type 10

Polikarpov I-16 Type 17

2m.

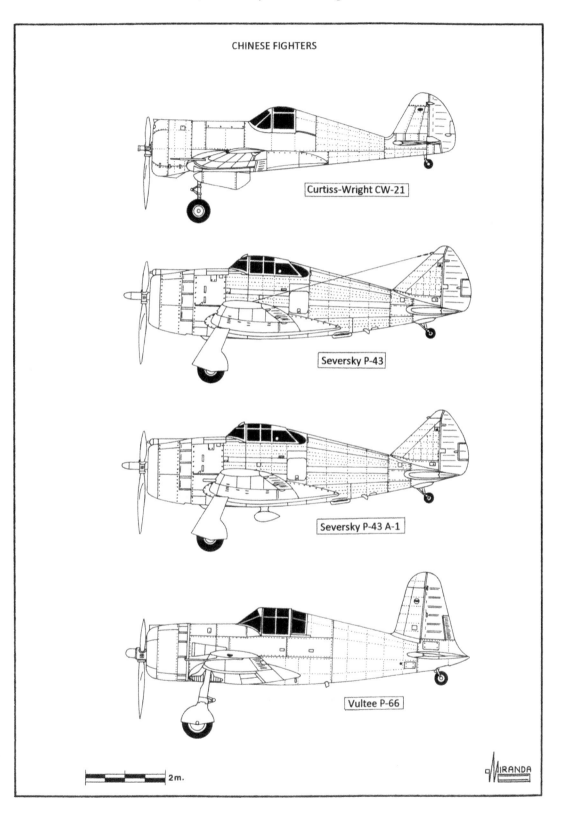

CHINESE FIGHTERS

Curtiss-Wright CW-21

Seversky P-43

Seversky P-43 A-1

Vultee P-66

2 m.

MIRANDA

226

Enemy at the Gates

CHINESE FIGHTERS

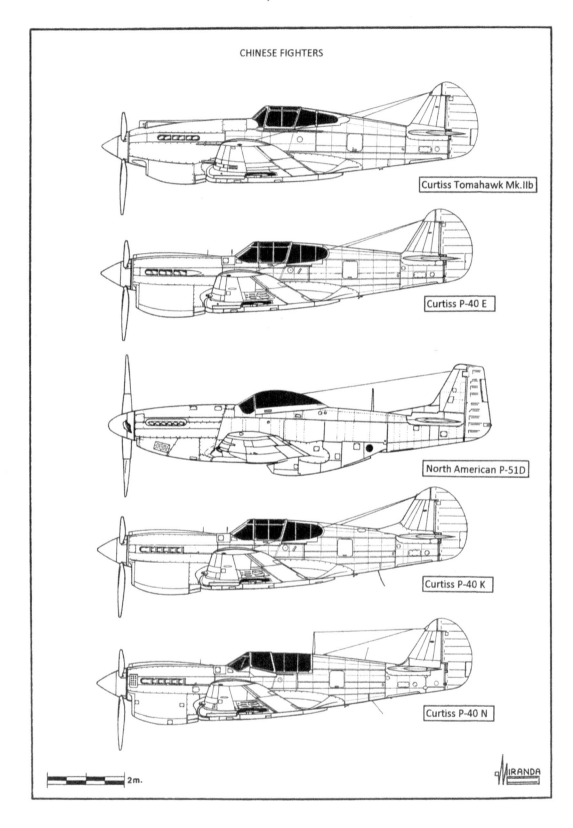

Curtiss Tomahawk Mk.IIb

Curtiss P-40 E

North American P-51D

Curtiss P-40 K

Curtiss P-40 N

2 m.

MIRANDA

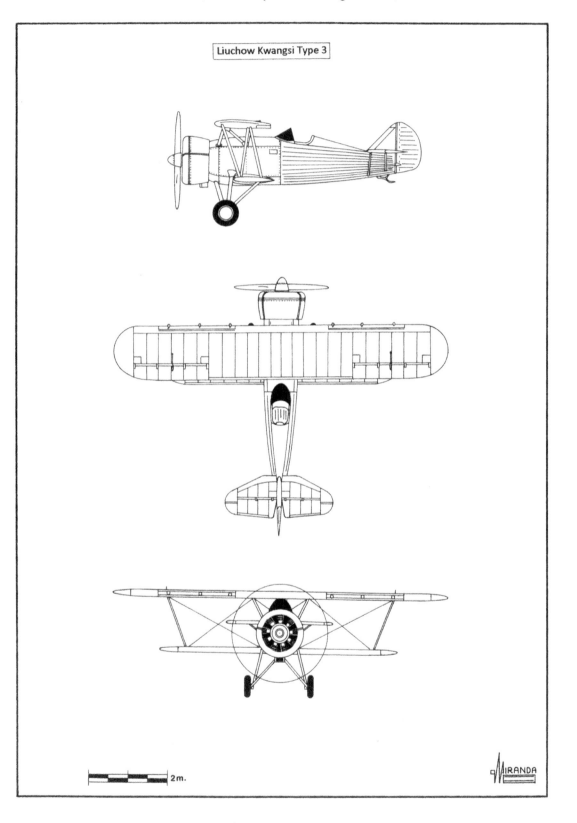

Liuchow Kwangsi Type 3

2m.

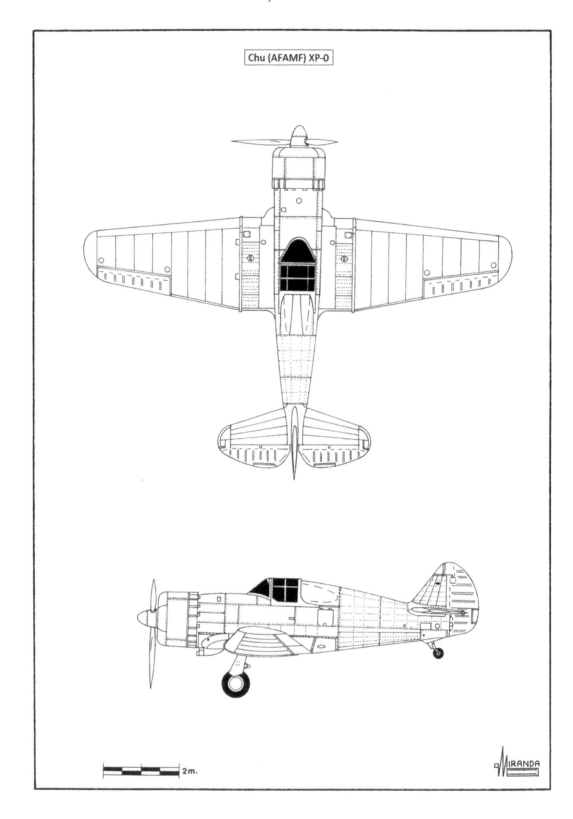

Chu (AFAMF) XP-0

2m.

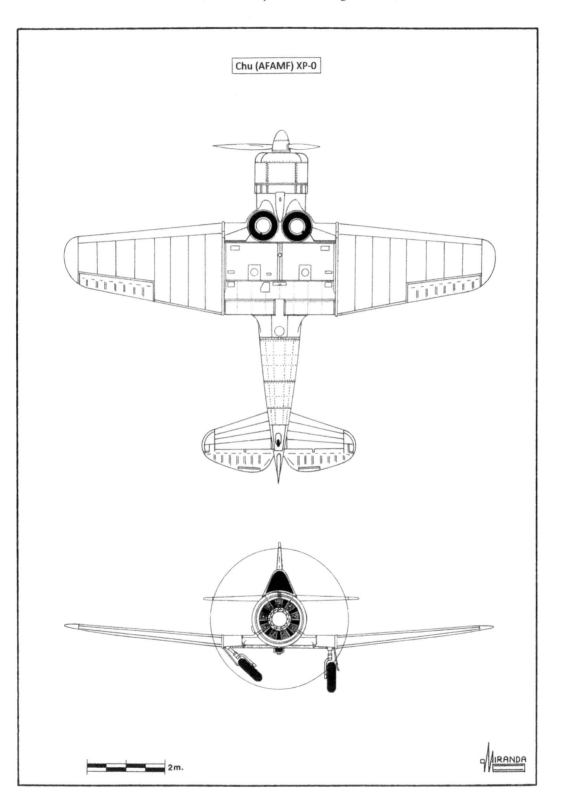

Chu (AFAMF) XP-0

2m.

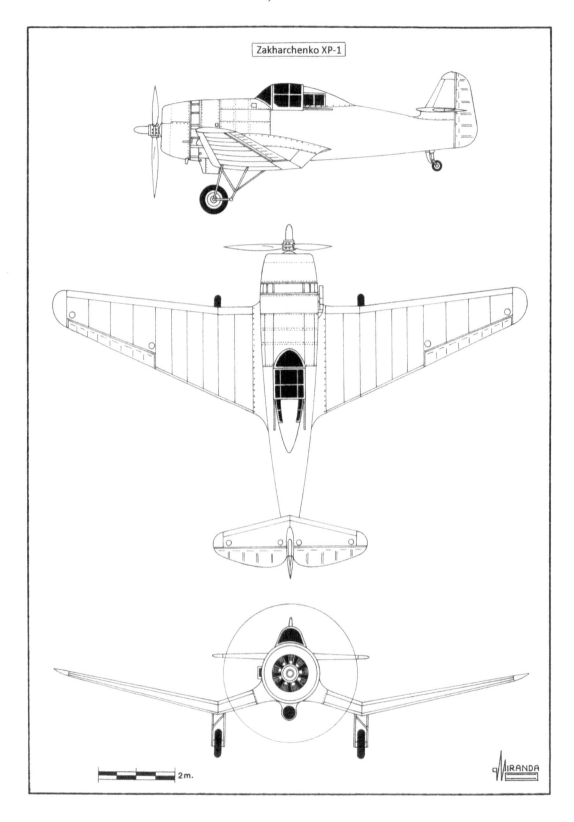

Zakharchenko XP-1

2m.

23

Khalkhin Gol/Nomonhan
(11 May–17 September 1939)

The Soviets were engaged in a war with Japan in the border of Outer Mongolia and Manchuria. The Soviet Air Force (VVS) used four fighter regiments equipped with Polikarpov I-152, I-153, and I-16 (Types 6, 10, 17, and 18) and two bomber regiments with Tupolev SB-2M-100 and Polikarpov R-5.

The Imperial Japanese Army (IJA) sent six Sentais to the combat zone, equipped with Kawasaki Ki.10 and Nakajima Ki.27 fighters and six more with Nakajima Ki.4, Mitsubishi Ki.15, Mitsubishi Ki.21, Mitsubishi Ki.30, Tachikawa Ki.36, and Fiat BR.20 bombers.

It was a confrontation for prestige reasons and without gain of territories, in which the pilots of the IJA behaved very aggressive, despite having air and technological superiority. It was their first chance to emulate the successes obtained by the Imperial Japanese Navy (IJN) in China.

According to reports from Soviet veteran pilots of the Sino-Japanese War, the pilots of the Ki.27 made numerous attempts to ramming from the first fighting. On 22 June, a Ki.27 piloted by the 2Lt Saito Shogo rammed the tail of the I-16 of Lt Vorozheikin, over Kalka River. On 5 August, a Ki.27 from the 11th Sentai, piloted by the 2Lt Taro Kobayashi, rammed an I-153.

The Soviets soon copied the tactic that they named *Taran*. On 20 July, 2Lt Viktor Skobarikhin of the 22nd IAP rammed a Ki.27 of the 11th Sentai with his I-16. On 3 August, Captain P. Kustov of the 56th IAP rammed a Japanese bomber. Two days later, a Ki.27 from the 11th Sentai, piloted by Tokuyaso Ishizuka, was rammed by the I-16 of Lt Aleksandr Moskin. On 20 August, 2Lt Viktor Rakhov of the 22nd IAP rammed a Ki.27 of the 11th Sentai with his I-16.

The clumsy and heavy I-152 were especially vulnerable in a dogfight. On 28 May, all aircraft of the 22/4 IAP who took part in a battle against the Ki.27 were downed. They were hastily replaced by the new I-153 that just managed to survive the Japanese fury by using evasive manoeuvres. On the other hand, the Ki.27 could evade the combat thanks to their greater speed, which even exceeded that of the I-16, despite the drag generated by the fixed undercarriage of the Japanese fighter. The only efficient tactic against the Ki.27 consisted in taking advantage of the superior climb rate and dive speed of the I-16 in 'hit and run' attacks, avoiding a dogfight with the agile Nakajima.

The Japanese fighters did not use the radio, communicating through movements of the wings. That made them especially vulnerable to an attack from above, while they were carrying out strafing missions. The Ki.27 used outdated tubular gunsights and during the firing of machine guns, the pilot could not watch around.

To compensate for the superior manoeuvrability of the Japanese fighters, the Soviets tried to increase the firepower with the introduction of the I-16 Type 17, armed with two 20-mm ShVAK cannons and 82-mm rockets. They could be carried under the wings of the fighters and used indiscriminately in air-to-air or ground attack configurations. The first use of unguided rockets in combat, launched from an aircraft, occurred on 20 August, when five I-16 fighters launched RS-82 rockets against a flight of Ki.27, shooting down two of them.

The Polikarpov Type 17 was particularly vulnerable in dogfights due to the extra weight of its weapons. For the Japanese, the weight was all-important, so they used to dismantle the radio, the masts of the antennas, and the enclosed cockpits. Some pilots even avoided using parachutes to gain additional manoeuvrability.

With the start of the Second World War in the West, the Soviets decided to find an easier enemy in the defeated Poland and requested an armistice. On 16 September, the hostilities ceased. The VVS lost 249 aircraft, of which 196 were fighters, and the IJN lost 220 aircraft, including ninety-seven fighters.

AIR ACTIONS OVER KHALKIN GOL FRONTIER

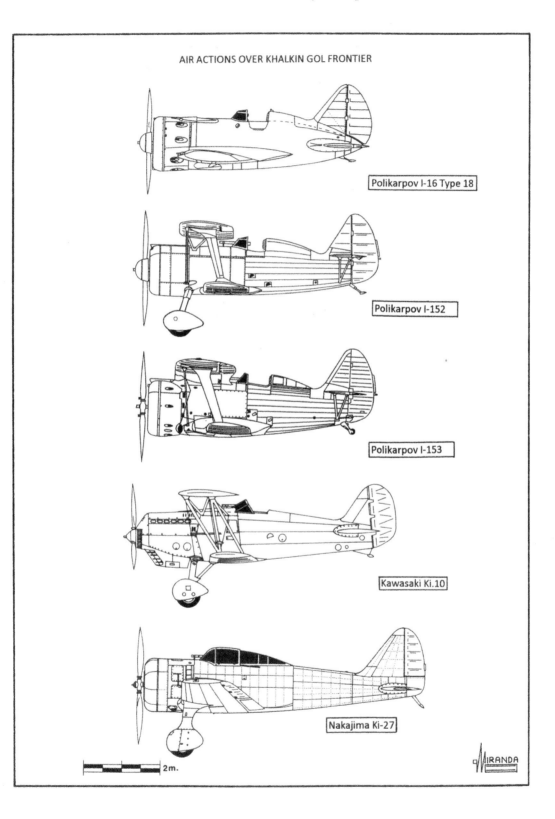

Polikarpov I-16 Type 18

Polikarpov I-152

Polikarpov I-153

Kawasaki Ki.10

Nakajima Ki-27

2m.

MIRANDA

24

Thailand
(8–21 December 1940)

Coinciding with the attack on Pearl Harbor, 100,000 troops of the Imperial Japanese Army crossed the border into Thailand from newly acquired bases in southern Indo-China.

The 15th Army needed to pass over the Bangkok plain to attack Burma and the 25th Army had to attack Malaya via the Kra peninsula. The invasion was supported by five IJA Sentais with eighty-four Ki.27bs, three Sentais with fifty-nine Ki.43-Ias, and one Chutai with nine Ki.44 fighters.

The Thai defence was formed by five fighter squadrons with twelve Curtiss Hawk IIs (301 kph), forty-two Curtiss Hawk IIIs (387 kph), and nine Curtiss Hawk 75Ns (450 kph) that were neutralised almost without any fight. In the first Japanese attack, three of the Hawk 75Ns were destroyed by strafing. The fighting ceased at noon on 8 December 1940, when orders for an armistice to be arranged were received. A treaty of friendship with Japan was signed on 21 December 1940.

New fighter monoplanes models entering service during the second half of the 1930s required the retraining of many pilots who were not familiar with the use of the retractable undercarriage. This huge demand was answered by the North American firm in 1937 with the creation of the NA-26 model, a version of the NA-16 1935 trainer equipped with retractable landing gear.

The plane was a worldwide success and thousands of units were manufactured. The availability of many airframes and spares encouraged the manufacturer to design the NA-50, a low-cost light fighter based on the NA-26. The NA-50 could be sold for export to the air forces of smaller nations in need of faster fighters to combat against the new bombers Bristol Blenheim, Heinkel He 111, and Mitsubishi Ki.21 that were entering service.

These countries could not acquire such sophisticated bombers, but they needed fast and cheap attack aircraft. To meet both requirements, North American built seven units of the NA-50A, a small single seat fighter for the Peruvian Air Force, in 1938. Then, in 1939, they built six units of the NA-68, a more sophisticated version with 23-mm cannons, for the Royal Thai Air Force.

In July 1940, the NA-68 fighters were *en route* to Thailand when their export clearance was cancelled and seized by the US authorities in Hawaii. The cancellation was caused by the news that Thailand had acquired twenty-four Mitsubishi Ki.30 attack bombers and nine Mistsubishi Ki.21 medium bombers to Japan to attack the French forces in Indo-China. On 1941, the NA-68 was redesignated P-64 and delivered to the USAAC, for use as an advanced trainer at Santa Ana and Luke Field airbases.

Technical Data

Wingspan: 11.38 m.
Length: 8.51 m.
Height: 3.63 m.
Wing area: 21.13 sq. m.
Maximum weight: 2,713 kg.
Maximum speed: 452 kph.
Range: 1,140 km.
Power plant: one 875-hp Wright Cyclone R-1820-77 air-cooled radial engine
Armament: two 8-mm Colt machine guns in the cowl and two 23-mm Madsen cannons in underwing nacelles.

North American NA-69

The attack version of the NA-26 advanced trainer was designed in 1937 for export purposes. In November 1939, ten units were ordered by Thailand; in October 1940, they were seized by American authorities and impressed into USAAC service under the designation A-27. The aircraft were sent to the Philippines, where they were attached to the 24th Pursuit Group, operating together with the P-35A of the 17 Sqn as second line emergency fighters between December 1941 and March 1942.

Technical Data

Wingspan: 12.8 m.
Length: 8.84 m.
Height: 3.71 m.
Wing area: 23 sq. m.
Maximum weight: 3,035 kg.
Maximum speed: 402 kph
Range: 1,300 km.
Power plant: one 775-hp Wright R-1820-F52 air-cooled radial engine.
Armament: two 0.30 in machine guns in the cowl and one flexible 0.30-inch machine gun in the rear cockpit.

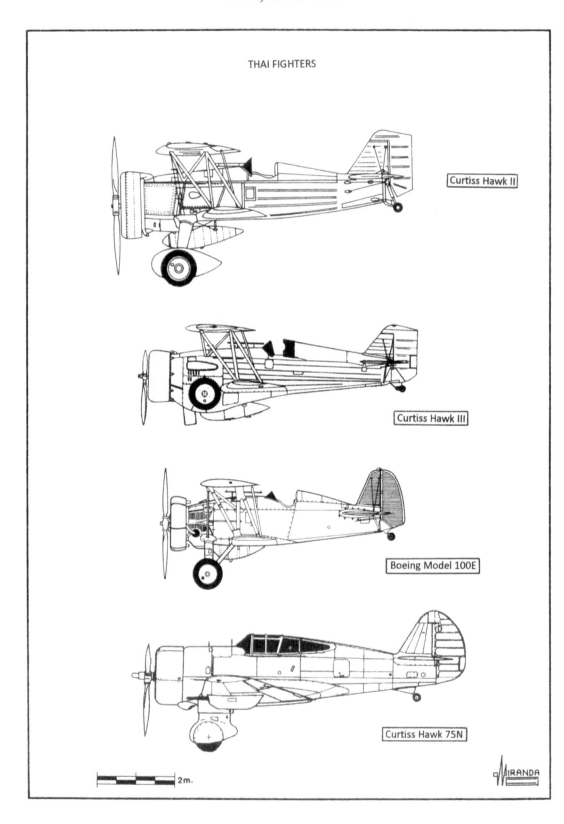

THAI FIGHTERS

Curtiss Hawk II

Curtiss Hawk III

Boeing Model 100E

Curtiss Hawk 75N

2m.

MIRANDA

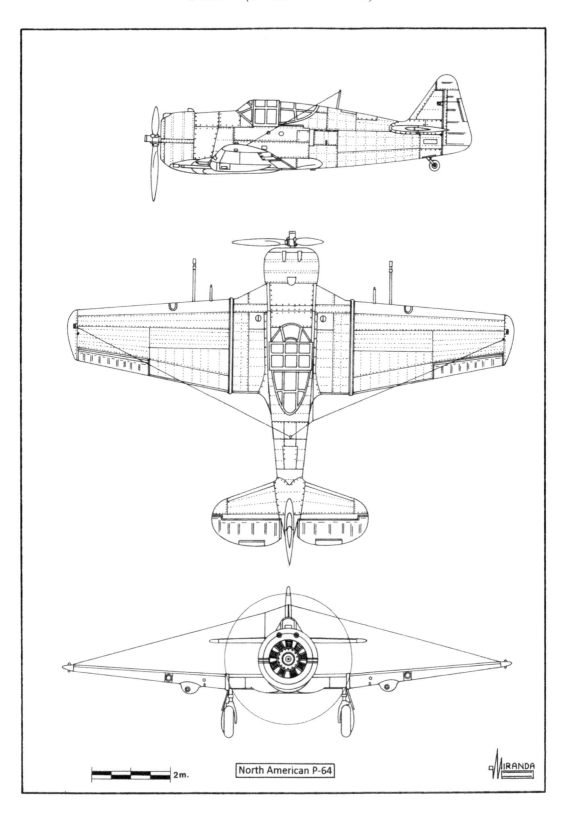

2m.

North American P-64

MIRANDA

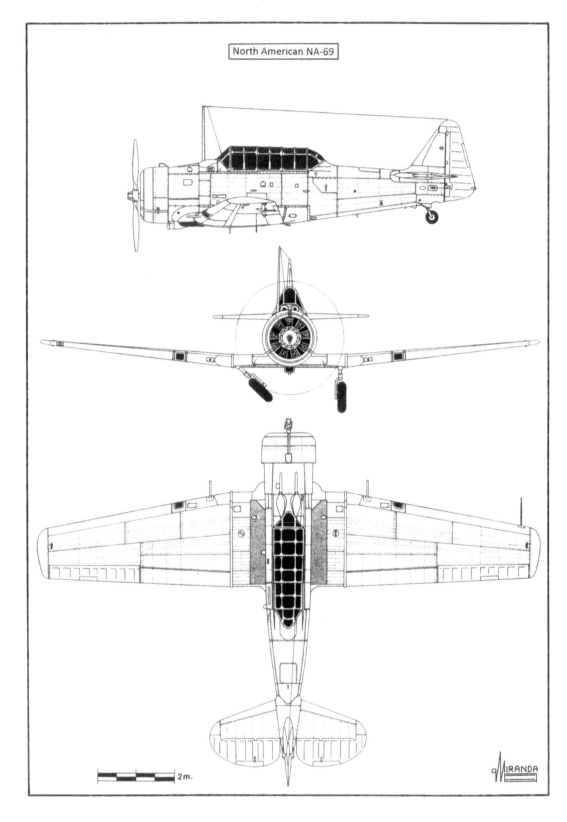

North American NA-69

2 m.

MIRANDA

25

Pearl Harbor
(7 December 1941–4 March 1942)

On 7 December 1941, the American defences in Hawaii consisted of four Curtiss P-40C, eighty-five Curtiss P-40B, thirty-seven Curtiss P-36A, six Boeing P-26A, and eight Boeing P-26C fighters based at Wheeler airfield; eight Curtiss P-40Cs and two Curtiss P-36As based at Haleiwa airfield; two Curtiss P-40Bs based at Bellows airfield; eleven Grumman F4F-3s based at Ewa Air Station; and eight Brewster F2A-3s, five Grumman F4F-3s, and five Grumman F4F-3A based at Ford Island Air Station, together with five radar stations with SCR-270B sets.

After the Japanese attack, out of the 402 military aircraft in Hawaii, 188 were destroyed and 159 damaged. On 8 December, there were only eighteen P-40B, two P-40C, sixteen P-36A, six P-26A, six P-26C, and three F4F-3 fighters in flying condition.

The Japanese Fleet still could operate with 311 aircraft and had been recovered seventy-four planes damaged but repairable. Fearing a third attack, the few fighters available in Hawaii were constantly in flight. However, they did not have IFF devices installed and the radar operators could not distinguish them from enemy aircraft. The visual detection depended on an observer corps, mainly made up of civilian volunteers. The identification errors and continuous alarms raised the attrition rate of the aircraft and exhausted pilots. In this situation, the Americans decided to use the obsolete P-26, armed with one 0.50-inch and one 0.30-inch machine gun, as emergency night fighters.

Following the withdrawal of the Japanese Fleet, the P-26C, fitted with flaps and painted black, continued service to protect Pearl from long-range night intruders based in Marshall Islands. On 4 March 1942, three Kawanishi H8K1 flying boats from the Yokohama Kokutai, based in Wotje Island, attempted to bomb Pearl Harbor, refuelling from a submarine at French Frigate Shoals. The attack was finally aborted due the poor visibility over Oahu and the P-26 lost the opportunity to fight.

Technical Data

Wingspan: 8.5 m.
Length: 7.15 m.
Height: 3.04 m.
Wing area: 13.4 sq. m.
Max. weight: 1,585 kg.
Max. speed: 379 kph.
Range: 1,000 km.
Power plant: one 600-hp Pratt & Whitney R-1340-33 air-cooled radial engine.
Armament: one 0.30-inch and one 0.50-inch machine gun in the cowl.

PEARL HARBOR DEFENDERS

Boeing P-26C

Curtiss P-36 A

Curtiss P-40 B

Grumman F4F-3

2 m.

MIRANDA

26

The Philippines
(8 December 1941–9 April 1942)

Ten hours after the attack on Pearl Harbor, 107 Japanese naval bombers, escorted by eighty-four *Zeros* from Taiwan, carried out a devastating attack on Clark and Iba airfields, on the Island of Luzon. The bombing and subsequent strafing caused the destruction of nearly half of US Far East Air Force, including fifteen Curtiss P-40E fighters and twelve Boeing B-17E heavy bombers.

The attackers were twenty-seven Mitsubishi G3M *Nell* and twenty-six Mitsubishi G4M *Betty* medium bombers, from Takao and Kanoya Kokutais, together with forty-two Mitsubishi A6M2 *Zero-Sens* from Tainan Kokutai. The Japanese planes were tracked by the radar station at Iba, and eighteen fighters took off to intercept them, believing that they were heading to Manila. During the attack on Clark Field, the control centre was destroyed, causing the complete breakdown of communications with other bases.

When 3rd Squadron's P-40E returned to Iba for refuelling, they found that the base was being attacked by fifty-four Bettys from Takao Kokutai and forty-two Mitsubishi A6M2 *Zero-Sens* that shot down five American fighters. At the same time, fifteen Nakajima B5N2 Kate bombers, escorted by three Mitsubishi A5M4 *Claude* fighters from IJN *Ryujo* carrier, attacked the naval bases at Davao and Mindanao, destroying two PBY seaplanes. The defence of the Philippines consisted of eighteen P-40Es from 3rd Sqn, based at Iba Field; eighteen P-40Es from 20th Sqn, based at Clark Field; eighteen P-40Es, six P-35As, and ten NA-69s from 17th Sqn, based at Nichols Field; eighteen P-40Bs from 21st Sqn, based at Nichols Field; eighteen P-35As from 39th Sqn, based at Del Carmen Field; and fourteen P-26As and two P-12Es, from 6th Sqn of Philippine Army Air Corps, based at Batangas Field.

The fighters that survived the first attack were reserved for reconnaissance tasks, but on 13 and 16 December, they were forced to combat, suffering new losses. Eight days later, only sixteen P-40 were serviceable on Bataan airfields. On 17 January 1942, there were only seven; on 14 February, only four; and only two by March. On 20 and 25 December 1941, the IJN *Ryujo* carrier supported the landings at Davao City and Jolo with sixteen *Kates* and twenty-two *Claudes*.

The involvement of the IJA during the first days of the invasion was limited by the short range of the ninety Nakajima Ki.27b fighters of the 4th, 24th, and 50th Sentais, based in Taiwan, as they just provided air cover for amphibious assault forces operating to the North of 16 degrees latitude.

On 12 December, the 24th and 50th Sentais, with eighteen aircraft each, were based at Vigan and Aparri airfields, located on the north of Luzon Island. The 27th Sentai was moved to Del Carmen airfield to support the offensive of Bataan escorting the Mitsubishi Ki.51 *Sonia* dive bombers.

Seversky P-35A

On 24 October 1940, the US War Department declared an embargo of the second batch of sixty Seversky EP-1-106 fighters acquired by Sweden.

On February 1941, forty-five of them were transferred to the US Far East Air Force, under the name P-35A. The planes arrived to the Philippines with Swedish instruments and cockpit placards. Their maintenance was complicated by the absence of replacement engines and by flying user guides written in Swedish. Ten aircraft were destroyed in accidents before the Pacific War started.

On 7 December 1941, the Far East Air Force had twenty-four P-35A in flying condition: six in the 17th Pursuit Squadron and eighteen in the 34th PS. During combat on 10 December, twelve aircraft were destroyed and six damaged by the *Zeros*. Two days later, only eight were left in flying condition, five in January 1942, and one in May. The P-35A was inferior to the *Zeros* during dogfights, and it was therefore mainly used on strafing missions.

Technical Data

Wingspan: 10.97 m.
Length: 8.17 m.
Height: 2.97 m.
Wing area: 19.8 sq. m.
Max. weight: 2,775 kg.
Max. speed: 452 kph.
Range: 1,529 km.
Power plant: one 1,050-hp Pratt & Whitney R-1830-45 air-cooled radial engine.
Armament: two 0.30-inch machine guns in the cowl and two 0.50-in heavy machine guns in the wings.

North American NA-69

This attack version of the AT-6 advanced trainer was designed in 1937 for export purposes. On November 1939, ten units were ordered by Thailand; in October 1940, they were seized by American authorities and impressed into USAAC service under the designation A-27. These ten aircraft were sent to the Philippines and attached to the 24th Pursuit Group, operating together with the P-35A of the 17th Sqn as second line 'emergency fighters' between December 1941 and March 1942.

Technical Data

Wingspan: 12.8 m.
Length: 8.84 m.
Height: 3.71 m.
Wing area: 23 sq. m.
Max. weight: 3,035 kg.
Max. speed: 402 kph.
Range: 1,300 km.
Power plant: one 775-hp Wright R-1820-F52 air-cooled radial engine.
Armament: two 0.30-inch machine guns in the cowl and one flexible 0.30-inch machine gun in the rear cockpit.

Boeing P-26A 'Panic Fighter'

In November 1940, the USAAC had twenty-eight of these obsolete aircraft in Philippines, attached to the 3rd and 17th Pursuit Squadrons based at Nichols and Clark airfields.

In April 1941, all Boeing fighters were transferred to the Philippine Army Air Corps. Attached to the 6th Pursuit Squadron based on Batangas Field, they entered combat against Japanese planes on 10, 12, 14, and 23 December. Seven P-26 were shot down in the unequal struggle against the *Zeros*, although they were successful against the Mitsubishi G3M *Nell* on 12 December. The Filipino pilots continued the fight operating from Zablan airfield until the fall of Bataan.

Technical Data

Wingspan: 8.5 m.
Length: 7.18 m.
Height: 3.04 m.
Wing area: 13.45 sq. m.
Max. weight: 1,524 kg.
Max. speed: 377 kph.
Range: 1,020 km.
Power plant: one 600-hp Pratt & Whitney R-1340-27 air-cooled radial engine.
Armament: two 0.30-inch machine guns in the cowl.

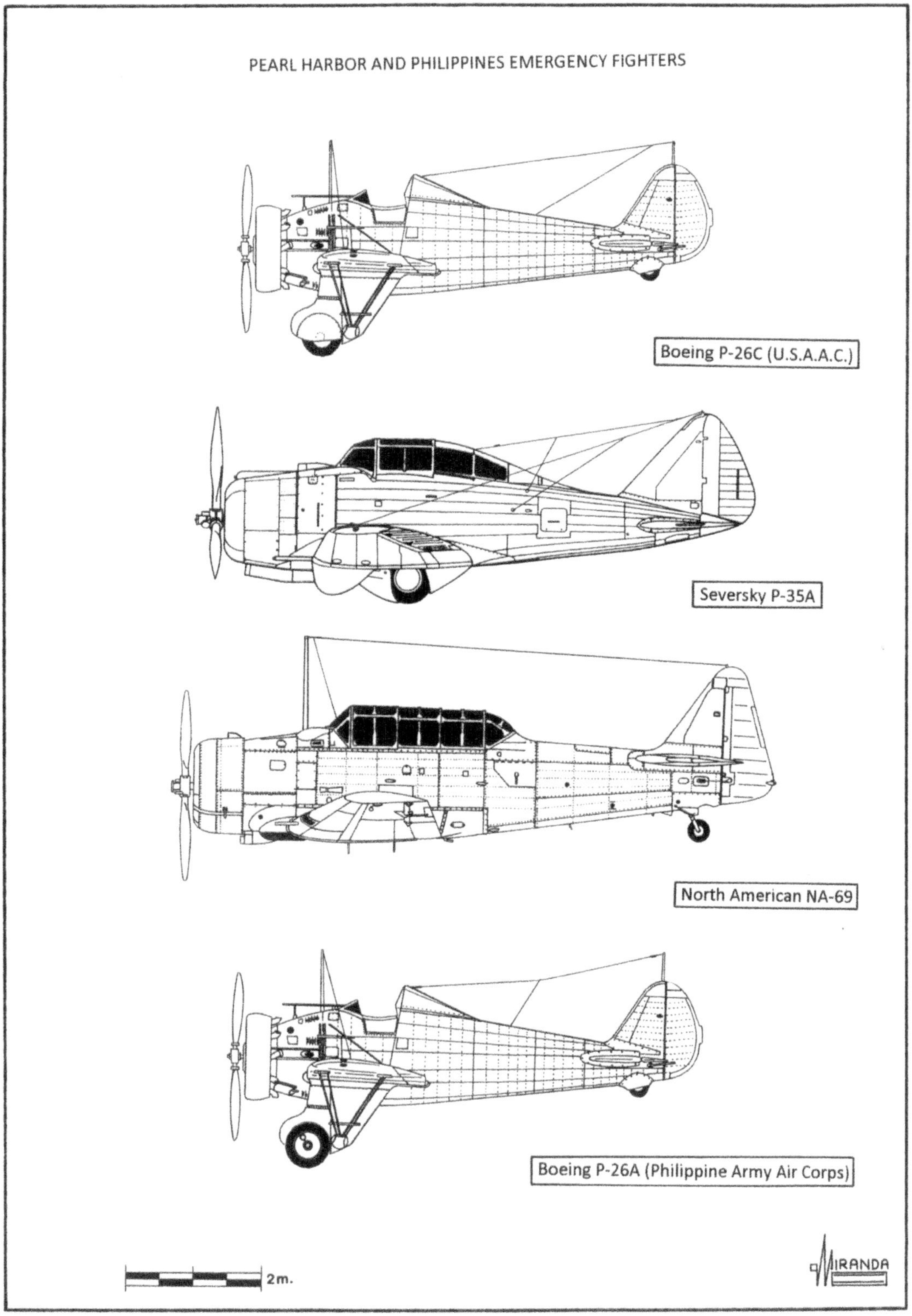

PEARL HARBOR AND PHILIPPINES EMERGENCY FIGHTERS

Boeing P-26C (U.S.A.A.C.)

Seversky P-35A

North American NA-69

Boeing P-26A (Philippine Army Air Corps)

2 m.

MIRANDA

27

Malaya/Singapore (8 December 1941–15 February 1942)

At the time of the Japanese attack, the British naval base of Singapore and the Malayan Peninsula were defended by 114 fighters Brewster B-339 E Buffalo.

Forty-eight of them were in Singapore, scattered among the Squadrons 453rd RAAF, 243rd RAF, 488th RNZAF, and No. 4 PRU flight RAF. The 21st RAAF (with twelve aircraft) and the 243rd (Det) RAF (with just two) were based in Northern Malaya. The remaining fifty-two Buffaloes were a reserve element.

The British version of the Buffalo was powered by a 1,100-hp Wright 1820-G105A engine, driving a Hamilton Standard Hydromatic propeller. Although in theory they could fly at 504 kph, the weight of the equipment added by the British in the original model just allowed them to reach 473 kph, with a rate of climb of 11.4 m/second and a service ceiling of 8,300 meters.

The fuel tanks were sealed with Goodyear Linatex, the telescopic gunsight was replaced by one Mk III reflector gunsight and the pilot was protected by armoured windshield and dorsal plates. The armament consisted of two 0.5-inch Colt M-40 heavy machine guns and two 0.303-inch Browning light machine guns with 500 rounds each.

The strength of Japanese fighters in the area was limited to eighty-seven Nakajima Ki.27bs (470 kph), fifty-nine Nakajima Ki.43-Ias (550 kph), and nine Nakajima Ki.44-Ias (580 kph) belonging to the 1st, 11th, 59th, and 64th Sentais and the 47th Dokuritsu Hiko Chutai of the Imperial Japanese Army (IJA); ninety-two Mitsubishi A6M2 *Zero-Sens* of the 23rd Koku Sentai of the Imperial Japanese Navy (IJN); and some Mitsubishi A5M4 from the IJN *Ryujo* aircraft carrier.

The Buffaloes entered into combat for the first time against the Ki.27b on 9 December 1941, while the A6M2 did it on 17 December, together with the Ki.43 on 22 December and the Ki.44 on 25 December, being surpassed in all cases by the manoeuvrability of the aircraft and the experience of the Japanese pilots.

After the initial shock, the British tried to improve the performances of the B-339 E, eliminating the wireless mast and rear vision mirrors to reduce air resistance; the gun camera, armour, and other unnecessary equipment were also removed, the heavy machine guns were replaced by Brownings, and the fuel and ammunition loads were also reduced to save 454 kg.

Yet the Buffaloes subjected to the stress of combat showed new shortcomings: the engines installed by the manufacturer had previously belonged to the Douglas DC-3 airliners. As they were heavily used, they tended to overheat and lose power over 3,000 m, which prevented the Buffaloes from intercepting the Mitsubishi Ki.21 bombers. The inadequate fuel pumps from 800-hp *Hornet* engines caused frequent fails of the fuel pressure system, the undercarriage often remained down in locked position by the malfunction of the Constantinescu hydraulic system, and the tropical corrosion of the electric-firing solenoids affected the machine guns, which tended to fail during service.

In their retreat to the south, the British evacuated their radar equipment to protect their secret, thus losing its unique technological advantage. The consequences were disastrous. During nine weeks of fighting, twenty-two Buffaloes were shoot down, fifty-five were destroyed in the ground by air raids, and twenty-nine in crashes. During the second week of January 1942, only eight aircraft could reach Sumatra, along with five B-339D of the Dutch 2-VI.G.V Squadron, which had been sent to the north as a reinforcement.

The urgent request for help to the mother country was answered by sending fifty-one 'panic fighters' Hawker Hurricane Mk IIb trops (equipped with Vokes tropical dust filters as its original destination was Iraq) that came to Singapore on 13 January 1942. By that time, the Buffaloes had been virtually overwhelmed.

Veteran pilots of the Battle of Britain also arrived, being formed into 232nd Squadron. The 488th (NZ) Squadron changed their Buffaloes for Hurricanes. On 29 January, the 258th Squadron arrived, equipped with fifteen Hurricanes. Fifteen additional units arrived with the 263rd Squadron on 29 February. The Mk IIb was propelled by one 1,460-hp Rolls-Royce engine driving a Rotol constant-speed propeller and armed with twelve 0.303-inch Browning machine guns, with 332 rpg each. Its maximum speed was of 518 kph, its climb rate of 11.9 m/second, and its service ceiling was of 11,100 meters. The additional equipment made them slow and unwieldy to manoeuvre.

To help improve climb rate and manoeuvrability, the dust filters and the two outer Browning were removed from each wing. Unfortunately, though, the improvement did not work, and the Hurricanes began to suffer heavy losses in dogfight when their pilots tried to use the same tactics employed in Europe against Germans and Italians. Forty-five Hurricanes were lost for various reasons in Malaya after causing the destruction of nearly 100 enemy planes.

On 5 February, eight surviving aircraft of the 232nd Sqn, thirteen of the 258th Sqn, and five of the 488th Sqn were forced to evacuate to Sumatra, followed by another ten of the 263rd Sqn five days later. On 15 February, Singapore formally surrendered.

28

Burma
(14 December 1941–26 April 1942)

On 14 December 1941, the 15th Imperial Japanese Army started the occupation of Burma with an attack against Victoria Point.

Nine days later, fifty-four Mitsubishi Ki.21 bombers from 60th, 62nd, and 98th Sentais, along with twenty-seven Mitsubishi Ki.30 attack bombers from 31st Sentai, attacked Rangoon escorted by twelve Nakajima Ki.27b and eight Nakajima Ki.43-Ia fighters from 77th and 59th Sentais.

The city was defended by thirty Brewster B-339 E Buffalo Mk I fighters from 67th Sqn RAF and eighteen Curtiss Hawk 81-A2 (P-40B) Flying Tigers from 3rd Squadron AVG (American Volunteer Group), based at Mingaladon air base. The Japanese formation was intercepted by twelve Hawks and thirteen Buffaloes, who managed to knock down fifteen bombers and eight fighters at the cost of three of their own aircraft. During the subsequent bombing of Mingaladon, two Buffaloes and three Hawks were destroyed on the ground.

On 25 December 1941, the IJA repeated the attack by sending sixty-three Ki.21 from 12th Sentai, escorted by twenty-five Ki.43 from 64th Sentai, an elite unit. They were intercepted by fourteen Hawks and fifteen Buffaloes that shot down twenty-four bombers and one fighter, losing four Buffaloes and two Hawks.

On the 28th of the same month, Mingaladon fighters were caught while refuelling by ten Ki.21s and twenty Ki.43s. After the attack, there were only four P-40s and twelve B-339 Es in flying condition. Two days later, the 3rd AVG was relieved by the 2nd AVG with seventeen new aircraft. On 4 January 1942, six Curtiss fought against thirty Japanese fighters, losing three aircraft. On the 13th, eight new Curtiss from 1st AVG arrived in Mingaladon. Ten days later, twenty Allied fighters managed to shoot down twenty-one Japanese planes, losing one of their own over Rangoon.

During the month, thirty Hawker Hurricane Mk IIb (Trop) fighters from 17th and 135th RAF Squadrons arrived to Burma. On the 24th, Allied fighters shot down six Ki.21s in a combat over Mingaladon. Four days later, a fighter sweep of thirty-seven Ki.27s was intercepted by sixteen Curtiss and two Buffaloes. The Japanese lost three planes in the combat and the Americans lost two.

On 29 January, another similar attack carried out by twenty Ki.27s from 70th Sentai was intercepted by eight Hawks from 1st AVG and two Hurricanes from 17th Sqn, bringing down four Japanese fighters without the loss of their own. The next day, the AVG lost a Curtiss in combat against thirty-five enemy planes. By early February, the IJA secured air superiority over Rangoon.

On 3 February, eighteen Hurricanes were destroyed during a ferry flight between Calcutta and Lashio airfield. By mid-February, only ten Curtiss were still in flying condition at Burma. On the 25th, the Japanese launched a fighter sweep over Mingaladon with twenty-one Ki.27s from 50th Sentai, twenty-three Ki.27s from 77th Sentai, and three pre-production Nakajima Ki.44s from 47th Independent Chutai. They were intercepted by three Curtiss and six Hurricanes. None of the planes were downed.

Shortly afterwards, the same fighters returned escorting twelve Ki.48 bombers from 8th Sentai and were intercepted again by ten Curtiss and twelve Hurricanes from 17th and 135th Sqn RAF. Two Ki.27 fighters were knocked down during the combat. Two days later, the RAF retreated to Kyedaw airfield with its radar equipment and the AVG withdrew to bases in northern Burma on 1 March. Rangoon was occupied a week later.

For one month more, the Allies continued fighting from Akyab, Magwe, and Kyedaw airfields against 270 Japanese aircraft, including 115 fighters. On 11 March, the six surviving Buffaloes moved to Calcutta, India. The 67th Sqn achieved the destruction of twenty-seven Japanese aircraft, at the cost of losing eight Buffaloes of its own in combat.

On the 21st, Magwe was destroyed by 170 bombers escorted by 100 fighters. Six days later, a raid against Akyab destroyed seven Hurricanes. On 23 March, the last three Curtiss retreated into China via Loiwing and the four last Hurricanes in flying condition withdrew to India. The arrival of the monsoon rains paralyzed the advance of the Japanese troops at the end of April.

The 'Panic Fighter' of Burma was the Curtiss P-40B. It achieved the destruction of 115 Japanese aircraft in ten weeks of aerial combat. The P-40B was powered by one 1,090-hp non-supercharged Allison V-1710-33 (C-15) engine and armed with two 0.50-inch Colt Browning M-2 heavy machine guns in the top cowl and four 0.30-inch Colt Browning MG-40 light machine guns mounted in the wings.

Its maximum speed was 565 kph, its climb rate 13.6 m/second, and its service ceiling 9,000 m. The sturdy airframe, the armoured cockpit, and the protection of the fuel tanks allowed this aircraft to survive the weak armament of the Japanese fighters and the crash landings.

The fantastic agility of the Ki.27b had been a surprise for the AVG pilots and its 'climb and turning' ability made it difficult to shoot down. After studying one of these fighters captured by the RAF, the Allies could devise more effective tactics of combat.

29

Dutch East Indies
(23 January–28 March 1942)

On December 1941, the fighter strength of the Royal Netherlands East Indies Army (ML-KNIL) consisted on twenty Hawk 75 A-7s of 1-VI.G.IV. Squadron, thirty-six Brewster B-339 D Buffalos of 1-VI.G.V., 2-VI. G.V., and 3-VI.G.V., and twenty-four Curtiss CW-21B Demons of 2-VI.G.IV.

On 23 January 1942, Japanese bombers attacked Palembang-Sumatra for the first time. The defences of the island consisted of sixteen Hawk 75s, five B-339Ds, four B-339 Es of the 453rd Sqn RAAF, and twenty-six Hawker Hurricane Mk IIbs of the 232nd RAF, 258th RAF, and 488th RNZAF Squadrons. On 30 January, the Japanese conquered Ambon. On 1 February, all the B-339 D units had been ordered back to Java. These aircraft differed from the British model in their more powerful 1,200-hp Wright R-1820-G205A engine. They were also lighter, and some planes of the 2-VI.G.V. were equipped with ex-British armoured windshields in Singapore.

On 7 and 8 February, Japanese bombers attacked the P1 airfield at Pangkalan Benteng-Sumatra, destroying thirty-four British aircraft, leaving fifteen serviceable Hurricanes on the island. On the 9th, the Japanese conquered Celebes. Between 10 and 14 February, ten Hurricanes from 263rd Squadron, twenty-three from 266th Squadron, and eight from 488th Squadron arrived in Sumatra. On the 13th, the Japanese conquered Borneo.

The following day, Kawasaki Ki.56 and Mitsubishi Ki.21 transports, escorted by Nakajima Ki.43 fighters, launched paratroopers over the Royal Dutch Shell oil refineries at Palembang-Pladjoe and P1 airfield in Sumatra. On 15 February, the Japanese invasion force-landed off the mouth of Musi River; the air support was provided by Mitsubishi A5M4 (435 kph) fighters of the IJN 3rd Air Group from carrier *Ryujo*. The same day, the RAF retired to Western Java (with eighteen Hurricanes and four Buffaloes) after suffering strong losses against the Ki.43-Ia of the 59th and 64th Sentais of the IJA.

The Western defences of Java consisted of forty-eight Hurricanes of the 242nd, 605th, 232nd, 258th, 488th, 263rd, and 266th Squadrons and four Buffaloes of the 453rd Squadron operating with the help of two radar sets. Thirty-one Brewster B-339 Ds, eight

Curtiss H-75s, fourteen Curtiss CW-21Bs, and sixteen Hurricane Mk Is and Mk IIs of the 2-VI.G.IV were based at the eastern area, together with thirty Curtiss P-40Es (555 kph) of the 17th Pursuit Squadron USAAC.

The Hawk H-75 (500 kph) had very worn Wright Cyclone R-1820-G205 engines and were wiped out by the *Zeros* during the fighting on 3 and 4 February and 1 March. On 16 February, the 2-VI.G.IV, based in Kalijati, had sixteen Hurricanes. Two were destroyed in crashes. The P-40E fought against the Ki.27 on 17 February. They lost seven aircraft against the *Zeros* on the 19th, and three more the next day. Twenty more were strafed in Ngoro-Blimbing airfield. After the combat, the 17th Squadron withdrew to Australia with just nine aircraft left.

On 25 February, seven Hurricanes of 232nd RAF Squadron fought against twenty-four Ki.43s and Ki.48s over Andir and Lembang, losing two planes. That same day, the Dutch lost six Hurricanes in Bandoeng, taken by surprise by the Ki.43 during landing. Other two aircraft were strafed on 28 February and two more on 2 March. The Hurricanes of Java also managed to destroy thirty enemy planes.

The 'Java Panic Fighter' was the Curtiss CW-21B Demon, which differed from the Chinese version in the undercarriage retraction system and armament. It was powered by a 1,000-hp Wright Cyclone R-1820-G5 engine and armed with four 7.9-mm Browning M-36 machine guns. Its maximum speed was 505 kph, and its service ceiling was of 10,500 meters. With a maximum weight of 2,041 kg only and a climb rate of 22.9 m/second, the Demon would have been able to overcome any Japanese fighter in combat, had it been used according to the AVG tactics (diving down, zooming away, and back to altitude). However, its pilots made the mistake of getting involved in dogfights at medium altitude without having numerical superiority.

The Demon was not designed for this type of combat. It lacked structural strength, armour, and self-sealing fuel tanks; its hydraulic system was not duplicated; and a single impact was enough to prevent the deployment of the undercarriage and flaps, a defect that caused the destruction of 25 per cent of the aircraft in crash landings. Another 37 per cent was shot down by impacts to the pilot or fuel tanks, which would not have occurred in other better-protected Curtiss models such as the H-75 or the P-40.

Dutch pilots were good but lacked experience in combat when they faced two elite squadrons (the 64th Sentai and the Tainan Kokutai) in which veterans of Khalkhin Gol, the Philippines, and China flew. Other factors that decreased the effectiveness of the Demon were the deficient Dutch raid warning organisation and erroneous tactics of the ML-KNIL that split into small units the scarce available fighters, being systematically overcome in number by the attackers.

On 3 February 1942, the Demon entered combat for the first time during a raid carried out by aircraft of the IJN against Soerabaja, Maospati, and Singosari airfields. The attackers were thirty-seven Mitsubishi G4M bombers of 21st Kanoya Kokutai and twenty-seven G4Ms of the Takao Kokutai, based more than 1,000 km away in Kendari-Celebes. The escort fighters were sixteen Mitsubishi A6M2 Model 21 *Zero-Sens* (535 kph) of the 251st Tainan Kokutai and twelve more *Zeros* from the 3rd Kaohsiung Kokutai, from Balikpapan-Borneo.

The large formation of Japanese aircraft was intercepted over Madura island by twelve Demons based in Perak, eight Curtiss H-75s of Singosari, and four Curtiss P-40Es of the

17th USAAC Pursuit Squadron based at Ngoro-Blimbing. The Tainan *Zeros* shot down three Demons and damaged six more (four of which were destroyed in crash landings) and the 3rd Kokutai fighters shot down other two. In this battle, the Allies also lost three Curtiss H-75s and three Curtiss P-40s; the Japanese lost three *Zeros* and twenty other aircraft by battle damage during the return flight.

The following day, the IJN repeated the attack using forty G4M bombers from the 4th Kokutai and twenty-seven *Zeros* from the Tainan Air Group. They were intercepted by four Demons, two H-75s, and seven P-40s; the Japanese lost two *Zeros* and the Allies one Demon, one P-40, and two H-75s. On 19 February, seven Demons based in Bandoeng faced for the first time the IJA aircraft that, coming from Sumatra, attacked Semplak airfield. The attackers were nine Kawasaki-Ki.48-II bombers of the 90th Sentai escorted by twenty-eight Nakajima Ki.43-Ia fighters of the 59th Sentai. One Demon suffered battle damage and was destroyed in a crash landing.

On the same day, another group of five Ki.48-IIs of the 75th Sentai, escorted by nineteen Ki.43-Ias of the 64th Sentai, attacked RAF and ML-KNIL installations in Buitenzorg and Andir bases, destroying another Demon in the ground. On 23 February, the Buffaloes went into combat with the Tainan *Zeros*, resulting massacred.

The following day, seven British Hawker Hurricane Mk IIbs of the 232nd Squadron and four Demons intercepted a strafing raid of the IJA over Lembang, carried out by twenty-seven Ki.43 fighters of the 59th and 64th Sentais from Sumatra. One Demon was shot down in combat, another by the Dutch anti-aircraft artillery, one in a crash landing, and one more destroyed in Andir by the Ki.48-II of the 90th Sentai.

On 1 March, fifty Ki.48-II bombers of the IJA 27th Air Group, which were attacking Bandoeng escorted by Ki.43 fighters of the 59th and 64th Sentais, were intercepted by four Hurricanes and four Demons, one of which was shot down. The next day, four Curtiss Hawks, four Buffaloes, and two Demons entered combat against Nakajima fighters from 64th Sentai, with one of the Demons being shot down.

On 3 March, the last three Demons in flying condition carried out a strafing mission against the Kalidjati airfield, destroying a Type 97 bomber. After the surrender of Java, two Demons were captured by the Japanese and sent to the Tachikawa Test Centre to study the secrets of its construction. Sumatra surrendered on 28 March.

On 20 February 1940, the US Air Corps Materiel Division issued circular request data for R-40C, calling for new fighter designs capable of facing the new European fighters. The projects considered suitable for immediate construction essentially were modifications of existing production models propelled by Allison V-1710 or Continental XIV-1430 engines.

The Bell firm proposed its Model 13 and Curtiss its Model 88 and the P-248-01 project that satisfied the need to complement the deficiencies of the Curtiss P-40E in ceiling and climb rate. The first two projects were cancelled in June 1940 due to the unavailability of the Continental engine.

The P-248-01 was a version of the Curtiss CW-21B powered by a 1,150-hp Allison V-1710-E9 engine, with a two-stage supercharger, but it did not comply with the safety conditions of the US Air Corps as it lacked protection for the pilot and fuel tanks. An export version was proposed, but its construction was dismissed after the bad results obtained by the Demon in China and Java.

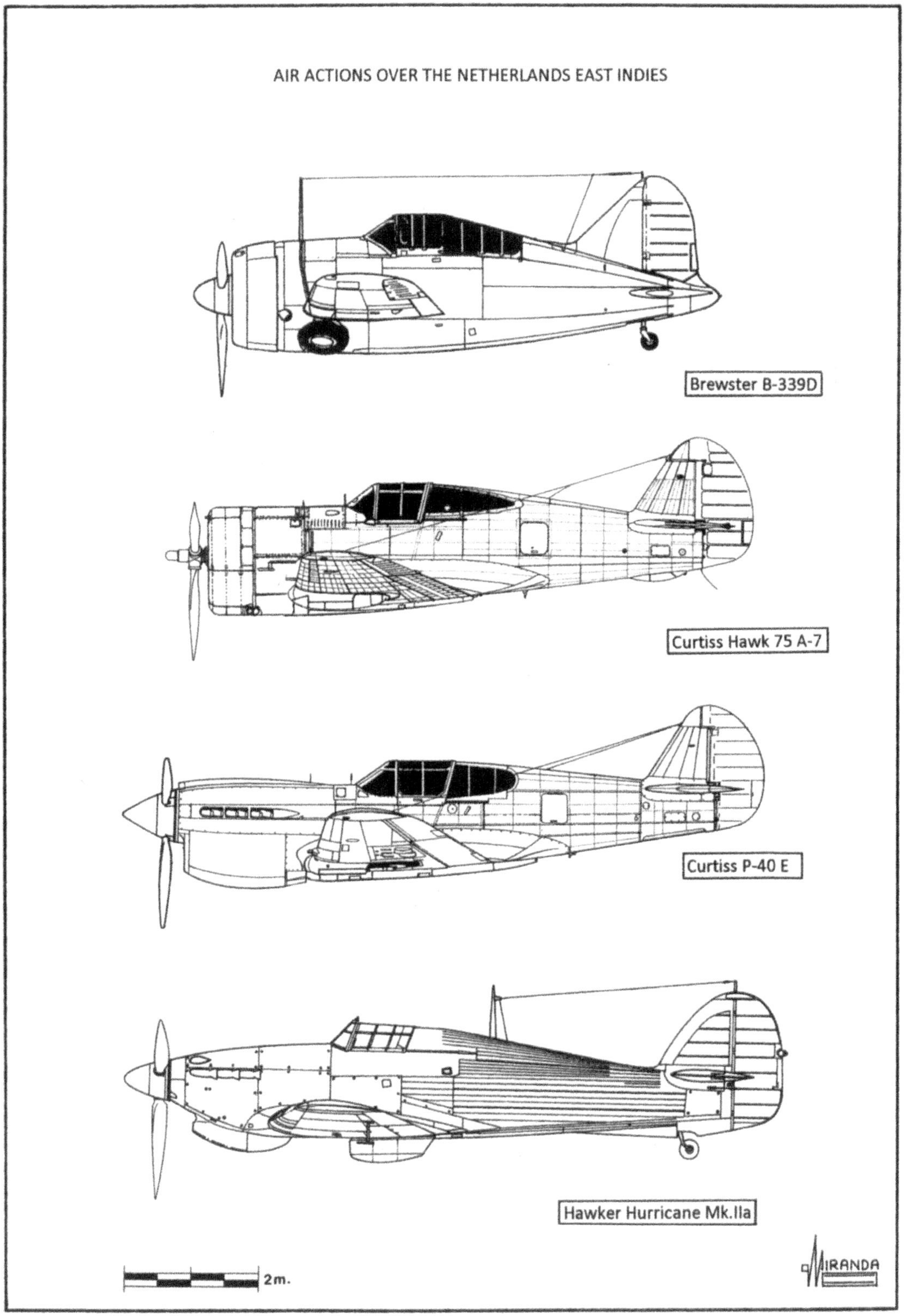

AIR ACTIONS OVER THE NETHERLANDS EAST INDIES

Brewster B-339D

Curtiss Hawk 75 A-7

Curtiss P-40 E

Hawker Hurricane Mk.IIa

2m.

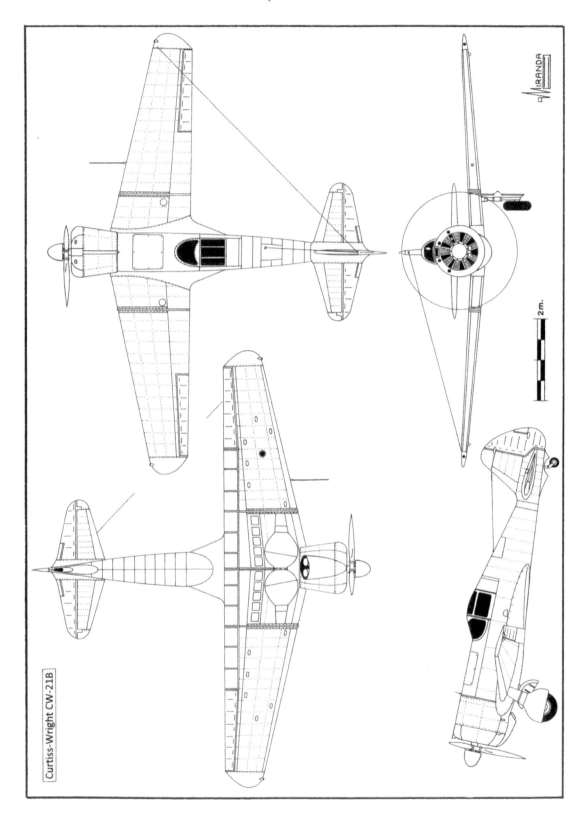

Curtiss-Wright CW-21B

30

Ceylon
(5–12 April 1942)

In early April 1942, two powerful Japanese fleets penetrated the Indian Ocean with the mission to annihilate the British Eastern Fleet based in Ceylon.

The Malay Force—formed by an aircraft carrier with thirty-eight aircraft, six cruisers, and four destroyers—left Burma on 1 April to attack merchant shipping in the Bay of Bengal. This force sank twenty-three merchant ships by gunfire in three days, while sixteen B5N2 *Kate* bombers and twenty-two A5M4 *Claude* fighters from *Ryujo* carrier attacked Cocanada and Vizagapatam ports on the east coast of India. On 7 April, the Malay Force retired to Rangoon.

On 26 March, the 1st Air Fleet, formed by five aircraft carriers with 247 aircraft, departed from Kendari-Celebes with an escort of seven cruisers, eleven destroyers, five submarines, and six tankers, starting their raid in the Indian Ocean on 1 April. Four days later, fifty- three B5N2 *Kate* bombers, thirty-eight D3A1 *Val* dive bombers, and thirty-six A6M2 *Zero-Sen* fighters attacked Colombo, sinking three British cruisers and one destroyer. They also shot down twenty-one Hawker Hurricanes, six Fairey Fulmars, and six Fairey Swordfishs, losing one *Zero* and six *Vals* of their own.

The defences of Colombo consisted of twenty-one Hawker Hurricane Mk IIbs from 30th Squadron, twenty-four Fairey Fulmar Mk IIs from 803rd and 806th Squadrons based at Ratmalana airfield, ten Hawker Hurricane Mk IIbs and seven Hawker Hurricane Mk Is from 258th Squadron based at Racecourse airfield, and one AMES Type 9 mobile radar station, which was poorly located among hills and so was unable to detect the attacking aircraft.

On 9 April, ninety-one B5N2s and thirty-eight A6M2s attacked Trincomalee. They sank one aircraft carrier, one destroyer, one corvette, and two tankers. They also destroyed eight Hurricanes, two Fulmars, and five Blenheims in combat and eleven Fairey Albacores on the ground, losing three *Zeros* and two *Kates* of their own. Three days later, the 1st Air Fleet retreated to Malacca straits.

The defences of Trincomalee consisted of sixteen Hawker Hurricane Mk IIbs from the 261st Squadron, sixteen Fairey Fulmar Mk Is and Mk IIs from the 273rd Squadron, and three Martlets (unserviceable) from the 888th Squadron, based at China Bay and Kokkilai airfields. On this occasion, the Type 9 radar did locate the attackers giving the alarm.

These attacks were intended to force the intervention of the Eastern Fleet, formed by three aircraft carriers with ninety-one aircraft, five battleships, seven cruisers, and sixteen destroyers. Despite having the advantage of radar and their superiority in artillery, the British evaded a confrontation with the Japanese Fleets and the overwhelming Carrier Force. The Eastern Fleet remained hidden in Addu Atoll, a secret base located 1,000 km to the south-west of Ceylon, until the attacks ceased. On 15 April, ignoring the Japanese withdrawal, they moved to Kilindini-Mombasa on the east African coast.

The 'Panic Fighter' of Ceylon was the Fulmar, a two-seat heavy fighter designed to protect the British Fleet against the attacks carried out, far from the coast, by German and Italian bombers that operated without fighter escort.

In 1942, the Eastern Fleet already had several American Martlets and gave part of their Fulmars to the RAF to reinforce the few Hurricanes available in Ceylon. The Fulmar had the same engine and armament as the Hurricane but was slower and less manoeuvrable due to its excessive weight (4,950 kg). If they could avoid being exterminated by the *Zeros* in Ceylon, it was thanks to the support of the Hurricanes that suffered the greatest losses. The Fulmar Mk II had a maximum speed of 417 kph, a climb rate of 7.8 m/second, and a service ceiling of 7,300 m.

31

Australia
(21 December 1941–15 August 1945)

In July 1940, the hounded British Government warns the Australians of an imminent embargo of any aviation materials. On 10 December 1941, the capital ships of the Royal Navy HMS *Prince of Wales* and HMS *Repulse* were sunk by Japanese aircraft. On 21 December, the firm Commonwealth Aircraft Corporation (CAC) received the order from the Australian Government to design a 'Panic Fighter' starting from the 'Wirraway' trainer airframe (the Australian version of the North American T-6 produced under licence by the CAC) and from the most powerful engine available in the country, the 1,200-hp Pratt & Whitney R-1830 S3C4-G.

On 15 February 1942, Singapore surrendered to the Imperial Japanese Army. On 18 February, the Australian War Cabinet authorised an order for 105 units of the new 'stop-gap' fighter under the designation CA-12 'Boomerang' (490 kph). The next day, Japanese naval aircraft attacked Port Darwin, causing serious damage. On 9 March, the island of Java was invaded by Japanese troops and the Allies dissolved the naval force 'ABDA'. On 9 April 1942, Japanese naval aircraft attacked Ceylon, and the British Eastern Fleet moved to the base of Kilindini in the eastern coast of Africa.

The 'Boomerang' first flight tests were performed on 29 May 1942. The new fighter showed excellent performance for low altitude flight, being superior to their American equivalents: the NA-50 and the NA-68. On the other hand, its engine (originally designed to go with the Beaufort torpedo bombers) was optimised to operate at low altitude and reached highest power at 4,900 feet. However, the 'Boomerang' proved to lack the right performances for medium altitude interception of standard Japanese bombers and was used for ground attack duties only.

In August 1942, the RAAF received four P-43 A-1s and two P-43D 'Lancers' from the USAAF, plus two more P-43Ds in November. These aircraft had the same engine as the 'Boomerang', but they were also equipped with a belly-mounted turbo-supercharger General Electric B-2 that considerably improved its performances at high altitude. Unfortunately, the Americans had been extremely reluctant to provide B-2 superchargers,

125 of which had been approved by Lend-Lease at the beginning of 1942. The reasons behind this political attitude were the plans of the North American company to manufacture the P-51 Mustang, propelled by a British Merlin engine, in Australia.

Even so, the CAC continued improving the 'Boomerang', afraid the unstoppable advance of the *Teikoku Kaigun* through the Pacific could interrupt the supplying routes with the USA. By the end of 1942, the CA-12 was modified by installing a B-2 turbocharger (coming from a 'Liberator') and a Harrison intercooler (coming from a 'Fortress') mounted in the rear fuselage on the starboard side. The prototype flew on 13 January 1943 as CA-14, reaching a maximum speed of 560 km/h at 8,600 m, powered by one 1,700-hp Wright Cyclone R-2600 engine, driving a 3.35-m diameter Curtiss Electric three-bladed, constant-speed propeller. By comparison, the standard CA-12 could achieve just 490 km/h at 4,700 m.

In May 1943, the engine was replaced by a non-turbocharged R-2000 (basically a wartime modification of the R-1830 extended to 2000 cubic inch capacity) with a General Electric B-9 turbocharger, square fin and rudder and geared engine cooling fan 'Fw 190 style'. This version was named CA-14A.

On 28 May 1942, the CAC proposed to build an 'improved Boomerang' named XP-17, with modified tail surfaces and completely new wing, propelled by a 1,700-hp Wright Cyclone R-2600-12 (with ten-bladed cooling fan and B-9 ventral turbo-supercharger) driving a Hamilton Standard four-bladed wooden propeller.

On 8 August 1942, the P-176 project saw the light—a new and more conservative model based on a 'Boomerang' airframe with new streamlined leading edges, a 1,900-hp R-2600-20 engine, a four-bladed wooden propeller, a cooling fan, and a B-13 ventral turbocharger. The project was discontinued in February 1943.

To meet RAAF Specification 2/42, the CAC was instructed to design a new fighter named CA-15 in October 1942 to be propelled by the 2,000-hp Pratt Whitney R-2800-21 air-cooled radial engine with single-stage/single-speed supercharger and General Electric B-9 exhaust-driven turbocharger. It would soon be available as it used the same power plant as the American Thunderbolts, Hellcats, Corsairs, and Marauders. On 4 November 1942, 'Report No. A-87' was published depicting a first design of the CA-15, fitted with semi-elliptical wings, a R-2800-21 engine with four-bladed wooden propeller, four 0.303-inch Browning Mk II machine guns, and two 20-mm Hispano Mk II cannons.

As it turned out, the R-2800-21 was not available by the beginning of 1943 and the design was modified to adapt it to the 2,100-hp R-2800-43 engine, optimised for medium altitude operations, with a single-stage, two-speed supercharger and a liquid-cooled Airesearch intercooler. The engine cowling adopted a more streamlined shape, the propeller was three-bladed, and the 'Boomerang' standard armament was replaced by four 20-mm Hispano Mk II cannons and two 0.303-inch Browning Mk II machine guns.

By early 1943, the CA-15 was redesigned as a high-altitude interceptor, with NACA 66 laminar flow wings and a 12.19-m wingspan. The power plant was one 2,180-hp R-2800-10W (with two-speed/two-stage General Electric Type C turbocharger and liquid-cooled intercooler) driving one CAC four-bladed, hydraulically operated, constant speed, wooden propeller of 3.89 m in diameter. The proposed armament was six 0.50-inch Colt Browning machine guns mounted on the wing and the estimated maximum speed was of 702 kph.

To meet RAAF Specification 2/43, calling for a low–medium-altitude long-range fighter, the CAC proposed the August 1943 design, the turbocharger was removed, and the engine was fitted with a single-stage, two-speed supercharger. Four months later, the supercharger site was changed, being installed under the engine in one enormous cowling with large exhaust pipe under the fuselage, a configuration that had already been tested in the Curtiss XF14C.

On May 1944, the CAC was disappointed to learn that the 10W engine was no longer in production and considered its replacement by a 2,800-hp R-2800-57W with single-speed/ single-stage supercharger and GE Type CH-5 turbo-supercharger. On June, the cooling fan was replaced by a 'Thunderbolt style' airscoop placed under the engine. The estimated maximum speed was 796 kph.

On August, the CA-15 prototype was around 50 per cent complete and the availability of 57W engine became doubtful. The 2,500-hp Bristol *Centaurus* engine was considered but its performance would have been substantially reduced from that of the R-2800-57W. They finally selected the 2,440-hp Rolls-Royce Griffon 125 twelve-cylinder, Vee, liquid-cooled engine (with two-stage/three-speed supercharger) driving three-bladed contra-rotating airscrews. For its installation in an airframe that had been designed for a radial engine, it was necessary to build a new streamlined cowling.

The cooling system consisted of a Morris single-row intercooler, with a three-row main radiator and was packaged in a large 'Mustang style' ventral fairing with frontal scoop. The Griffon 125 turned out to have the smallest frontal surface, but when the CA-15 prototype was completed, the engine had not yet reached its serial production stage and Rolls-Royce decided to replace it by two copies of the weaker version Griffon 61. The two available engines arrived in Australia in April 1945.

The Griffon 61 (2,035 hp) was fitted with two-stage/two-speed supercharger and drove a Dowty-Rotol compressed wood, four-bladed propeller of 3.81 m in diameter. Its installation in the CA-15 reduced the overall length from 11.51 m to 11.04 m. By February 1946, the prototype was completed, performing its first flight on 4 March. It was used for a very limited test programme and gained a speed record by achieving 808.2 kph flying over Melbourne on 25 May 1948. The CA-15 would have ranked among the best fighters in the Pacific had the war been prolonged. Superseded by the jet age, it was scrapped in 1950.

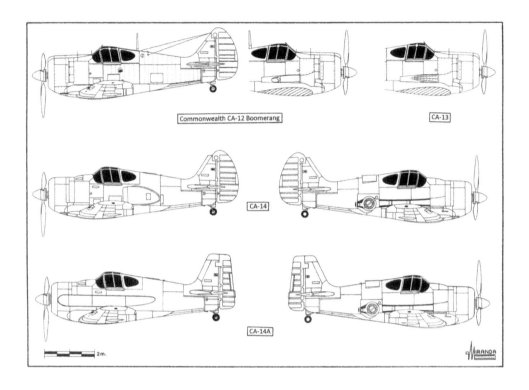

Commonwealth CA-12 Boomerang

CA-13

CA-14

CA-14A

2m.

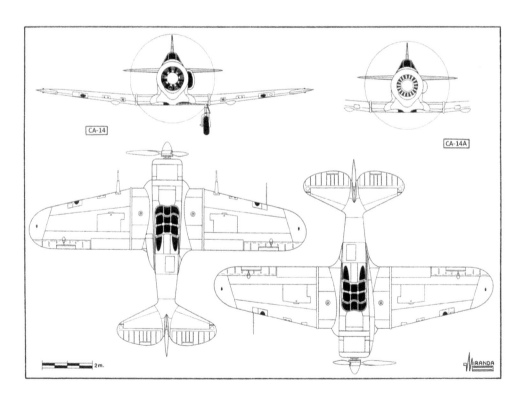

CA-14

CA-14A

2m.

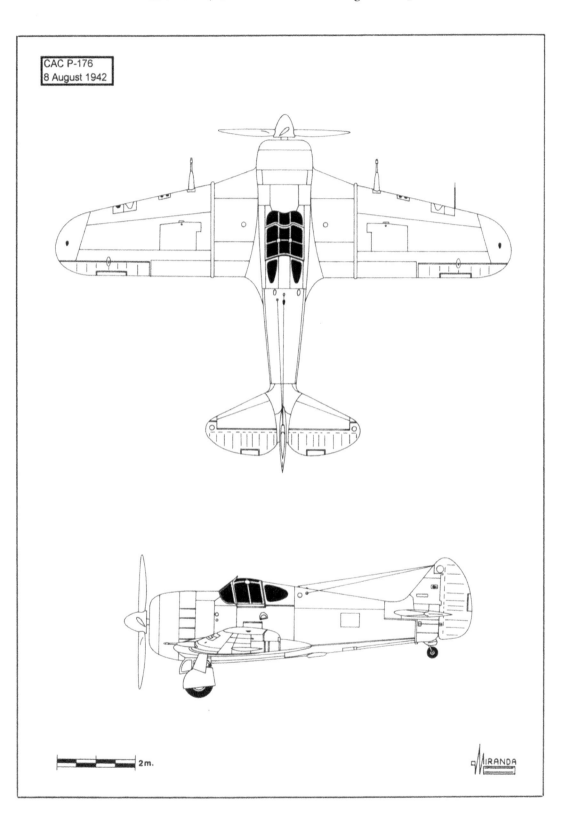

CAC P-176
8 August 1942

2m.

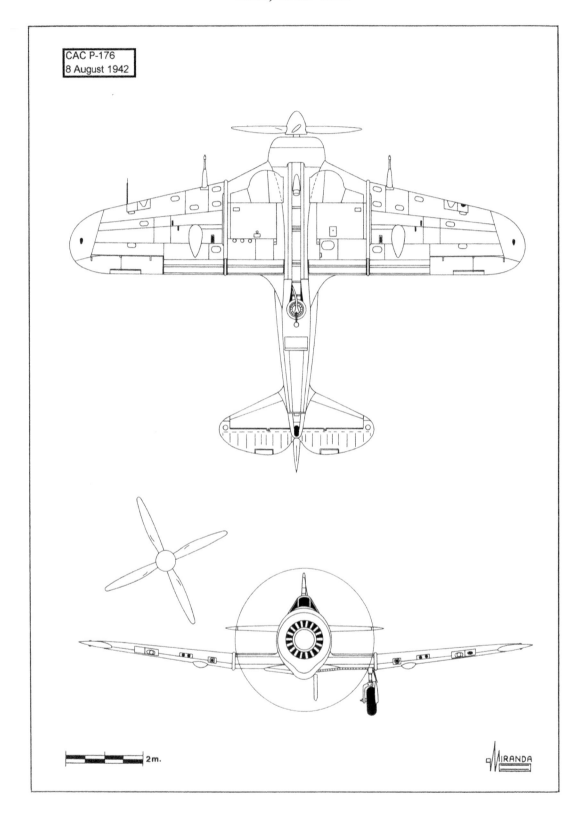

CAC P-176
8 August 1942

2m.

MIRANDA

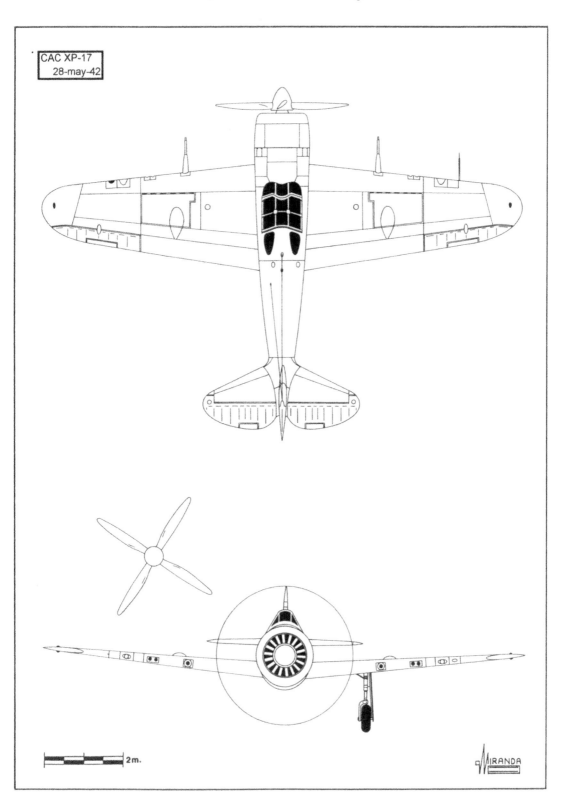

CAC XP-17
28-may-42

2 m.

MIRANDA

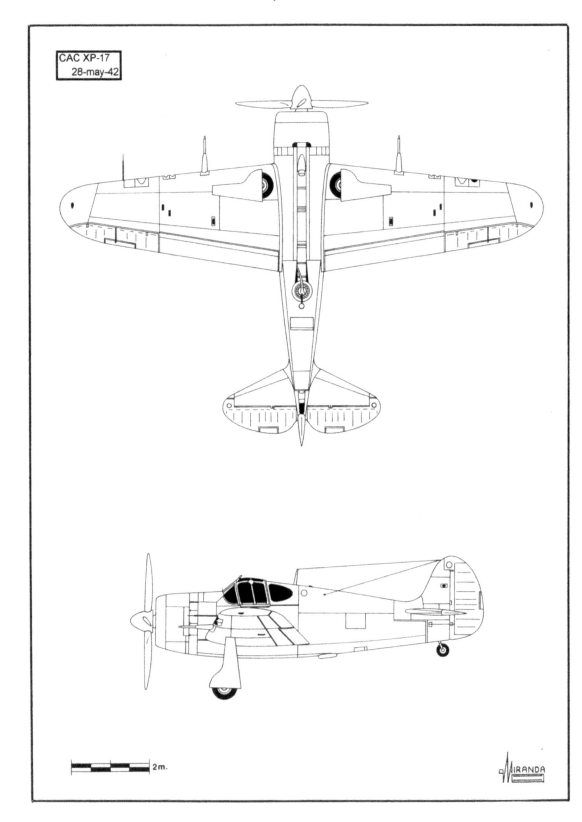

CAC XP-17
28-may-42

2 m.

MIRANDA

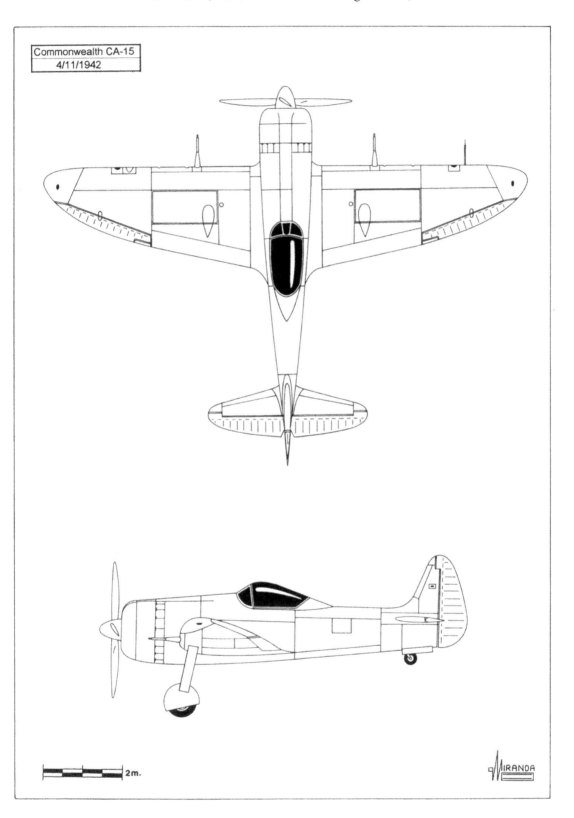

Commonwealth CA-15
4/11/1942

2m.

Enemy at the Gates

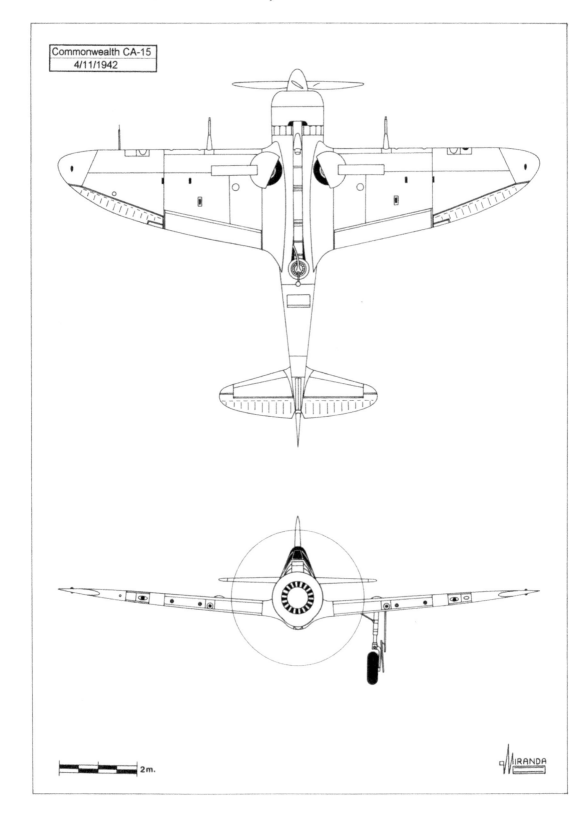

Commonwealth CA-15
4/11/1942

2 m.

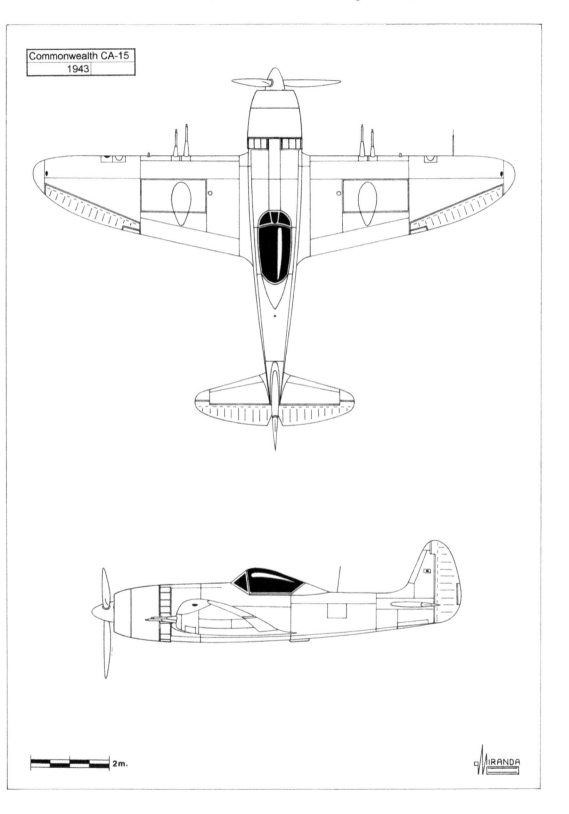

Commonwealth CA-15
1943

2m.

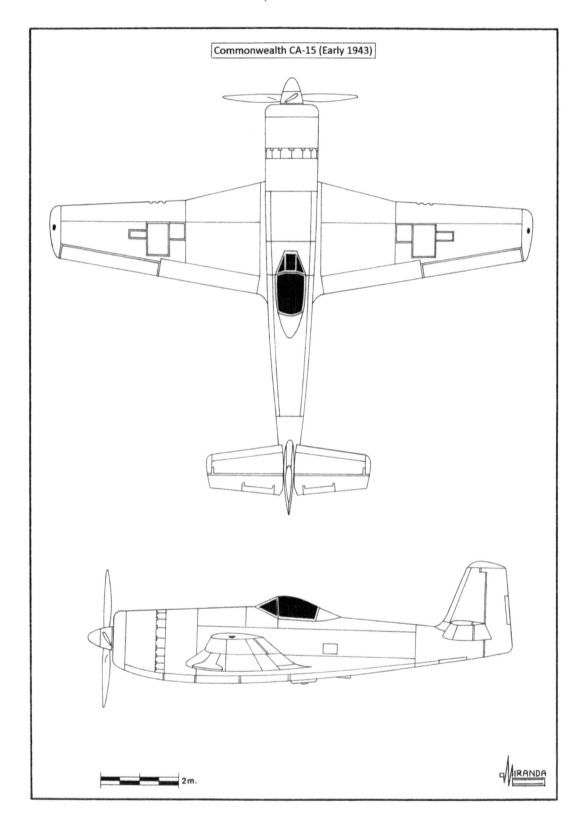

Commonwealth CA-15 (Early 1943)

2 m.

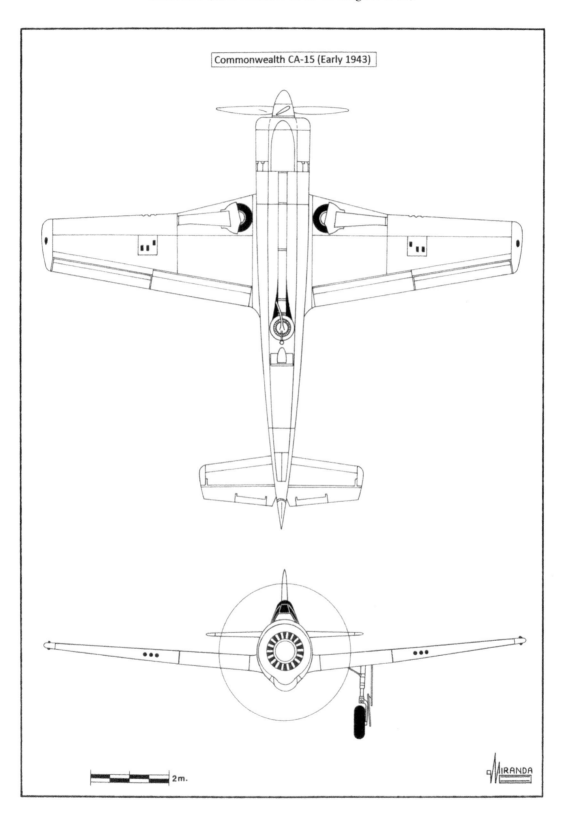

Commonwealth CA-15 (Early 1943)

2m.

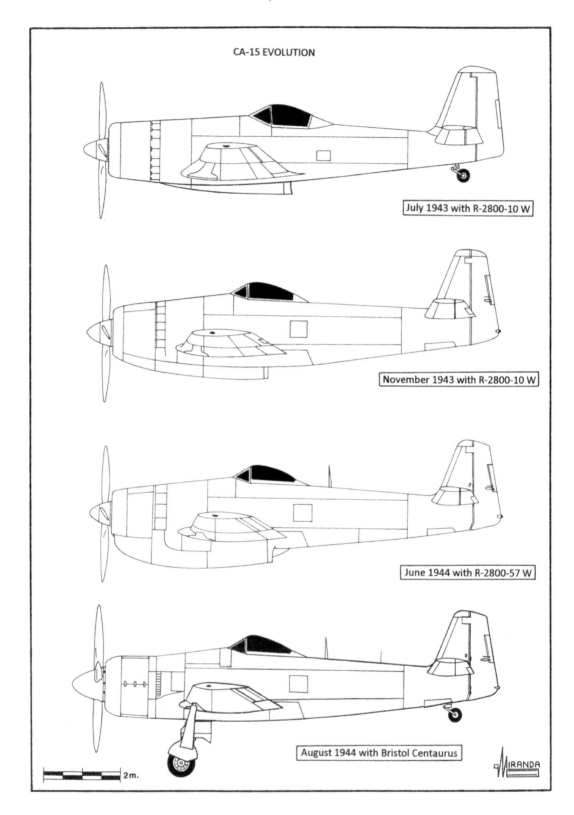

CA-15 EVOLUTION

July 1943 with R-2800-10 W

November 1943 with R-2800-10 W

June 1944 with R-2800-57 W

August 1944 with Bristol Centaurus

2 m.

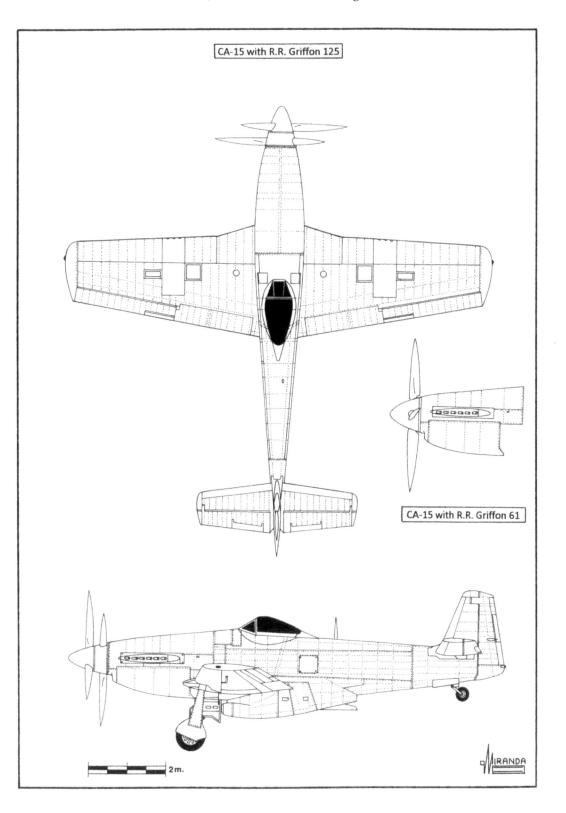

CA-15 with R.R. Griffon 125

CA-15 with R.R. Griffon 61

2m.

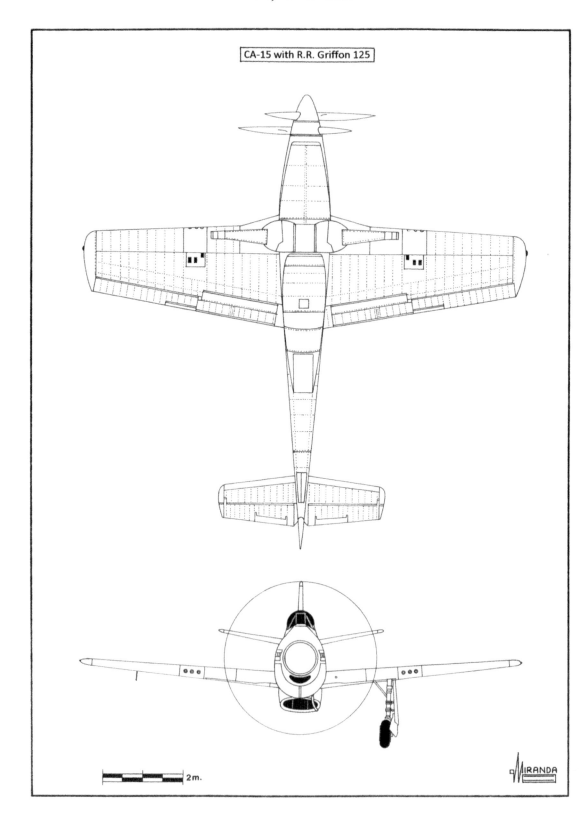

CA-15 with R.R. Griffon 125

2 m.

32

With Enemy Core

The lack of the right engines in the international market during the Second World War caused the appearance of many different prototypes of hybrid fighters. Engines and aircraft of both bands were exchanged with experimental purposes.

In 1938, the Yugoslavian Government acquired twenty-four Hawker Hurricane fighters, together with the manufacturing licence to allow production of another 100 units in the factories of Zmaj and Rogožarski. However, by the time of German onslaught on April 1941, only twenty Hurricanes had been delivered to the Royal Yugoslav Air Force. When entering the war, the British Government suspended the exports of Merlin engines, required for their own defence.

As an alternative, the engineers Ilic and Sivcev of the Ikarus-Zemun factory experimentally installed the German Daimler Benz DB 601A engine in a Hurricane IK-Z of local manufacturing. New engine bearers had to be built for the transformation, as well as a redesign of the electrical and cooling systems.

The new machine was named LVT-1 (Lovac Vazduhoplovno Tehnički-1) and flight tested by the captain pilot Milos Bajagic in the summer of 1940, proving a better take-off performance and climb rate that either the Hurricane Mk I of the Bf 109 E.3. The Ikarus LVT-1 'Hurrischmitt' was a bit faster than the Hurricane IK-Z although not as much as the Bf 109 E.3.

By early 1941, several proposals were made for the installation of alternative power plants in the Hawker Hurricane Mk II, to alleviate possible shortages of Merlin engines. The Rolls-Royce Griffon IIA, Napier Dagger, and Bristol Hercules engines were considered.

Britain had provided the Soviet Union a total of 2,952 Hurricanes and there were strong rumours that at least one of them was powered by one 1,250-hp Shvetsov ASh-82 radial engine and armed with two 20-mm ShVAK cannons and four 0.5 in UBT machine guns.

By early 1942, a 1,200-hp Jumo 211 in-line engine from a Savoia-Marchetti SM. 79B bomber was mounted into the IAR 80 c/n 111 Romanian fighter, but during flight tests, the aircraft experimented destructive vibration problems and the experiments were discontinued. At the end of 1943, a DB 601 Aa from Bf 109 E-3 was installed in the IAR 80 c/n 13, performing some test flights. On 29 June 1943, the IAR 81C c/n 326 was fitted with a 1,475-hp DB 605A engine on an experimental basis.

By mid-1942, a number of Curtiss P-40E that had been provided to the Soviets, under the Lend-Lease arrangements, were re-engined with one 1,100-hp Klimov M-105 engine and pressed into service with several Aviation Regiments. On April 1942, one Rogožarski IK-3 prototype was converted from HS.12Y-29 to a Daimler Benz DB 601 engine.

On 18 November 1942, the Spitfire Mk Vb (EN 830) of the 131st Sqn of the RAF was captured virtually intact by the Germans after a forced landing in France. It was sent for experimentation purposes to the Daimler Benz test centre of Echterdingen, south of Stuttgart, in 1943. One DB 605 A-1, with a new engine support, was installed. To that purpose, fuel and oil tanks and new refrigeration system had to be redesigned; the electrical system and starter were also changed into a 24 V.

The propeller was a standard VDM with a diameter of 3 m. The conversion was completed at the Sindelfingen factory with the installation of one Bf 110G engine cowling with the carburettor scoop from a Bf 109 G. The 'Spitschmitt' received the radio code letters CJ+ZY, performing its comparative flight tests against a Bf 109 G in the Rechlin Test Centre. It proved its superiority on both visibility and handling on the ground as well as in the climb rate, compared to the standard Bf 109 G. The maximum speed was also estimated above 11,000 feet, but the maximum power of the engine could not be tested due to deficiencies in the air coolant system.

The Spanish Government ordered the modification of the Bf 109 E-3 (6-119) in 1942, replacing the engine by one 1,300-hp Hispano-Suiza HS.12-Z89. The prototype, named HA-1109 J1, was flight tested in Muntadas-Barcelona by Lt Lacour in October 1942, revealing problems of overheating. By the beginning of 1945, one HS.12-Z89 was installed in the Bf 109 G-2 airframe imported from Germany. The new model was named HA-1109 J1L, flying for the first time with a three-bladed Hamilton Standard propeller on 2 March 1945, without solving the engine overheating problem.

In 1951, it was decided to replace the engine by the HS.12-Z17 variant, considered more secure. The new HA-1109 K version was equipped with a three-bladed de Havilland PD-63 propeller and went into service for the *Ejercito del Aire* in a number of thirty units. Other Bf 109 G-2s were converted into the HA-1112 M by installing the British R.R. Merlin 500/45 engines with four-bladed Rotol R-116 propellers from the summer of 1953 onwards. None of these transformations (profoundly disgusting for Willy Messerschmitt) produced any satisfactory result.

In Finland, forty-one ex-French Morane-Saulnier M.S.406 fighters were re-engined in June 1944 as *Mörkö Moraani* (525 kph) with one 1,100-hp Klimov (Hispano-Suiza) M-105 P driving one VISh-61 constant-speed airscrew; it was armed with one engine-mounted 20-mm MG 151 cannon and two wing-mounted 7.7-mm (belt feed) Browning machine guns.

In 1946, one Focke-Wulf Fw 190 F-8 was re-engined with one 1,250-hp Shvetsov ASh-82 radial engine in the LII VVS (Soviet Air Force Test Flying Institute) and kept in flight condition until 1951.

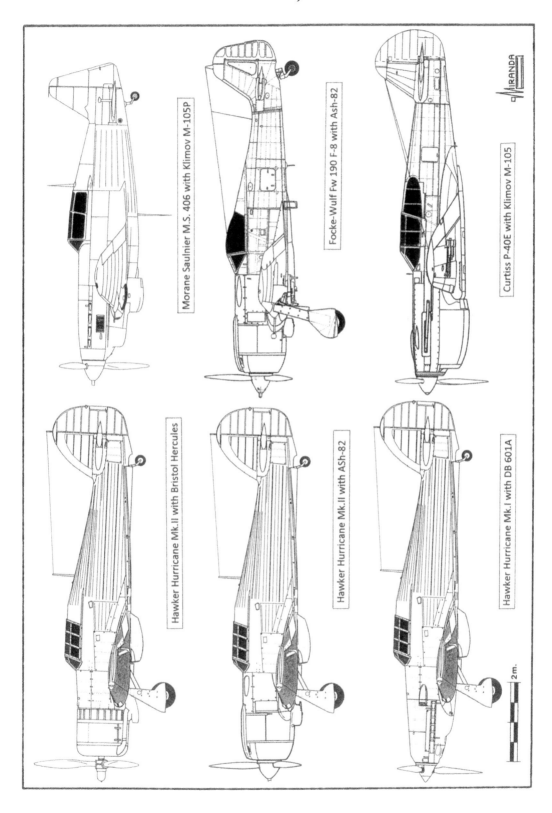

Morane Saulnier M.S. 406 with Klimov M-105P

Focke-Wulf Fw 190 F-8 with Ash-82

Curtiss P-40E with Klimov M-105

Hawker Hurricane Mk.II with Bristol Hercules

Hawker Hurricane Mk.II with ASh-82

Hawker Hurricane Mk.I with DB 601A

2 m.

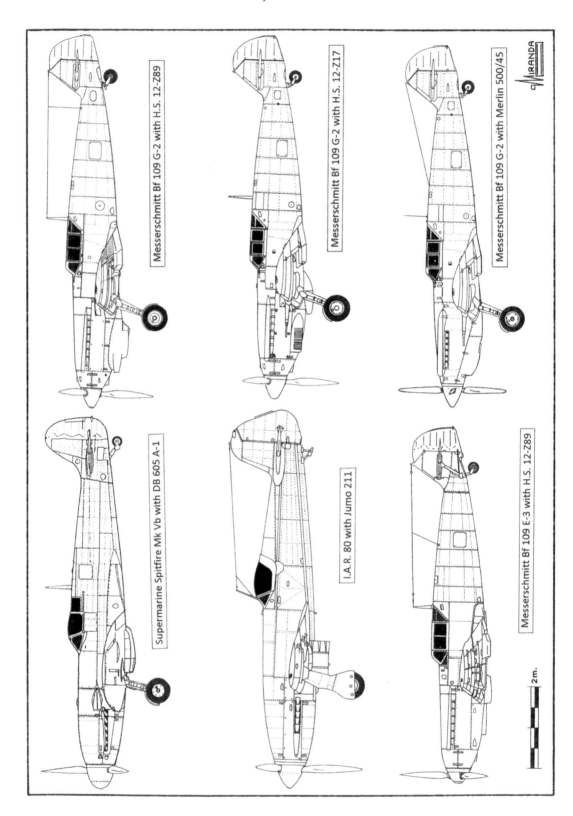

Messerschmitt Bf 109 G-2 with H.S. 12-Z89

Messerschmitt Bf 109 G-2 with H.S. 12-Z17

Messerschmitt Bf 109 G-2 with Merlin 500/45

Supermarine Spitfire Mk Vb with DB 605 A-1

I.A.R. 80 with Jumo 211

Messerschmitt Bf 109 E-3 with H.S. 12-Z89

2 m.

Bibliography

CZECHOSLOVAKIA

Books
Bílý M., Bernád D., and Kučera P., *Avia B-35, B-135* (MBI Publications 2003)
Green W., *Warplanes of the Second World War, Fighters, Volume One* (MacDonald, 1963)
Němeček V., ČESKOSLOVENSKÁ *Letadla 1918–1945* (Naše vojsko- Praha, 1983)

Publications
'*Les Avia B.35/135 de František Novotný*', *Le Fana de l'Aviation*, No. 190

POLAND

Books
Cynk, J., *Polish Aircraft 1893–1939* (Putnam, 1971)
Cynk, J., *Siły Lotnicze Polski i Niemiec*, WKŁ (Warszawa, 1989)
Duleba, L., *Samoloty RWD*, WKŁ (Warszawa, 1980)
Glass, A., *Polskie Konstrukcje Lotnicze 1893–1939*, WKZ (Warszawa, 1976)
Green, W., *Warplanes of the Second World War, Fighters, Volume Three* (MacDonald, 1961)
Koniarek, J., *Polish Air Force 1939–1945* (Squadron/Signal Publications, 1994)
Krzyzan, M., *Miedzynarodowe Turniieje Lotnicze*, WKŁ (Warszawa, 1988)
Liss, W., *The P.Z.L. P.11* (Profile Publications, No. 75)
Malak, E., *Prototypy Samolotow Bojowych, Polska 1936–1939* WUW (Wrocław, 1990)
Morgała, A., *Samoloty Wojskowe, Polsce 1924–1939*, Bellona (Warszawa, 2003)
Sołtyk, T., *Polska Mysl Technierna w Lotnicze*, WKŁ (Warszawa, 1983)

Publications
Cynk, J., 'Les intercepteurs P.Z.L. P.7 et P.11', *Le Fana de l'Aviation*, nos 72 to 77
Dobrzelecki, M., 'The Polish Air Force in September 1939', *SAFO*, vol. 13, no. 4 (October 1989)
Cynk, B., 'P.Z.L. P.50 *Jastrząb*', *Air Pictorial* (December 1962)
Kowalski, T., '4 Pulk Lotniczy', *SAFO*, vol. 3, no. 1 (March 1978)
Cynk, J., 'Blitzkrieg', *Airpower* (June 1983)
Davis C., 'P.Z.L. P.50 *Jastrząb*', *Aero Plans* (August 1988)

Musialkowski, P., 'The Pulawski Fighters', *SAFO* (July 1989)
Dildy, D., 'Jadenastka', *SAFO*, vol. 15, no. 1 (June 1991)
Dobrzelecki, M., 'First Kills Over Poland', *SAFO*, vol. 15, no. 3 (July 1991)

DENMARK

Books
De Jong, P., *Le Fokker D.21* (Lela Presse, 2005)
Dildy, D., *Denmark and Norway 1940: Hitler's Boldest Operation* (Osprey, 2007)
Mason, F., *Gloster Gauntlet* (Profile Publications, No. 10)
Nigel, T., *Hitler's Blitzkrieg Enemies 1940: Demark, Norway, Netherlands & Belgium* (Osprey, 2014)

Publications
Aphopenia, A., 'Indigenous Danish Fighter?' secretprojects.co.uk/forum/index.php?topic=5357.30
Larsen, G., 'Hawker Danish Nimrod', *Wingpan* (June 1993)
Larsen, G., 'OV-J-1 Dansk Marinejagerprojekt 1940' *Flyvehistorisk Tidsskrift from Danks Flyvehistorisk Forening*, vol. 3 (1993)
natureandtech.com/?p=3057
tapatalk.com/groups/aaminis/orlogsv-rftet-j-1-jager-naval-fighter-t48088.html
Willadsen, K., 'Denmark: April 1940', *Aircraft of the Small Air Forces (SAFO)*, April 1990, vol. 14, no. 2

NORWAY

Books
Crawford, A., *Gloster Gladiator* (Mushroom Magazine Special, 2002)
Cuny, J., *Curtiss Hawk 75*, Docavia no. 22 (Editions Larivière, 1985)
Mason, F., *The Gloster Gladiator* (Profile Publications, No. 98)
Mason, F., *The Hawker Fury* (Profile Publications, No. 18)
Thomas, A., *Gloster Gladiator Aces* (Osprey Publishing, 2002)

Publications
Dildy, D., 'Operation Wesertag', *SAFO*, vol. 13, no. 3 (July 1989)
Hagen, K., 'Norwegian Air Services, April 1940', *SAFO*, vol. 14, no. 3 (July 1990)
Kadari, Y., '*Marinens Flyvevesen & Haerens Flygevåpen*', *Aéro Journal*, no. 61 (2017)
Kent, R., 'Camouflage and Markings of Gloster Gladiator', *IPMS Stockholm Magazine*
Olrog, M., 'The Gloster Gladiator in the Norwegian Army Air Service', *Håkans Flygsida*, surfcity.kund.dalnet.se/gladiator_norway.htm.

NETHERLANDS

Books
De Jong, P., *Le Fokker D.21* (Lela Presse, 2005)
Green, W., *Warplanes of the Second World War: Fighters, Volume Three* (MacDonald, 1962)
Postma, T., *Koolhoven, Nederlands Vliegtuigbouwer in de Schaduw van Fokker* (Romen-Haarlen, 1981)

Publications
Hazewinkel, H., 'Koolhoven FK.55', *Le Fanatique de l'Aviation*, No. 129
Hazewinkel, H., 'Fokker D.XXIII', *Le Fanatique de l'Aviation*, No. 60
Hazewinkel, H., 'Koolhoven FK.58', *Le Fanatique de l'Aviation*, No. 205

Correspondence with Hannu Valtonen (1999) and Harm J. Hazewinkel (1992)
Hazewinkel, H., 'De Schelde S.21', *Air International* (February 1974)

BELGIUM

Books
Green, W., *Warplanes of the Second World War, Bombers Volume Seven* (MacDonald, 1963)
Green, W., *Warplanes of the Second World War, Fighters Volume One* (MacDonald, 1962)
Mali, C., *Les Avions S.A.B.C.A., prototypes & projects* (Fonds National Alfred Renard, 2003)
Pacco, J., *Het Militair Vliegwezen 1930–1940* (J.P. Publications, 2003)

Publications
De Maeyer, P., 'Built in Belgium', *Air-Britain Digest* (July–August 1980)
De Vinck, H., 'Les Fairey Fox', *Le Fanatique de l'Aviation*, nos 23 and 24
De Wulf, H., 'Renard neutrality fighters', *Air International* (April 1977)
Garcia, D., 'Air Force on the Edge', *Air Enthusiast*, No. 96 (2001)
Hauet, A., 'Le Chasseur Renard R.36 et ses Dérivés', *Le Fanatique de l'Aviation*, No. 32
Hauet, A., 'Le Renard R.31', *Le Fanatique de l'Aviation*, nos 37 to 49
Hauet, A., 'Les Derniers Chasseurs Renard', *Avions*, No. 153.
Huntley, I., 'Fairey's Elusive Fox', *Aeroplane Monthly* (January 1979)
Laureau, P., 'Le Fairey Firefly', *Air Magazine* (May–June 2001)
Mali, C., 'Renard R.37', *Fonds National Alfred Renard*
Sgarlato, N., 'Le Fiat CR.42', *Le Fanatique de l'Aviation*, nos 166 to 169
Thagon, P., 'l'Aéronautique Militaire Belge Durant la campagne de Mai–Juin 1940', *Ciel de Guerre*, no. 8
    (December 2005)
Thagon, P., 'l'Aéronautique Militaire Belge en Mai–Juin 1940', *Avions Hors Série*, No. 18
Verstraeten, W., 'History of the Belgian Air Force', *SAFO*, vol. 15, no. 2 (April 1991)

FRANCE

Books
Comas, M., *Le Morane-Saulnier 406* (Lela Presse, 1998)
Cuny, J., *Le Dewoitine D.520*, Docavia No. 4 (Ed. Larivière, 1980)
Facon, P., *L'Armée de l'Air dans la Tourmente* (Economica, 2005)
Green, W., *Warplanes of the Second World War: Fighters* (Macdonald, 1962)
Joanne, S., *Le Bloch M.B.152* (Lela Presse, 1998)
Ketley, B., *French Aces of World War II* (Osprey Publishing, 2000)
Klein, B., *Airplane Five Views* (B.C.F.K. Publications, 1974)
Marchand, P., *Les Moteurs à Piston Français* (D'Along, 2003)
Marchand, P., *Morane-Saulnier M.S. 406 C1*, Les Ailes de Gloire No. 7 (D'Along, 2002)
Shores, C., *Armée de l'Air* (Squadron/Signal Publications, 1976)

Publications
Belcarz, B., 'L'Armée de l'Air durant la Campagne de 1940', *Ciel de Guerre*, no. 8 (2010)
Belcarz, B., 'Le G.C. I/145', *Air Mag, Hors Série*, no. 6 (2009)
Breffort, D., 'L'Armée de l'Air en 1939–1942', *Wing Masters, Hors Série*, no. 1 (1991)
Correspondence with Paul Deweer, Jean Cuny, and Bernhard Klein
Coste, A., 'Le Spad 510 s'en va-t-en guerre', *Avions*, no. 128 (2003)
Cuny, J., 'Bloch M.B.150 à 157', *Le Fana de l'Aviation*, nos 8 to 11
Cuny, J., 'Les Chasseurs Arsenal VG 30 à VG 70', *Le Fana de l'Aviation*, nos 197 to 200
Ehrengardt, C., 'Arsenal VG 33 et dérivés', *Aéro-Éditions*, Aéro Files no. 1
Facon, P., 'L'Armée de l'Air en 1939–1940', *Le Fana de l'Aviation, Hors Série*, no. 7 (1997)

Facon, P., '*Le Sacrifice des Bombardiers Français*', *Le Fana de l'Aviation*, no. 558 (2016)
Leyvastre, P., 'Bloch's Fighters', *Air International* (April 1978)
Michelet, G., '*Des idées originales*', *l'Aérophile* (October 1938)
Michulec, E., 'Jagdwaffe *en France*', *Ciel de Guerre*, no. 8 (2011)
Mihaly, E., '*Il a failli être le T6 français en 1940*', *Le Fana de l'Aviation*, nos 78 and 423
Mihaly, E., '*Les Chasseurs Légers Caudron-Renault*', *Le Fana de l'Aviation*, nos 33 to 36
Moulin, J., 'C.A.P.R.A. R.30 *ou* R.300', *l'Aérophile* (2010)
Moulin, J., 'Loire 43, 45 & 46', *Document'air No. 3, Avia Editions* (1998)
Němeček, V., 'Potez 230', *Letectvi + Kosmonautika*, 22/85
Němeček, V., 'Roussel 30', *Letectvi + Kosmonautika*, 5/86
Nicole, F., 'Payen: *un rêve de vitesse*', *Le Fana de l'Aviation*, no. 266
Pelletier, A., 'Paper Darts to Deltas', *Air Enthusiast*, No. 68 (April 1997)
Ricco, P., '*Le Bloch M.B. 700 dernier des* Spads', *Le Fana de l'Aviation*, no. 341
Roux, R., 'Bugatti 100P& 110P', *Le Fana de l'Aviation*, nos 7 and 328
Roux, R., '*Les Avions* Payen', *Le Fana de l'Aviation*, nos 5, 6, and 7
Roux, R., 'M.Bloch 700', *Le Fana de l'Aviation*, no. 8
Watteeuw, P., '*Les Pertes de la Chasse de Jour Allemande en France* 1939–45', *Avions, Hors Série*, nos 10 and 15 (2005)

GREAT BRITAIN

Books
Bishop P., *The Fighter Boys* (Harper Perennial, 2007)
Bungay S., *The Most Dangerous Enemy* (Aurum Press, 2010)
Buttler T., *British Secret Projects, Fighters & Bombers 1935–1950* (Midland Publishing, 2004)
Cull B. and Lander B., *Diver! Diver! Diver!* (London, Grub Street, 2008)
Goulding J., *Interceptor* (Ian Allan, 1986)
Graham T., *Terror from the Sky* (Pen & Sword Aviation, 2008)
Green W., *War Planes of the Second World War, Vol. 4: Fighters* (London; Macdonald, 1963)
Lambert B., *Miles Aircraft since 1925* (London: Putnam, 1970)
Lewis P., *The British Fighter since 1912* (London: Putnam, 1967)
Mason T., *The Secret Years, Flight Testing at Boscombe Down 1939–1945* (Hikoki Publications, 1998)
Mondey D., *The Hamlyn Concise Guide to British Aircraft of World War II* (London: Chancellor Press, 1997)
Morgan E. and Shacklady E., *Spitfire: The History* (Key Publishing, 2000)

Publications
Aero Plastic Kit Revue No. 51
Bowyer M., 'Rammers', *Airfix Annual for Aircraft Modellers* (1978)
Museum of Berkshire Aviation Newsletter, Vol. 2, no. 13 (2007)
Rammer Plane (patent by I. Shamah, 1939)
Correspondence with Kevin Coyne and Brian Miller
The Aeroplane Spotter (January 1945 and February 1948)
Model Aircraft (July 1963)
Air Enthusiast (December 1971)
Jarret P., 'Nothing Ventured', *Aeroplane Monthly* (January 1992)
Scale Aircraft Modelling (October 1997)
Air International (January 1994 and August 1999)

SWITZERLAND

Books
Green, W., *Warplanes of the Second World War, Volume One: Fighters* (MacDonald, 1960)

Publications
Gaudet, E., 'A Dream Come True', *Aeroplane* (June 2002)
Gunti, P., 'Alpine Avenger', *Air/Enthusiast*, no. 47
Gunti, P., 'Morane *Sur l'Helvetie*', *IPMS Schweiz magazine, Xe Anniversaire* issue
Gunti, P., 'Neutral Warriors', *Air/Enthusiast*, no. 43
Guttman, J., 'Switzerland's two-seater soldiered through World War II', *Aviation History* (July 1998)
Klein, B., 'Morane-Saulnier M.S. 460', *Airplanes Five-View Album* (1974)
Meister, J., 'The Swiss Battle of Britain', *World War Investigator* (July 1988)
Moulin, J., '*Un project de chasseur* Morane-Saulnier M.S. 540', *l'Aérophile* (2010)
Moulin, J., '*Un project de chasseur* Morane-Saulnier M.S. 640', *l'Aérophile* (2010)
Osche, P., 'Swiss Bf 109', *SAFO*, no. 49 (January 1989)
Théroz, J., 'Bataille *au dessus des Alpes*', *Le Fanatique de l'Aviation*, no. 36

ROMANIA

Books
Bernád, D., *Heinkel He 112 in action* (Squadron/Signal Aircraft no. 159, 1996)
Bernád, D., *Rumanian Air Force, The Prime Decade 1938–1947* (Squadron/Signal, 1999)
Dabrowski, H., *Heinkel He 112* (Schiffer, 1998)
Green, W., *Warplanes of the Second World War, Fighters, Volume Three* (MacDonald, 1961)
Morosanu, T., *Rumanian Fighter Colours 1941–1945* (MMP Books, Redbourn)
Robanescu, M., *L'Aviation Roumaine pendant la Seconde Guerre Mondiale*, (Editions TMA)

Publications
Craciunoiu, C., 'Rumanian Aeronautics in the Second World War', *Modelism* (2004)
Axworthy, M., 'On three fronts', *Air Enthusiast*, No. 56 (winter 1994)
Cortet, P., '*Les Chasserus Roumains I.A.R.80*', *Le Fanatique de l'Aviation*, no. 244
Bernád, D., 'Rumanian Round-Out', *Air Enthusiast*, No. 59 (September–October 1995)
Green, W., 'The Polygenetic Rumanian', *Air International* (July 1976)

HUNGARY

Books
Bonhardt, A., *A Magyar Királyi Honvédség Fegyverzete* (Zrínyi Kiadó, 1984)
Punka, G., *Hungarian Air Force* (Squadron/Signal, 1994)

Publications
Baczkowski, W., 'Sojusznicy Luftwaffe', *Books International* (1998)
Bernád, D., 'Heinkel He 112 in action', *Aircraft* no. 159 (Squadron/Signal, 1996)
Cattaneo, G., *The Reggiane Re 2000*, Profile no. 123
Di Terlizi, M., 'Reggiane Re 2000 Falco, Hejja, J.20', *Aerolibri* Special no. 6 (IBN editore, 2002)
Punka, G., 'Reggiane Fighters in Action', *Aircraft* no. 177 (Squadron/Signal, 2000)
Sárhidai, G., *Hungarian Eagles* (Hikoki Publications, 1996)
Winkles, L., *A Magyar Repülés Története* (Müszaki Könyvhiadó, 1977)

YUGOSLAVIA

Books
Cirovic, D., *Vazduhoplovne Zrtve 1931–1945* (Beograd, 1970)
Green, W., *Warplanes of the Second World War, Fighters, Volume Four* (MacDonald, 1961)
Mason, F., 'The Hawker Fury' (Profile no. 18)
Oštric, Š., 'IK fighters, Yugoslavia 1930-40s' (Profile no. 242)
Shores, C., *Air War for Yugoslavia, Greece and Crete* (Grub Street, 1987)
Weale, E., *Combat Aircraft of World War Two* (Lionel Leventhal Ltd, 1977)

Publications
Ciglic, B., 'La Force Aérienne Royale Yougoslave dans la Deuxième Guerre Mondiale', *Le Fanatique de l'Aviation*, nos 503, 504, and 505
Hall, A., 'Hawker Fury and Nimrod', *Scale Aircraft Modelling* (December 1993)
Kolka, B., 'Aircraft of the Yugoslav Air Force', *SAFO* vol. 18, no. 1 (March 1994)
Miklusev, N., 'Ikarus LVT-1 Hurrischmitt', *Yasig*, vol. 2, nos 1–4 (1999)
Miklusev, N., 'Rogožarsky Ik-3, *un Dewoitine 520 à la mode Yougoslave*', *Air Magazine*, no. 53
Miklusev, N., 'Rogožarsky Ik-3', *Avions* No. 149. Miklusev, N., 'Ik fighters', *Yasig* (March 1998)
Ognjević, A., 'Le Hawker Fury *dans les Balkans*', *Avions*, no. 210
Petrovic, O., 'Ikarus Ik-2, *La Mouette Yougoslave*' *Avions*, nos 201 and 223
Zoran, J., 'Emil Versus the Luftwaffe', *Air Enthusiast* (September 1971)

GREECE

Books
Cristeco, M., *The Bloch 151 & 152* (Profile Publications no. 201)
Cynk, J., *The P.Z.L. P.24* (Profile Publications no. 170)
Krybus, J., *The Avia B.534* (Profile Publications no. 152)
Manson, F., *The Gloster Gladiator* (MacDonald, 1964)
Marchand, P., *Bloch 150, 151*, Les Ailes de Gloire No. 3 (Editions d'Along)
Shores, C., *Airwar for Yugoslavia, Greece and Crete* (Grub Street, 1987)

Publications
Joanne, S., 'Le Bloch MB 152', *Collection Histoire de l'Aviation no. 13* (Lela Presse, 2003)
Napier, S., 'Le P.Z.L. P.24 en Grèce', *Air Magazine* no. 34
Cynk, J., 'P.Z.L. P.24 *dernier chasseur à aile* Pulawski', *Le Fanatique de l'Aviation*, nos 95, 96, and 97.
Napier, S., 'The Hellenic Gladiators', *Mushroom Model Magazine* (April 2015)
Leyvastre, P., 'Bloch´s Fighters, the Contentious Combatants', *Air International* (April 1978)
Dildy, D., 'Air War over Greece', *SAFO*, vol. 15, no. 4 (October 1991)

FINLAND

Books
Bowers, P., *The Curtiss Hawk 75* (Profile no. 80)
Comas, M., *Le Morane-Saulnier M.S.406*, Histoire de l'Aviation No. 5 (Lela Presse, 1998)
Cuny, J., *Curtiss Hawk 75*, Docavia no. 22 (*Editions Lariviere*, 1985)
Geust, K., *Baltic Fleet Air Force in Winter War*, Red Stars 5 (Apali, 2004)
Geust, K., *The Winter War in the Air*, Red Stars 7 (Apali, 2011)
Green, W., *Warplanes of the Second World War, Fighters, Volume Four* (MacDonald, 1961)
Jong, P., *Le Fokker D.21*, Collection Profils Avions no. 9 (Lela Presse, 2005)
Keskinen, K., *Curtiss Hawk 75* (Tietoteos, 1984)

Keskinen, K., *Finnish Air Force 1939–1945* (Squadron/Signal Publications, 1998)
Keskinen, K., *Suomalaiset Hävittäjät* (Suomen Ilmavoimient Historia no. 14, 1990)
Keskinen, K., *Suomen Ilmavoimien Historia 18 LeR3* (Uudenmaan Paino, 2001)
Keskinen, K., *Suomen Ilmavoimien Historia LeR2* (Edita OYJ, 2001)
Luukkanen, E., *Fighters over Finland* (MacDonald, 1963)
Maas, J., *F2A Buffalo in Action* (Squadron/Signal Publications no. 81, 1987)
Stenman, K., *Finnish Air Aces of World War II* (Osprey Aircraft Aces no. 23, 1988)
Stenman, K., *Mersu Messerschmitt Bf 109G in Finnish Service*, Koala-Kustannus, 2017)
Vergnano, P., *Fiat G.50*, Ali d'Italia (La Bancarella Aeronautica, 1997)

Publications
Correspondence with Hannu Valtonen (1999)
Good, M., '*Un Fantôme Venu du Froid*', *Wingmaster Magazine* (January 2000)
Gréciet, V., 'Morane-Saulnier M.S. 406 C1', *Aèrojournal* No. 20
Guttman, J., 'Aerial Oddities', *Aviation History* (May 1998)
Hazewinkel, H., 'Fokker C.X', *Le Fanatique de l'Aviation* no. 50
Heinonen, T., 'V.L. Pyörremyrsky', *Ilmailu Magazin*, nos 4 and 10 (1948)
Hurme, M., 'Flygflottilj 19, the Swedish Volunteer Air Unit' *SAFO*, no. 53 (January 1990)
Keskinen, K., 'The Finnish Air Force in the Winter War', *SAFO*, vol. 14, no. 2 (April 1990)
Millot, B., 'Brewster Buffalo', *Le Fanatique de l'Aviation*, nos 92 to 95
Muikku, E., '*Pyörremyrsky*', *IPMS Mallari*, no. 16 (1975)
Partonen, K., 'Mörkö-Moraani', *IPMS Mallari* (1984)
Raunio, J., 'V.L. Puuska', *Suomen Ilmailuhistoriallinen*, Lehti 2/1998.
Raunio, J., '*Pyörremyrsky*', *Lentäjän Näkökulma* (1991)
Stenman, K., '38 to 1 the Brewster 234 in Finnish service', *Air Enthusiast*, No. 46.
Stenman, K., 'A violent Finnish Wind', *Air Enthusiast* (October 1971)
Stenman, K., 'Finland's Fighter Finale', *Air Enthusiast*, no. 23
Stenman, K., '*Le Morane Sort ses Griffes*', *Le Fanatique de l'Aviation*, no. 554 (January 2016)
Timonen, J., '*Pyörremyrsky osa 2*', *IPMS Mallari* No. 115, 5/1996
Uolamo, S., '*Pyörremyrsky Entisöinti osa 1*', *Suomen Siivet*, nos 1 and 2 (1973)
Valtonen, H., 'Guidebook', *Keski-Suomen Ilmailmuseo* (1999)

LITHUANIA

Books
Comas, M., *Le Morane Saulnier M.S.406, Histoire de l'Aviation* no. 5 (Lela Presse 1998)
Humberstone, R., *Lithuanian Air Force 1918–1940* (Blue Rider Publishing, 1996)
Marchand, P., *Dewoitine D.500, D.510, Les Ailes de Gloire* no. 3 (Editions d'Along, 2004)

Publications
Bezouska, P., 'Lithuanian Adenda', *Air Enthusiast*, No. 30
Dulaitis, D., 'Color schemes and insignia of Lithuanian aircraft at the beginning of the WWII' *SAFO*,
    vol. 14, nos 3 and 4 (October 1990)
Jasiunas, E., 'Lithuanian Aviation 1918–1940', *SAFO*, no. 39 (July 1986)
Passingham, M., '*Les Inconnus de la Baltique, l'Industrie Aéronautique Lituanienne*', *Le Fanatique de
    l'Aviation*, no. 271

ESTONIA

Books
Humberstone, R., *Estonian Air Force 1918–1940* (Blue Rider Publishing, 1999)

Publications
Gerdessen, F., 'Estonian Air Power 1918-1945', *Air Enthusiast*, No. 18
Lennurägi, E., 'Estonian Air Force', *SAFO*, vol. 15, no. 3 (April 1991)
Lennurägi, E., 'Estonian Air Force', *SAFO*, vol. 16, no. 2 (April 1992)

LATVIA

Books
Humberstone, R., *Latvian Air Force 1918–1940* (Blue Rider Publishing, 2000)
Irbitis, K., *Of Struggle and Flight, The History of Latvian Aviation* (Canada Wings, 1988)
Mason, F., *The Gloster Gladiator* (MacDonald, 1964)

Publications
Branke, P., 'Latvian Bulldogs', *SAFO*, vol. 14, no. 3
Davis, C., 'Latvia's Little Hawk', *Air Enthusiast*, no. 48
Irbitis, K., 'Latvia 1940', *SAFO*, vol. 14, no. 3
Passingham, M., '*La construction aéronautique de Lettonie*', *Le Fanatique de l'Aviation*, no. 283 (June 1993)
Thomas, A., 'Iron Cross Gladiators', *Håkans Aviation Page*

SWEDEN

Books
Cattaneo, G., *Fiat C.R. 42* (Profile No. 16)
Cattaneo, G., *Reggiane Re.2000* (Profile No. 123)
Crawford, A., *Hawker Hart Family* (Casemate Publishers, 2008)
Davis, C., *Aircraft Three View Drawings for Collectors* (B.C.F.K. Publications, 1989)
Davis, L., *P-35*, Mini in action no. 1 (Squadron/ Signal publications, 1994)
Di Terlizi, M., *Reggiane Re.2000 Falco, Héja, J.20*, Aviolibri Special 6 (IBN Editore, 2002)
Punka, G., *Reggiane Fighters in action*, Aircraft no. 177 (Squadron/ Signal publications, 2001)
Wildfelt, B., *The SAAB 21 A & R* (Profile No. 138)

Publications
Billing, P., 'A fork tailed Swede', *Air Enthusiast*, no. 22
Drawings from Bo Wildfelt, Chuck Davis, and Torstein Landström
Drawings from SAAB Svenska Aeroplan Aktiebolaget, Linköping (1946)
Green, W., 'A SAAB half-century', *Air Enthusiast*, no. 33
Knutsson, G., 'SAAB J 23', Flyg Specialnummer no. 20 (1945)
Sgarlato, N., '*Le Fiat C.R. 42*', *Le Fanatique de l'Aviation*, nos 166 to 169
Waligorsky, M., 'Adventures into the Esoteric', *IPMS Stockholm Magazine* (2002)

CHINA

Books
Apostolo, G., *Fiat C.R.32*, Ali d'Italia 4 (La Bancarella Aeronautica, 1996)
Bowers, P., *Curtiss Navy Hawks in action*, no. 128 (Squadron/Signal publications, 1992)
Cheung, R., *Aces of the Republic of China Air Force* (Osprey aircraft of the Aces 126, 2015)
Cuny, J., *Curtiss Hawk 75*, Docavia no. 22 (Editions Lariviere, 1985)
Green, W., *The Complete Book of Fighters* (Salamander Books, 2001)

Publications

Anderson, L., 'Chinese Junks', *Air Enthusiast* (Autumm 1994)

Demin, A., 'Soviet Fighters in the Sky of China', *Aviatsiia Kosmonavtika* (2000)

Gustavsson, H., 'Sino-Japanese Air War 1937–1945'

Hackett, B., 'Rising Storm-The Imperial Japanese Navy and China 1931–1941',
    combinedfleet.com/Rising.htm (2012)

Hooton, E., 'Airwar Over China', *Air Enthusiast*, no. 34.

Johnson, R. 'Before the Tigers: China's Air Forces in the Struggle Against Japan', worldatwar.net/
    chandelle/v2/v2n2/china30s.html

Sakaida, H., '*La Guerre des deux Soleils* 1937–1941', *le Fanatique de l'Aviation* (July 1996)

surfcity.kund.dalnet.se/sino-japanese-1937.htm

Demin, A., 'Changing from Donkeys to Mustangs', *Aviamaster* 6/2000,
    Twin Cities Aero Historians.

O'Leary, M., 'Boeing P-26 Peashooter', *Aeroplane* (August 2006)

KHALKHIN GOL/NOMONHAN

Books

Bueschel, M., *Nakajima Ki.27 A-B*, Aircam Aviation Series no. 18 (Osprey, 1972)

Hillman, N., *Ki.27 'Nate' Aces* (Osprey, 2013)

Liss, W., *Polikarpov I-16* (Profile no. 122)

Maslov, M., *Polikarpov I-15, I-16 and I-153 Aces* (Osprey, 2010)

Polak, T., *Stalin's Falcons* (Grub Street, 1999)

Sakaida, H., *Japanese Army Air Force Aces 1937–45* (Osprey, 1997)

Sewell, J., *Polikarpov Fighters in Action, Part II*, Aircraft No. 162 (Squadron/Signal, 1996)

Stapfer, H., *Polikarpov Fighters in Action, Part I*, Aircraft No. 157 (Squadron/Signal, 1995)

Publications

Baëza, B., '*Les Aigles Sauvages de l'Armée Impériale Japonaise*', *Avions*, nos 217 to 220.

Green, W., 'End of an Era, Polikarpov's Chaika' *Air Enthusiast* (June 1971)

Izawa, Y., '*Les As de l'Armée Impériale Japonaise 1937–45*', *Aéro Journal*
    (October–November, 2014)

Maslov, M., 'Polikarpov I-153, *un biplan au combat*', *Le Fana de l'Aviation*, no. 570 (May 2017)

THAILAND

Books

Beauchamp, G., *Curtiss Hawk 75*, Docavia no. 22 (*Editions Lariviére*, 1985)

Bowers, P., *The Boeing P-12E* (Profile no. 2)

Bowers, P., The Curtiss Hawk 75 (Profile no. 80)

Bowers, P., *The Curtiss Navy Hawks* (Profile no. 1169)

Young, E., *A History of Aviation in Thailand* (Smithsonian Institution Press, 1995)

Publications

Kadari, Y., 'Royal Thai Air Force', *Aérojournal*, no. 59 (2017)

Pelletier, A., 'North American P-64', *Le Fanatique de l'Aviation*, no. 339 (1998)

Gwynn, T., 'Forgotten Air War Over Indochina', *Aviation History* (September 2000)

Wixey, E., 'Hawk Dynasty', *Air Enthusiast* (September–October 1997)

Guttman, R., 'Aerial Oddities', *Aviation History* (March 2000)

PEARL HARBOR

Books
Bowers, P., *Boeing Aircraft Since 1916* (Naval Institute Press, 1989)
Bowers, P., *Boeing P-26* (Aerofax Minigraph 8, 1964)
Davis, L., *Boeing P-26* (Squadron Signal in Action Mini Series no. 2, 1994)
Maloney, E., *Boeing P-26 Peashooter* (Aero Series 22, 1973)
Maloney, E., *History of the Famous Boeing P-26 Peashooter* (Challenge Publications Inc. 1965)

Publications
Green, W., 'Boeing's Fighter Finale, The Peashooter Chronicle', *Air Enthusiast*, no. 14

PHILIPPINES

Books
Beauchamp, G., *Curtiss P-40* (*Le Fanatique de l'Aviation*, nos 130 to 147)
Bowers, P., *Aircraft in Profile*, vol. 1, no. 14 (Doubleday, 1965)
Bueschel, R., *Mitsubishi A6M1/2/2N Zero-Sen*, Aircam Aviation Series no. 16 (Osprey, 1970)
Bueschel, R., *Nakajima Ki.27 A-B*, Aircam Aviation Series no. 18 (Osprey ,1972)
Caidin, M., *Zero Fighter* (Ballantine's, 1969)
Crosby, F., *Boeing P-26 Fighter Aircraft* (Lorenz Books, 2002)
Davis, L., *P-35* (Squadron/Signal Aircraft Mini no. 1, 1994)
Davis, L., *Texan in Action* (Squadron/Signal Aircraft no. 94, 2002)
Morton, L., *The War of the Pacific, the Fall of the Philippines. United States Army in World War II*
    (Center of Military History, United States Army)
Munson, K., *Fighters 1919–39* (Blanford Press, 1970)
Shores, C., *The Drift of War to the Fall of Singapore* (Grub Street, 1992)
Wagner, R., *American Combat Planes* (Doubleday, 1968)

Publications
Dorr, R., 'Boeing P-26 Peashooter', *Air International*, Vol. 48, No. 4 (1995)
Tremble, B., 'Peashooter', *Scale Modeller*, Vol. 9, No. 11 (November 1974)

MALAYA/SINGAPORE

Books
Shores, C., *The Brewster Buffalo* (Profile no. 217)
Shores, C., *The Drift to War to the Fall of Singapore* (Grub Street, 1992)
Wagner, R., *Curtiss P-40 Tomahawk* (Profile no. 35)

Publications
Shores, C., 'The Agile Asian, Japan's Type 97 Fighter', *Air Enthusiast*, no. 6
Minnich, M., 'Tiger in the Sky', *Air Enthusiast*, no. 4

BURMA

Books
Bueschel, R., *Nakajima Ki.27AB* (Aircam Aviation Series no. 18, Osprey, 1972)
Ehrman, V., *Curtiss P40* (MBI Praha, 1998)
Shores, C., *The Brewster Buffalo* (Profile no. 217)
Shores, C., The Defence of Sumatra to the Fall of Burma (Grub Street, 1993)

Publications
Beauchamp, G., 'Curtiss P40', *Le Fanatique de l'Aviation*, nos 130 to 147
Minnich, M., 'Tiger in the Sky, the Saga of the AVG', *Air Enthusiast*, no. 4
Shores, C., 'The Agile Asian, Japan's Type 97 Fighter', *Air Enthusiast*, no. 6

DUTCH EAST INDIES

Books
Angelucci, E., *The American Fighter* (Orion Books, 1987)
Balzer, G., *XP-55 le canard boiteux de Curtiss* (*Le Fanatique de l'Aviation*, no. 224)
Bowers, P., *Curtiss Aircraft 1907–1947* (Naval Institute Press, 1979)
Bowers, P., *The Curtiss Hawk 75* (Profile no. 80)
Bueschel, R., *Nakajima Ki.27 A-B* (Aircam Aviation Series no. 18, Osprey, 1972)
Cuny, J., *Curtiss Hawk 75*, Docavia no. 22, (Ed. Larivière, 1980)
Green, W., *The Complete Book of Fighters* (Smithmark, 1995)
Green, W., *Warplanes of the Second World War-Fighters-Volume Four* (MacDonald, 1961)
Maas, J., *F2A Buffalo* (Squadron/Signal Publications, in action no. 81, 1987)
Norton, W., *U.S. Experimental & Prototype Aircraft Projects* (Speciality Press, 2008)
Sakaida, H., *Japanese Army Air Force Aces 1937–1945* (Osprey, 1997)
Shores, C., *The Brewster Buffalo* (Profile no. 217)
Shores, C., *The Defence of Sumatra to the Fall of Burma* (Grub Street, 1993)

Publications
Baëza, B., 'La Chasse de l'Armée Impériale Japonaise', *Avions*, no. 220 (2017)
Casius, G., 'Brewster Benighted Buffalo', *Air Enthusiast*, no. 1
Casius, G., 'The St. Louis Lightweight', *Air Enthusiast*, no. 16
Farara, C., 'Hawker Hurricane Database', *Aeroplane* (October 2007)
Porter, R., 'Against Great Odds', *World War Investigator* (October 1988)
Shores, C., 'The Agile Asian, Japan's Type 97 Fighter', *Air Enthusiast*, no. 6

CEYLON

Books
Brown, D., *Fairey Fulmar Mks I & II* (Profile no. 254)
Bussy, G., *Fairey Fulmar* (Warpaint Series n. 41)
Sierra, L., *La Guerra Naval en el Pacifico* (Editorial Juventud, 1979)

Publications
Bussy, G., 'Fairey Fulmar, *Chasseur Malgré Lui*', *Le Fanatique de l'Aviation*, nos 458 to 460

AUSTRALIA

Books
Francillon, R., *The Commonwealth Boomerang* (Profile no. 178)
Green, W., *The Complete Book of Fighters* (Smithmark, 1994)
Pentland, G., *Aircraft of the RAAF 1921-71* (Kookaburra Publications, 1971)
Thetford, O., *Aircraft of the Fighting Powers*, Vol.7 (Argus Books, 1979)
Wilson, W., *The Wirraway, Boomerang & CA-15 in Australian Service*
   (Aerospace Publications, 1991)

Publications
Darbyshire, D., 'Full Red Circle', *Wingspan* (January 2002)
Donald, D., 'Commonwealth CA-15', *Wings of Fame*, vol. 4
Green, W., 'Antipodean Finale', *Air Enthusiast* (October 1972)
Guttman, J., 'Aerial Oddities', *Aviation History* (May 1997)
Hourigan, R., 'Vintage Australians', *APMA*, no. 3 (1995)
Millot, B., 'Le Commonwealth Boomerang', *Le Fanatique de l'Aviation*, nos 190 and 234
Vella, J., 'From Fisherman Bend', *Air Enthusiast*, no. 61